angles on

psychology

D0493509

dedications

This book is dedicated to my family.   *MJ*
To Em.   *JR*
To those that matter most: Pip, Jack, Rosie and Rob.   *CF*
To Mum and Dad with love and thanks.   *LD*

angles on psychology

Matt Jarvis Julia Russell Cara Flanagan Larry Dolan

First published in 2000 by:
Stanley Thornes (Publishers) Ltd

Reprinted in 2001 by:
Nelson Thornes Ltd
Delta Place
27 Bath Road
CHELTENHAM
GL53 7TH
United Kingdom

. 03 04 05 06 / 10 9 8 7 6 5 4

A catalogue record for this book is available from the British Library

ISBN 0 7487 5692 2

Line illustrations by Oxford Designers and Illustrators; cartoons by Shaun
Williams
Page make-up by Northern Phototypesetting Company Ltd

Printed in Great Britain by Scotprint

contents

acknowledgements

We would all like to acknowledge the unceasing efforts and invaluable help from everyone at Stanley Thornes, especially Rick Jackman, Rachel Warner and Louise Watson.

The authors and publishers are grateful to the following for permission to reproduce material:

- *The Guardian* (pp. 144–5)
- *The Times Educational Supplement* (p. 55)

Every effort has been made to contact copyright holders and we apologise if anyone has been overlooked.

Photo credits
- Associated Press (p. 42)
- Bettman Corbis (pp. 99, 133)
- Christie's Images (p. 19)
- George McCarthy/Corbis (p. 23)
- Matt Jarvis (pp. 128, 135)
- Alexandra Milgram (p. 181)
- Mirror Syndication International (p. 191)
- National Medical Slide Bank (p. 10)
- Pfizer Inc (p. 46)
- Photofusion/Christa Stadtler (p. 174)
- Photofusion/Paul Mattsson (p. 168)
- Ronald Grant Archive (p. 91)
- Julia Russell (p. 47)
- Science Photo Library (p. 16)
- Science Photo Library/Department of Clinical Radiology, Salisbury District Hospital (p. 155)
- Tony Stone Images/Mary Kate Denny (p. 51)
- Wellcome Library, London (p. 39)

introduction

Psychology is the study of the mind and behaviour. The aim of *Angles on Psychology* is to introduce you to the wide range of theory and research that make up the subject. One aspect of psychology that can take quite a bit of getting used to when you first come to study it is the way that different psychologists look at mind and behaviour from very different angles. We have therefore designed a book that considers each of the major psychological perspectives or *angles* in turn, looking at some of the key assumptions, theories, research methods and real-life applications of each. If you are studying psychology at any level, part of your course will almost certainly be to carry out research. We have therefore also included a chapter on how to conduct your own psychological research.

Angles on Psychology has been structured around the Edexcel AS-level specification, making it the ideal choice for your main course text. If you are taking the Edexcel AS-level course you will need to know that Unit I is covered by Chapters 3, 4 and 6 and Unit II is covered by Chapters 1, 2 and 5. Chapter 7 covers Unit III.

1

The Biological Approach

This chapter concerns the ways in which biological principles can be applied to understanding psychology. This is not a new idea, and before psychology emerged as a distinct discipline about a hundred years ago, biologists were investigating the relationship between the brain and human behaviour. The scientific study of biology requires a certain level of technology, however, and at the start of the twenty-first century we are making very rapid advances in understanding how our psychology is influenced by our biology. We will look here at behavioural genetics, the study of the origins of human characteristics, abilities and behaviour. We will also examine neuropsychology, the study of the role of the brain in determining the way we think, feel and behave. In particular we focus on the ways we are affected by bodily rhythms and the mechanisms of sleeping and dreaming. In our *real lives* section we examine the effects of shift-work and jet-lag, and in *talking point*, we consider the phenomenon of seasonal affective disorder, a type of depression linked to reduced sunlight in winter.

The biological approach is based on the following ideas.

- Biology is a pure science, and psychologists taking a biological perspective tend to see psychology as a science and to be highly scientific in their approach.

- Our genetic make-up is of considerable importance in determining our individual characteristics, abilities and behaviour.

- Our thinking, behaviour and feelings (both normal and abnormal) are strongly affected by the ways in which the human brain works.

- Biological psychologists are primarily concerned with investigating biological activity. This is in contrast to behaviourists who are primarily interested in observable behaviour, cognitive psychologists who look at thinking and related processes and psychodynamic psychologists who focus on feelings.

In this chapter we will be looking particularly at the importance of two areas of biology. Genetics is the study of inheritance, and neuropsychology is the study of the relationship between psychology and the functioning of the brain. Neuropsychology is a vast area, and in this chapter we will be looking at two related ways in which the workings of the brain affect human psychology – bodily rhythms and sleep.

Genetic influences

One of the most important developments in psychology in the last 20 years has been the recognition of the importance of genetic influences on individual differences between people (Plomin *et al.*, 1997). You may have noticed that, just as some families have a number of very tall or red-headed members, some psychological characteristics also appear to run in families. There are thus families in which there are an unusually large number of highly intelligent or particularly bad-tempered individuals. One way in which characteristics can pass from one generation to the next is through *genes*. Genes are units of DNA which contain the information required to build biological structures. The reason that as humans we share so many characteristics is that we share 99.9 per cent of our genes. It is relatively simple to understand how a characteristic like eye-colour can be under the control of genes because eye-colour is obviously physical in nature. The question of how genes might affect psychological characteristics is a more complex one. It appears that genetic differences between individuals produce biological differences between people (sometimes very subtle) that, in combination with their environment, lead them to develop into unique individuals.

Most psychological characteristics that have a genetic component depend on several genes, and in most cases we do not yet know all the genes involved. However, there are examples of psychological disorders that result from single gene abnormalities. An example is phenylketonuria (PKU), which causes a form of profound mental retardation. PKU is caused by a single gene. The allele (meaning a particular form of a gene) for PKU is *recessive*, so PKU will only result if a child inherits the PKU allele from both parents. The diagram below shows how the combination of two PKU alleles can result in PKU.

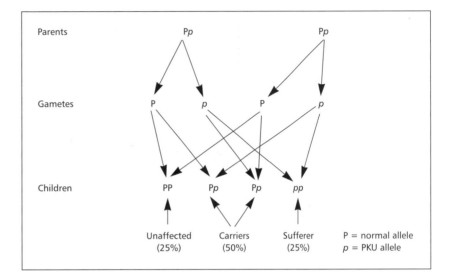

The genetic transmission of PKU
(from Plomin *et al.*, 1997)

If, as in the diagram above both parents are carriers of the PKU gene, each child has a 25 per cent probability of suffering the disease and a 50 per cent probability of carrying the gene but not developing symptoms. Our understanding of the genetic basis of PKU has allowed us to reduce greatly the number of people suffering mental retardation. The symptoms of PKU result from an inability to break down an amino acid called phenylalanine. A build-up of phenylalanine causes brain damage. We can now simply advise sufferers to avoid foods containing phenylalanine throughout childhood so that they never develop symptoms.

Behavioural geneticists are interested in genetic and environmental influences on individual differences in people. However, in real life it can be quite difficult to study genes and environment separately because people in the same family tend to share a similar set of genes and a similar environment. There are, however, various circumstances under which we can investigate the relative importance of genes and environment, including cases of twins and adoption.

Twin studies

We know that identical twins (properly called monozygotic twins or MZs) share 100 per cent of their genes. We also know that fraternal twins (properly called dizygotic twins or DZs) only share 50 per cent of their genetic material on average. These facts give us the basis for two types of *twin study*.

The first type of twin study involves comparing the similarity of MZs and DZs who have been reared together and hence have experienced a similar environment. If MZs, who share all their genes as well as having a similar environment, are more similar than DZs, this is powerful evidence for the importance of genes. An example of such a study comes from Gottesman (1991), who compared the concordance rates of MZs and DZs for schizophrenia, a serious mental disorder characterised by hallucinations, delusions and difficulty in thinking coherently. The term concordance refers to the probability of both twins sharing a characteristic like schizophrenia. Gottesman's results are shown in Table 1.1.

Twin type	Concordance for schizophrenia (%)
MZs	48
DZs	17

Table 1.1 Concordance rates of identical and fraternal twins (after Gottesman, 1991)

You can see from Table 1.1 that MZs have a much higher probability of sharing schizophrenia than DZs. This tells us that schizophrenia is at least partially a result of genetic factors. Of course, if schizophrenia were entirely a product of our genes, we would expect all the identical twins of sufferers to also have the condition. A number of environmental risk factors have been suggested, ranging from a dysfunctional family (Tienari

Identical twins

et al., 1992) to a difficult birth (Torrey *et al.*, 1994). These may account for the differences between MZs.

In the second type of twin study, we can compare the similarity of identical twins who have grown up in the same family or in different environments and see whether those who have grown up together are more alike than those who grew up apart. The fact that MZs reared apart show more differences than those reared together demonstrates the role of the environment, but the fact that even separated identical twins tend to be much more alike than two unrelated people demonstrates the importance of genes. Table 1.2 shows the similarity in personality of identical twins who have been reared together and apart. The correlations in the table represent how similar the twins were, with 0 meaning no relationship between the scores of the two twins and 1 being a perfect correlation between them.

Twin type	Correlation	
	Extraversion	**Neuroticism**
MZs reared together	0.51	0.46
MZs reared apart	0.38	0.38

Table 1.2 Similarity in personality between identical twins reared together and apart (from Loehlin, 1992)

The term *extraversion* refers to how impulsive and sociable the twins were. *Neuroticism* refers to how anxious and moody they were. Looking at Table 1.2, you can see that, although the twins reared apart are distinctly less similar than those reared together, they are still much more similar than we would expect if their genetic similarity were not a factor. Of course, this assumes that personality can be measured with sufficient accuracy to show up differences between different pairs of twins. Not all psychologists would accept this.

Twins studies provide a powerful argument for the role of genes in affecting individual differences amongst us with respect to intelligence, personality and mental disorder. However, there are problems with twin studies. In the case of separated identical twins, researchers must rely on data from a small group of people who have been separated at various ages and in a variety of circumstances. Some 'separated' identical twins may have spent considerable time in a similar environment *before* separation or been 'separated' but actually lived in very similar environments. They may also have been reunited for a considerable time before their personality and intelligence were assessed, so that they had a chance to share an environment for a time and to become more alike. When researchers compare the environments of MZs and DZs reared together, they make the assumption that MZs and DZs grow up in equally similar environments. In fact, because MZs look more alike than DZs, people may treat them in a much more similar manner and hence give them a more similar environment as well as the same genes. This means that when we compare the similarity of MZs and DZs we cannot know to what extent we are seeing the influence of genes and to what extent the effect of environment.

for and against

twin study methods

+ Twin studies have generated a very large volume of data, which points towards an important role for both genetic and environmental factors in individual development.

− Twins reared apart have been separated at a variety of times and in a variety of circumstances and often not assessed for similarity until they are reunited. They may also have experienced a similar environment during the period of separation. This means that it is difficult to know if similarities between twins reared apart are a result of genes or environment.

− Studies showing that MZs reared together are more similar than DZs reared together also have the latter problem. If MZs share a more similar environment than DZs, it may be this as well as the identical genes that leads to the greater similarity between MZs.

Adoption studies

The most direct way to isolate the influences of genes and environment involves adoption. If children are adopted into a different environment from that of their birth family we have a situation where the children have the genes of the biological parents and the environment created by the adoptive parents. Any similarity between child and biological parents suggests a role for genes, whilst any similarity between child and adoptive parents suggests a role for environment. Prior to the 1960s it was generally accepted that schizophrenia was the result of early experience. However, a classic adoption study by Heston (1966) demonstrated the importance of genes.

classic
research

is there a genetic component to schizophrenia?

Heston, L.L. (1966) Psychiatric disorders in foster home reared children of schizophrenic mothers. *British Journal of Psychiatry*, 112, 819–25

Aim: Prior to the 1960s, there had been evidence from twin studies which suggested that schizophrenia was at least partly a result of genetic factors. However, no adoption studies had been carried out, so there was a lack of direct evidence for a role for genes in schizophrenia. The aim of this study was to see how many adopted children of biological mothers with schizophrenia would go on to develop schizophrenia themselves. If a significant number did so, this would constitute powerful evidence for a role for genes in schizophrenia.

Method: Forty-seven adults were identified who had been adopted at birth because their mothers were suffering from schizophrenia. A matched group of 47 adoptees whose mothers were believed to be mentally healthy were also identified. The 94 adults were interviewed in order to see whether any had gone on to develop schizophrenia themselves. It had been previously established that the risk of developing schizophrenia if one parent had it was about 10 per cent. The incidence in the population at large is about 1 per cent. The rationale of this study was that if there were no genetic influences on schizophrenia, we would expect none or perhaps one of the people with a biological mother with schizophrenia to go on to develop the condition. If schizophrenia were entirely the result of genetic factors we would expect about 10 per cent of the children to develop it. A control group of adoptees without a parent suffering from schizophrenia was essential because, given the concern that early environment might cause schizophrenia, it was necessary to eliminate the possibility that the adoption itself was responsible for the high incidence of schizophrenia in the sample.

Results: The results were unequivocal. Of the 47 adults interviewed whose mother suffered schizophrenia, five had been hospitalised with schizophrenia. Three of these were chronically ill. Thus 10 per cent of the adopted children of schizophrenic mothers developed schizophrenia – exactly the number that we would have expected to develop it had they not been adopted but brought up by the biological mother. None of the control group developed schizophrenia, indicating that the experience of adoption was not a factor in schizophrenia.

Conclusion: The results provided powerful evidence for the role of genes in schizophrenia. No evidence emerged from this study of any role at all for environmental factors in the development of schizophrenia.

Since Heston's research, more sophisticated adoption studies (for example, Tienari *et al.*, 1992) have confirmed the importance of genetic factors in the development of schizophrenia, but, unlike Heston, they have also discovered possible environmental variables that influence the probability of an individual adopted child going on to develop schizophrenia. Adoption studies have also cast light on the role of genes in individual intelligence and personality.

Adoption studies, like twin studies, have their problems. One issue concerns the *representativeness* of adopted children in relation to the population. For example, if we look at the Heston study, clearly not all mothers with schizophrenia have their children adopted. It is thus possible that there was something different about these particular mothers or their babies that led to the adoptions and also contributed to the development of schizophrenia. A further problem with some adoption studies is *selective placement*. When children are adopted they are frequently placed in a family as similar as possible to their biological family. This means that it is difficult to see whether apparent similarities to the biological family are in fact caused by the influence of the similar adoptive family.

for and against

adoption studies

+ Adoption studies provide us with the most direct comparison of the influences of genes and environment.

+ Adoption studies have provided us with useful information concerning the role of genes in individual differences.

– There is an issue of representativeness of samples. Obviously, most people are not adopted, hence by definition people who are adopted are not representative of the whole population.

– Selective placement means that frequently people very similar to their biological families adopt children. This makes untangling the influences of genes and environment difficult.

what's new?

molecular genetics

We have already seen that twin and adoption studies have fairly serious methodological weaknesses. They are of course still practised and more recent studies tend to have rather fewer flaws than older ones. It may be that the future of separated twin and adoption studies is not a rosy one – considerably fewer twins are now separated and adoption has become much rarer with a growing acceptance of single parenthood. We may in time simply run out of participants for these studies. However, technological developments have allowed a new line of research – *molecular genetics*. Molecular genetics looks at the association between particular genes and psychological characteristics. Genetic material is extracted from individuals or in some cases whole families and associations are calculated between variations in particular genes and the psychological characteristics of the individuals or families.

The simplest way to establish that a particular gene may be implicated in affecting a characteristic is to look at whether people who exhibit that characteristic are more likely to have the gene. A recent study by Chorney *et al.* (1998) has attracted much attention. They claim to have, for the first time, isolated a gene linked to intelligence. In this study, two matched groups of children were established, a 'superbright' group (average IQ = 136) and a matched group of children the same age but with an average IQ (average IQ = 103). The researchers extracted DNA from the cells of members of the two groups and analysed their genetic make-up. The aim of the analysis was to see whether particular genetic variations were associated with the 'superbright' group. There was a significant difference between the two groups in the frequency of a single gene, situated on chromosome 6. Twice as many (33 per cent) of the 'superbrights' as opposed to 17 per cent of the control group had a particular allele of the gene IGF2R. This indicated that IGF2R is one of the genes associated with cognitive ability. The researchers have suggested that IGF2R accounts for about 2 per cent of the variance in intelligence. At the time of writing, IGF2R is the only gene that has been identified as associated with cognitive ability.

Some aspects of individual personality may be associated with genes. Two recent studies, Benjamin *et al.* (1996) and Ebstein *et al.* (1995) have found associations between alleles of the gene DRD4 and novelty-seeking behaviour. Other studies have found associations between DRD4 and drug-taking and hyperactivity, both of which could be related to a tendency for novelty-seeking. Molecular genetic studies have also isolated genes that are associated with mental disorders. Straub *et al.* (1995) analysed the genetic material of 265 families and isolated a variation on the short arm of chromosome 6 (6p24-22), that was present in around a quarter of families which included a number of individuals suffering from schizophrenia.

Molecular genetics promises great advances in the new century. We are rapidly heading towards an understanding of which genes impact on different psychological characteristics and to what extent. In parallel, our ability to intervene on a genetic level is also increasing. This knowledge may bring with it great medical advances, as we become able to modify or select embryos in order to eliminate faulty genes and hence inherited disease. However, we will also become capable of more sinister modifications. No one will object if we become able to reduce the incidence of schizophrenia by genetically modifying vulnerable embryos, but suppose we find a way to alter people's genetic make-up to make them more obedient, conforming and hard-working? There would be a tremendous incentive to do so in terms of industrial productivity and law-and-order, but would we still have (or want!) any notion of individual freedom or democracy?

where to now

The following are good sources of further information regarding behavioural genetics:

▶ **Plomin, R., DeFries, J.C., McClearn, G.E. and Rutter, M. (1997)** *Behavioural Genetics*. **New York: Freeman** – a state-of-the-art account of the field of behavioural genetics, including chapters on molecular genetics and genetic influences on intelligence and mental disorder

▶ **Rose, S., Kamin, L.J. and Lewontin, R.C. (1984)** *Not in Our Genes*. **Harmondsworth: Penguin** – puts well the case against the over-riding importance of genes in behaviour. This is well worth reading as counterpoint to the positive attitude expressed here towards behavioural genetics.

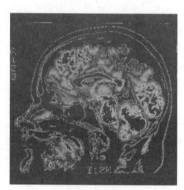

An MRI scan (see page 13) of the human head (vertical section), showing the structure of the brain

Neuropsychology

The human brain is a remarkable organ. It is composed of a huge number of interconnected nerve cells or neurones, which send electrical messages to each other across gaps called synapses using chemical messengers, called neurotransmitters. The brain is responsible for all cognitive processes, and can cope with more information than the most advanced computers (see Chapter 3 for a discussion of information processing in the brain).

A detailed discussion of the brain is not within the scope of this chapter. However, we will look at some of the methods used to study the brain and focus in detail on two ways in which human psychology is powerfully affected by the biological functioning of the brain – bodily rhythms and sleep.

Techniques for studying the brain

Electroencephalogram (EEG) recording

An *electroencephalograph* is a machine which records brain-waves, i.e. the patterns of electrical activity in the brain. It detects the activity of groups of neurones, as the output of one cell is too small to measure. The recordings are taken from participants using *macroelectrodes* stuck to the scalp with conductive jelly; they are very sensitive, detecting signals of only 0.00001 V. A neutral electrode (usually on the earlobe) completes the electrical circuit. Signals from each electrode are amplified, displayed on a screen and printed out, as an *electro-en-cephalo-gram* (electric-in-head-writing) or EEG. The wires from each electrode can be held together, forming a pony tail, to enable the participant to sleep. The recording consists of a rising and falling trace from each electrode or group of electrodes (see the example below), which change in terms of the frequency and amplitude of waves.

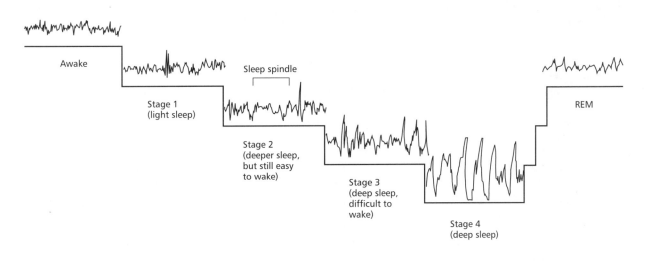

An EEG trace showing brain activity recorded when awake and in different stages of sleep (see page 20)

Electrooculogram (EOG) recording

One of the major applications of electrical techniques like EEG has been in recording patterns of brain-waves in sleep. The *electrooculogram* or EOG is also used to study sleep, taking advantage of the fact that when we dream our eyeballs move. The EOG records the electrical potential across the eyeball (rather than muscular activity) which changes as the eyeballs rotate. The movements of our eyes tend to be synchronised, but it is usual to record from both eyes. The EOG is used to detect the rapid eye movement (REM) associated with dream sleep but identifies only changes in movement, not the direction. Since the movement of the eyeballs under the lids can be readily seen, the direction of eye movements can be observed directly or via video.

for and against

electrical recording techniques

+ Measuring brain-waves has allowed us to distinguish between different states of consciousness and stages of sleep, and given us reliable information on the relative levels of brain activity in these different states.

– Electrical techniques provide clues from which we can only infer activity in the brain. We cannot see directly everything that takes place, for example we cannot electrically track a thought.

Lesioning and ablation

The action of brain areas on sleep and dreaming can be investigated by observing changes in behaviour when parts of the central nervous system (CNS) are destroyed. *Ablation* means to carry away and is used to refer to the removal or destruction of neural tissue, by suction, heat (cauterisation) or surgery. A *lesion* is a cut through a neural tract or region, which separates it from other brain areas. An early study involving lesioning comes from Hetherington and Ranson (1939), who lesioned part of the hypothalamus of a rat and observed that it ate until it had trebled its body weight.

Clearly there are good reasons why we cannot use lesioning or ablation techniques in human participants. It causes irreparable damage! This

for and against

lesioning and ablation

+ Ablation and lesioning can be carried out on live animals (*vivisection*) to observe their effects on the sleep–wake cycle.

+ Ablation and lesioning enable us to identify the regions of the brain responsible for different aspects of sleep control.

– The control of sleep in animals may not be identical to that of humans.

– The sleep state is in part a subjective experience, which animals cannot report.

– Vivisection is invasive and causes suffering to the animal subjects.

type of study is always carried out on animals. However, sometimes lesions occur as a result of strokes or injury and neuropsychologists can study the effects of lesions in particular parts of the brain.

Scanning techniques

There are now a variety of techniques that produce images of sections of the human body. Such techniques have many medical applications but they have become best known for brain-scanning. There are two broad categories of brain scan – *structural* and *functional*.

- **Structural imaging** techniques include *computerised axial tomography* (CAT) and *magnetic resonance imaging* (MRI). These produce images of sections of the brain, either on a slide or a TV monitor and these appear as if we have cut through the brain and taken a photograph. An example of an MRI image is shown on page 10.

  CAT and MRI work in quite different ways. CAT scans take x-ray photographs from several angles and these 'slices' are then computer-assembled into a single image. MRI scanning uses a powerful magnetic field instead of x-rays to produce a series of images that are likewise assembled by computer into an image. MRI is capable of producing much clearer images than CAT. MRI and CAT are of some value to psychologists because they allow us to compare the structure of brains that are functioning normally and abnormally and hence help to establish whether a physical abnormality is responsible for a symptom.

- **Functional imaging** techniques are often more useful to psychologists because they allow us to visualise events that are actually happening in the brain. *Positron emission tomography* (PET) scanning involves injecting a radioactive isotope into the blood. This ceases to be radioactive quickly and so does not harm the participant. However, by measuring the radiation levels in different parts of the brain we can determine where the most blood is flowing to and hence which parts are most active. If the participant is performing a particular task at the time, this tells us what parts of the brain are involved.

  A difficulty with PET scanning is that many tasks cannot be performed whilst in a scanner. One way around this is to use SPET (*single photon emission tomography*). This also involves a radioactive isotope entering the blood, but the difference is that once this type of isotope enters brain tissue it becomes trapped for some time. We can thus give someone a task in a suitable environment and scan them later.

for and against

scanning techniques

+ Structural scans can be used to identify abnormalities in the brain, and to link particular brain abnormalities with particular psychological problems.

+ Functional scans can give us some idea of how the brain functions.

− Currently scanning techniques are not sufficiently refined to tell us as precisely as we would like what is going on in the brain. We cannot for example track a thought through the brain.

where to now?

The following are good sources of further information regarding techniques for studying the brain:

▶ **Stirling, J. (1999)** *Cortical Functions*. **London: Routledge** – a clear and simple account of all the methods described here for studying the brain

▶ **Carlson, N. (1997)** *The Physiology of Behaviour*. **New York: Allyn & Bacon** – an advanced undergraduate text which covers the major methods of studying the brain in great detail.

Biological rhythms

An extra-terrestrial looking at the rush hour traffic would observe a profound daily rhythm. Each morning Earthlings move around, apparently randomly, then come to rest. This activity is repeated at dusk. Why should this be? Many physiological and behavioural responses of animals are controlled by a regular cycle of bodily changes. These bodily rhythms may be endogenous, dictated by internal events, or exogenous, controlled by external events. More commonly, control is exerted by interaction of the two factors.

Cyclical changes occurring more often than daily are described as *ultradian* rhythms (*ultra* = more [often than once per] *dies* = day). Our heart beat, for instance, is an ultradian rhythm and like other functions it is affected both intrinsically, by the pace-maker, and by external factors, such as air quality or exercise. Similar rhythmicity can be seen in psychological functions, such as appetite and awareness. Cyclical changes occurring over the course of periods longer than one day are called *infradian* rhythms. In this chapter we are most concerned with *circadian* rhythms, those that last about one day.

Circadian rhythms

Our most familiar behavioural rhythm is the sleep–wake cycle, that repetitive programme which insists that we go to sleep each night and wake up the next day, raves notwithstanding. Whilst we can 'lie in', we can't make ourselves stay asleep indefinitely, nor can we stay endlessly awake. Our patterned sleeping and waking runs on a *circadian* rhythm, one which lasts *circa-dies*, about a day (hence, circadian).

Tied to our 24-hour sleep–wake cycle is a rhythmical variation in awareness. When our body clock expects us to be asleep, our cognitive processing reaches a trough. Between 1 a.m. and 6 a.m. our sensitivity to pain, manual dexterity and reaction time bottom out, regardless of whether we are sleep-deprived. So 4 a.m. might seem an ideal time to visit your dentist, but will they be safe? Some important consequences of our reduced task performance during the small hours relate to safety, on the road and in the workplace. These applications are considered on page 29. Other circadian rhythms are exhibited in behaviours such as eating, drinking and the metabolism of alcohol.

In addition to changes in awareness and cognitive functioning, people also experience daily rhythms in emotions. Totterdell (1995) tested mood fluctuations in 30 healthy participants over 14 days, recording mood every two hours. He found that the participants showed a circadian variation in cheerfulness and depression. This was more marked in participants who had higher levels of psychological distress.

Our circadian rhythms regulate behaviours such as sleeping and waking. By affecting the activity of neurotransmitters such as noradrenalin and serotonin in a cyclical way, the daily pattern of sleeping and waking is precisely regulated. In the typical day, sleep onset coincides with the absence of daylight, but even without this external cue the desire to sleep arises regularly. What happens to this cycle without exposure to daylight? Studies have been conducted with participants isolated from natural light–dark schedules in caves or in more comfortable experimental rooms (where they have exposure to light on demand, are able to request food or old newspapers at any time of day and can sleep whenever they like). Findings from such experiments suggest that the human biological clock maintains rhythmical activity but that the apparent day length extends (Czeisler *et al.*, 1989).

Experimental evidence with rats confirms this shift in circadian cycle. Groblewski *et al.* (1980) found that rats' circadian clocks advanced an hour a day if they were isolated from daylight schedules. In such isolation experiments with humans, participants maintain 'daily' activities but as with rats these begin to *free run* with a periodicity of about 25–30 hours instead of the normal 24. Daily exposure to bright light or to regular social cues such as a telephone call at the same time each day is sufficient to keep the human clock in time (Empson, 1993). Environmental factors other than light can also entrain (that is, set) the clocks of animals such as hamsters. They will maintain a 24-hour sleep–wake cycle without light cues in response to regular feeding (Jilge, 1991), exercise (Mistleberger, 1991) or social interaction (Mrosovsky, 1988).

Control of circadian rhythms

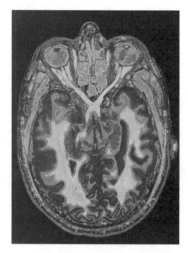

A section through the human brain. The SCN is located just above the point where the optic nerves cross

What controls a circadian rhythm such that it assumes a 24-hour cycle? Both internal and external factors seem to be involved. The most obvious cue to set the cycle, the *zeitgeber* (German for time-giver), is day length – the sun rises and sets every 24 hours. How do we process this external cue so that it can affect our behaviour? In humans, information about ambient light levels is passed from the eye to an area of the brain called the *suprachiasmatic nucleus* or SCN (a clump of cells in the hypothalamus) and then to the pineal gland. Evidence suggests that these structures are responsible for the control of circadian rhythms.

The role of the suprachiasmatic nucleus

Rats which have been blinded lose their periodic behaviour. They sleep for the same amount of time in total but they no longer have a clearly defined sleep phase. This confirms that visual information 'sets' the pattern but it would appear that once the cycle is established, it is self-perpetuating. Rats are nocturnal so, given an activity wheel, will run at night. This activity can be automatically recorded providing continuous data about periodic behaviour. Groblewski *et al.* (1980) kept rats under artificial illumination. Initially the lights were on for 12 hours during the day and the rats ran at night. When the lighting schedule was shifted so that the 12 hour light phase occurred six hours later in the day, the rats began to run later, stabilising their 'nocturnal' activity six hours later than previously. Finally, the rats were exposed to continuous light, but their patterned activity persisted. When allowed to free-run in this manner, however, their clocks ran a little slow, extending their day to 25 hours instead of the customary 24.

Miles *et al.* (1977) reported a case study of a young man who was blind from birth and had a circadian rhythm of 24.9 hours. He experienced considerable difficulties trying to keep in step with a 24-hour schedule, even with continual use of stimulants (in the morning) and sedatives (at night). This evidence, and that of Groblewski *et al.*, suggest that, whilst light 'sets the clock', i.e. acts as a *zeitgeber*, it is not essential for the maintenance of the cycle. So what internal mechanism maintains the endogenous rhythm once it is established?

Lesions of the SCN in animals abolish regularity in various behaviours such as drinking and activity (Stephan and Zucker, 1972). Ralph *et al.* (1990) confirmed the role of the SCN in the sleep–wake cycle by transplanting the SCN between hamsters with different 'free-running' clocks. First they transplanted the SCN from foetuses of a mutant strain of hamsters with free-running clocks of 20 hours, into the brains of normal adult hamsters whose cycles had been disrupted by lesions. Instead of reverting to their old 25-hour rhythm, the adult recipients assumed a new 20-hour 'day'. Likewise a second transplant, of SCN from adults free-running at 25 hours into animals of the mutant strain, produced individuals with a new cycle of 25 hours. It would appear that the circadian rhythm is intrinsic to the SCN.

The process by which the SCN generates its rhythm is, as yet, unclear. Assumptions that cycles result from interactions between neurones is opposed by the finding that circadian rhythms can be maintained by individual neurones. Michel *et al.* (1993) discovered that even isolated neurones from the eye of a marine mollusc (*Bulla gouldiana*) could display circadian changes in biochemical activity. This implies that endogenous rhythms may arise from cellular processes, rather than from neural interactions. This would be unsurprising given the endogenous rhythms demonstrated by cells within cardiac muscle which are myogenic – they generate their own rhythmic contraction.

The role of the pineal gland and melatonin release

The SCN responds to day length with neural messages to the *pineal gland* (Arendt, 1985). This small gland is part of the endocrine (hormonal) system but is tucked up inside the brain behind the hypothalamus and is insensitive to light. The cells of the pineal gland do, however, share characteristics with the rod-shaped photoreceptors of the retina, suggesting that its original role was as a light sensitive organ. Darkness causes the pineal gland to secrete the hormone *melatonin*, whilst daylight inhibits its production. As day length shortens towards winter, night-time excretion of melatonin increases, thus acting as an annual as well as a circadian clock. Surprisingly, the absence of light does not prevent cycling. Even in uninterrupted light or darkness melatonin levels continue to rise and fall daily. The absence of light as a *zeitgeber* does, however, cause the rhythm to 'free run' (usually at a slightly longer day length). Destruction of the SCN, in contrast, does prevent cycling. Melatonin is important in regulating the sleep–wake cycle. It also plays a role in determining our mood. We shall return to the latter issue later in this chapter when we look at seasonal affective disorder.

research
now

does early to bed, early to rise really make you healthy, wealthy and wise?

Roberts, R.D. and Kyllonen, P.C. (1999) Morningness-eveningness and intelligence: early to bed, early to rise will make you anything but wise! *Personality and Individual Differences*, 27, 1123–33

Aim: There has long been a popular belief that people who like to get up early in the morning are in some way advantaged as compared to individuals who prefer to get up later and continue working later. This belief is captured in the saying 'early to bed, early to rise makes you healthy, wealthy and wise'. This study was not concerned with health or wealth, but it did investigate the association between intelligence and preferences for early or late rising.

Method: A quasi-experimental design was used, in which the IQ of 'morning types' and 'evening types' was compared. Researchers asked 420 United States Air Force recruits, the majority of whom were women, to complete two questionnaires designed to measure their circadian rhythms. Participants were classified on the basis of these questionnaires as one of two *diurnal types*, called 'morning types' and 'evening types.' Morning types were identified as individuals who woke early and liked to get up and begin the day's activities early, being most active in the morning. Evening types, by contrast, rose later and were at their most active in the evening. Participants also completed two different IQ tests, the Cognitive Abilities Measurement (CAM) and the Armed Services Vocational Aptitude Battery (ASVAB), in order to assess their intelligence. The IQ of the two groups (morning types and evening types) was compared.

Results: A significant difference emerged between the intelligence of the 'morning' and 'evening' types. The evening group emerged as significantly higher in IQ than the morning group.

Conclusion: Based on these results, it appears that evening types are brighter than morning types. This is in direct contrast to popular stereotypes. The authors suggested a number of possible explanations for the results. One idea was that the ability to work in the evenings showed adaptability because of the extra difficulties involved, such as working in artificial light.

Sleep and dreaming

Sleep can be defined as a necessary state of altered consciousness experienced by animals with a central nervous system. It is characterised by rhythmical occurrence, limited sensitivity and reduced mobility. By its very nature, sleep is therefore difficult to study. What's it like to be asleep? It's a bit difficult to say, because as soon as I can reply to the question, I'm no longer sleeping. How can we find out about a state which is distinguished by a lack of awareness of and interaction with our surroundings?

After centuries of guesswork, psychologists can now use increasing powerful techniques to investigate some of the biological aspects of sleep.

Sleep reduces our sensory and motor functions, but alters our state of consciousness

Rhythms in sleep

A night's sleep is a well orchestrated sequence of psychological and physical changes. In general, we sleep once during each 24-hour period, a circadian rhythm. This is not, however, a single homogenous phase. Our sleep is broken into shorter, repeated rhythms during the night, called ultradian rhythms. This patterned activity has been traced using the methods previously described.

Asterinsky and Kleitman (1955) recorded the EEGs of sleeping participants and found that they sometimes consisted of *alpha* waves, resembling wakefulness. During these times the EOG was active, as it is when we are awake. Participants in this condition were hard to awaken but when roused they tended to report dreams. This 'paradoxical' stage, which shares characteristics with both very deep sleep and with wakefulness, was identified as a separate stage of sleep by Dement and Kleitman (1957). It has been variously described as *paradoxical sleep*, *dream sleep* or *REM sleep*, after the characteristic rapid eye movements (40–60 movements per minute) which occur throughout the stage. REM sleep is also identifiable by the loss of muscle tone, measured by an electromyogram (EMG). So while the EOG is active during REM sleep, the EMG is inactive; our bodies are effectively paralysed.

Most of the night is spent in 'orthodox' or non-REM (*nREM*) sleep. Even this, however, is not a homogeneous phase, but consists of four stages:

- **stage 1:** light sleep, where the sleeper is easily roused, has a slow heart rate and an irregular EEG, with little alpha activity

- **stage 2:** deeper sleep, where the sleeper is still fairly easy to wake. The EEG is interrupted by occasional *spindles* (high frequency low amplitude waves) and *K complexes* (occasional high amplitude waves)

- **stage 3:** deep sleep, where the sleeper is unresponsive, has a slow pulse, low blood pressure and a lowered body temperature. The EEG contains some slow waves (low frequency delta waves)

- **stage 4:** deep sleep, where the EEG consists mainly of high amplitude, low frequency *delta waves*.

The diagram below shows how we move from relaxed wakefulness into sleep and then through deeper sleep stages before returning through shallower nREM to reach our first REM phase. We then alternate between REM and nREM during the night. Several patterns can be seen in recordings from sleeping participants:

- the deepest sleep occurs early in the night

- REM phases increase in length during the night

- natural waking tends to occur during REM

- each 'cycle' from stage 1 back to stage 1 or REM takes about 90 minutes (an ultradian rhythm).

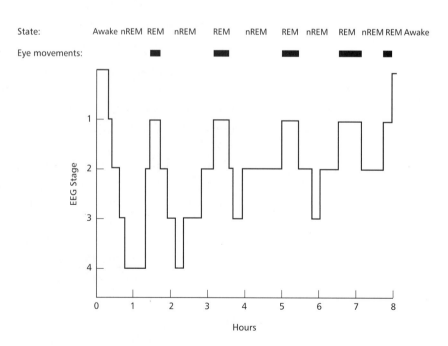

The stages of sleep

The nature of dream sleep

Paradoxical sleep is readily identifiable by changes in the EEG (to alpha waves) and the EOG (REMs), paralysis and a number of other changes. During REM sleep our pulse, respiration and blood pressure become irregular, and we are more likely to grind our teeth! The most psychologically interesting aspect of this stage of sleep, however, is our experience of dreams. Everyone has dreams, but we only recall them if we happen to wake up, even briefly, during REM. People who 'don't dream' simply always wake up in nREM and may have poor visual memories (Cory et al., 1975). On average, sleepers recall just over one dream a night, but this can vary between one every six months and three a night (Koulack and Goodenough, 1976).

To study dream content, participants may either be asked to keep a dream diary or to sleep overnight in a sleep laboratory. Here, a room within a psychology department is fitted with a bed and equipment to monitor the sleeping participant. They may be videoed or watched and may be interrupted during the night to test responses to stimuli and to answer questions. Dement (1978) woke participants when they were either in REM or in nREM sleep. Those in REM reported dreams on 80 per cent of occasions, those in nREM on only 15 per cent of the wakings. Dream reports from participants woken during nREM sleep were less visual and vivid and were described as 'thinking' rather than as active 'dreams'. The differences described between REM and nREM dreams are believed by Beaumont (1988) to be the due to the additional time it takes people to awaken from nREM sleep. When participants are slower to wake up they may forget more dream details.

An interesting question concerns why we remember so little about our dreams. Freud (1900), as we will see later, believed that we actively forget our dreams in order to protect ourselves from their content; this is the *repression hypothesis*. However, Reinsel et al. (1986) suggest that we actually recall emotional dreams better because they make more impact upon us. This enhanced memory for emotional dreams is called the *salience hypothesis*, suggesting that we forget dreams with unemotional content. Alternatively, we may fail to recall dreams because events which occur as we wake up, provide a source of interference. This *interference hypothesis* is supported by the observation that sudden awakening produces better dream recall than gradual awakening.

Ask someone to shut their eyes and pretend they are an umpire watching a tennis match. You should be able to see their eyes moving from side to side. In a classic study, Dement and Kleitman (1957) observed sleeping participants' REMs and woke them to ask about their dream content.

classic research

what do eye movements tell us about dreams?

Dement, W. and Kleitman, N. (1957) The relation of eye movements during sleep to dream activity: an objective method for the study of dreaming. *Journal of Experimental Psychology*, 53 (5), 339–46

Aim: Researchers were interested in the relationship of dream content and the REMs observed during periods of dreaming. There was a secondary aim of the study – to establish whether dreams take place in real-time, or whether they are condensed into a shorter period, as is popularly thought.

Method: Seven volunteers, five men and two women, took part in the experiment. Each participant turned up at the sleep laboratory shortly before their bedtime. They had instructions not to consume any drugs such as alcohol or coffee because these tend to reduce REM sleep. Each participant then went to bed in a dark, quiet room. A EEG and an EOG were run for the entire period of sleep. At a series of times during the night the participants were awakened by means of a bell, both from REM and quiet sleep. When awakened they were instructed to describe the nature of their most recent dream into a tape recorder. They were then allowed to go back to sleep. Participants were given no feedback about what period of sleep they had been awakened from. In order to see how closely the REMs corresponded with dream content the participants were woken following particularly distinctive eye movements. The researchers examined the accounts of dreams and the recordings of brain and eye activity, and looked for associations.

Results: Many more dreams were reported when participants were woken from REM sleep than nREM sleep. There was a significant correlation between the length of periods of REM and the length of the dreams reported by the participants. Participants were fairly accurate in estimating the length of their dreams. This was important because it indicated that the dreams were experienced in real-time. Of particular interest was a strong association between the distinctive eye movements noted and the content of dreams. For example one participant had a minute of very little eye movement followed by several large movements to the left. Their dream was of driving down the street and being crashed into by a car coming from the left. Another had been seen to have only vertical movements (as in looking up and down), and their dream was of climbing up and down ladders.

Conclusion: The results show that people dream in real-time, and that their REMs are closely related to the content of their dreams. The most fundamental finding was that people dream much more often and more vividly in REM sleep than in nREM sleep.

Oswald (1980) compared the dreams and REMs of six men, three who had been blind from birth and three who had been blind for three, ten and 15 years respectively. The previously sighted participants all 'saw' things in their dreams and had REMs. Those blind from birth had non-visual dreams but did have very slight REMs. This could suggest that REM is not related to dream content, since there could be no match to visual content.

Theories of the function of sleep

Empson (1993) suggests that a sleepless alien would (quite reasonably) conclude from the household space, furniture, rituals and time we devote to sleep, that for Earthlings this particular form of inactivity was a central preoccupation! Natural selection would only result in the evolution of a behaviour so dangerous and time-consuming as sleep if its benefits outweighed its costs. There are considerable costs associated with sleeping: we spend time asleep when we could be eating or reproducing and, because of the lowered level of sensitivity, we are at greater risk from the weather, competitors or predators. So what are the potential benefits which have made sleeping an evolutionarily worthwhile investment?

Ecological theory

According to ecological theory, the dormouse sleeps by day when it would otherwise be easy prey

Meddis (1977) argued that sleep is an instinctive behaviour which has evolved to keep animals 'out of trouble'. For humans, being out in the dark is dangerous, so we sleep at night. Cats and owls, on the other hand, have better night vision than us and can gain an advantage over their prey in the cover of darkness. They sleep during the day when their chances of successful hunting are lower. It is beneficial for small desert mammals to avoid the intense heat so they sleep during the day. In each case sleep occurs when the animal is least effective. Empson (1993) has described this as the 'waste of time' theory; animals are simply biding their time until the environment is more suitable.

The absence of motor activity during sleep can be accounted for by the ecological theory. Whilst 'keeping still' could explain the advantage of saving energy, being utterly inactive is even better: a motionless animal is less likely to attract the attention of predators. This can be extended to explain the reduction in sensitivity. For animals which rely on camouflage or concealment for protection, keeping completely motionless even when a predator is very near will lower the chances of detection. Being asleep ensures that the animal won't respond and blow its cover. It could even be argued that the reduction in brain activity ensures that the hiding animal is not motivated to seek out sources of stimulation.

If we wish to explain the existence of sleep through evolutionary adaptation, we need to be able to demonstrate that it has a long and common evolutionary history. Reptiles, believed to be the ancestors of modern birds and mammals, show various characteristics of sleep. Lizards display unequivocal signs of nREM and REM sleep, with loss of muscle tone and rapid eye movements (Tauber *et al.*, 1968), whilst in other reptiles REM sleep alone is seen. This observation may help to explain the appearance of REM sleep before nREM sleep in the human foetus. In embryological development, characteristics generally appear in phylogenetic (ancestral) sequence. Birds and mammals, which maintain a warm body temperature, have very similar nREM and REM sleep (Empson, 1993).

for and against

ecological theory

+ Ecological theory can explain why different species sleep at different times of day.

+ Ecological theory can account for the reduction of movement and sensitivity during sleep.

– Ecological theory cannot explain why there is such a huge variation in sleep requirement between species. Nor can it account for the absolute necessity to sleep, even when this is apparently maladaptive. The porpoise, for instance, sleeps with each brain hemisphere alternately (Mukhametov *et al.*, 1977).

+ Ecological theory can explain the reduction in cognitive activity during sleep.

– Ecological theory cannot explain other observations about sleep such as the cycles within sleep or the existence and content of dreams.

Restorational theory

Restorational theory, proposed by Oswald (1969), suggests that we need to sleep in order to conduct growth and repair functions. The processes of restoration and activity are mutually exclusive; we cannot 'recharge our batteries' whilst we are still running off them. Oswald (1980) reports that high levels of ATP, the energy currency of the cell, are only found during sleep as during wakefulness we are constantly using up the ATP. This is especially so for the brain; it represents only 5 per cent of our body weight but uses 20 per cent of our energy. This suggests that a special state of enforced quiescence may be needed to allow brain cells to recuperate from daytime activity. Enforced inactivity and insensitivity during sleep reduces the energy demands of the brain making ATP available for restoration. The same cannot be achieved by simply resting; the energy cost of sleeping is only about two-thirds of that at rest.

Bodily inactivity during REM sleep may be important for restoration of muscles. Adam (1977) found a correlation between the weight of participants and the time they spent in REM sleep; heavier people spent longer in REM sleep. This is perhaps because heavier participants would expend more energy maintaining posture and moving during the day, so would need more time to restore their muscles at night. More recently, Shapiro *et al.* (1986) have shown that body weight also correlates positively with time in nREM sleep. Zepelin and Rechtschaffen (1974) found a similar relationship between the activity levels of different animal species and the time they spent asleep.

Sleep deprivation and restoration

One way to test directly the restorational function of sleep is to deprive people of sleep and observe the effects. Systematic sleep deprivation experiments suggest that humans begin to suffer after relatively short periods of sleep deprivation. Dement (1960) deprived young volunteers of REM or nREM sleep on five successive nights. The REM sleep deprived participants became irritable, nervous, unable to concentrate and some reported hallucinations. When allowed uninterrupted sleep these individuals fell straight into REM sleep and spent up to 60 per cent more time in REM sleep; this is called a REM *rebound effect*. Similar effects have reported during total sleep deprivation such as experienced by Peter Tripp, a disc jockey who kept himself awake for 200 hours during a charity broadcast. Luce and Segal (1966) describe the decline in his cognitive ability and emotional stability, including his experiences of hallucinations and extreme paranoia.

Dement (1965) concluded that the severe effects of sleep deprivation reported in early research resulted from *experimenter effects*; the participants were expected to suffer bizarre sensations and these were duly reported. When warned of potential side effects and offered a round-the-clock psychiatrist, to whom unusual sensations could be reported, demand characteristics alone could have accounted for the hallucinations and paranoia experienced. More recent research suggests that even prolonged sleep deprivation, whilst reducing efficiency and concentration, has no more serious effects than to make the participants sleepy! (Webb and Cartwright, 1978)

The current *Guinness Book of Records* 'longest time without sleep' record is held by Robert McDonald, who stayed awake for over 453 hours in a rocking chair marathon in 1988. He could, however, have slept momentarily without being noticed. A previous holder, 17-year-old Randy Gardener, was closely observed by Gulevich *et al.* (1966). He showed none of the problems exhibited by other sleep-deprived participants other than sleepiness, successfully beating Dement at 100 straight games on a baseball machine on his first sleepless night! Following his 264-hour sleep deprivation, he slept for 15 hours and awoke feeling quite normal.

Sleep deprivation in animals can be maintained for much longer periods and the physical effects are much more severe. Early experiments were hindered by the confounding variable of forced exercise; it is necessary to keep the animal moving in order to keep it awake. Rechtschaffen *et al.* (1983) overcame this difficulty by designing a piece of apparatus in which pairs of animals could be housed and would experience identical exercise demands. One of the animals would be sleep deprived, the other not, so providing a well-matched control.

Some recent research has revived the interest in the negative effects of sleep deprivation. Maquet *et al.* (1997) studied the blood flow to different regions of the brain during sleep (using PET), as an indicator of which areas were most active. They found that the areas which were least active were the orbitofrontal cortex and the cingulate cortex, two regions involved in emotional behaviour, thus implying there may be some physiological basis for the effects of sleep deprivation on emotional stability. Studying the emotional responses of participants in experimental settings is, however, confounded by the novelty of the setting. This study can be further criticised in its exclusive use of male participants.

for and against

restorative theory

+ Growth hormone is released at night but only if we enter deep sleep. Growth hormone increases the level of protein synthesis and cell division. Growth hormone for children with stunted growth is more effective if injected at night than in the morning.

+ Restoration theory accounts for the cyclical nature of sleep as we cannot persist without regular restoration.

+ Athletes spend more time in deep sleep following intensive exercise.

+ Drug overdoses, withdrawal, brain damage or intensive ECT increase the time in REM sleep during which damaged brain tissue could be repaired.

− Restorative theory cannot account for our preference for sleeping at night.

− Restorative theory cannot explain the presence or content of dreams during sleep.

Theories of dreaming

'To sleep, perchance to dream' wrote Shakespeare. Perhaps the role of sleep is to dream, to provide a theatre for the mind. Certainly evidence from deprivation experiments suggest that REM sleep is essential. Participants deprived of sleep show a *REM rebound*, i.e. they spend proportionally more time in REM sleep when they next have the opportunity. In

Chapter 5 we will look at Freud's psychological theory of dreaming (see page 141). In this chapter we are concerned with physiological explanations.

Reorganisational theory

Reorganisational theories offer to the mind what restorational theories offer to the body, a chance to recuperate from the past day's activities and prepare for the next. Crick and Mitchison (1986) proposed a neurobiological theory of reorganisation. They suggested that dreams are the result of the random firing of neural networks (groups of neurones connected by synapses) which hold memories. These memories can be elicited by activating any part of the network (rather in the way that a spider can detect prey caught on any part of its web). The random activation serves to *debug* the networks, removing unwanted connections. 'Nonsense' in a network could obscure or interfere with essential information so removing waste and would increase the clarity of remaining memories. This is described as reverse learning, storage of important information is enhanced by the removal of cognitive debris. This is particularly important when neural nets become overloaded, because concepts which share a single feature are likely to become conflated, linked together by mistake. Debugging removes such 'parasitic associations'.

The purpose of Crick and Mitchison's debugging is to increase efficiency of brain function so it would be expected that failure to debug would impair learning. This prediction is supported by studies of sleep, and particularly REM, deprivation. Rideout (1979) tested the maze learning ability of sleep-deprived mice. Three deprivation conditions (total sleep, REM or nREM deprivation) were compared to non-sleep-deprived mice. Mice deprived of REM sleep, either selectively or by total sleep deprivation, were equally bad at maze learning compared to nREM or undeprived animals.

Smith (1995, 1996) has conducted a series of experiments with rats and human participants investigating the effects of learning on REM sleep requirements. Rats which learned to respond to a light and avoid an electric shock spent more time than usual in REM sleep. If they were deprived of REM sleep for four hours immediately after training, they only remembered the response half as well as those that slept normally. If the sleep deprivation was delayed for more than 20 hours after training, the rats showed no decrement in learning. They seemed to need the REM sleep in order to consolidate their memories.

In research with students, Smith found that in the week after revising for exams, requirement for REM sleep increased. In tests on REM sleep deprivation, memory for cognitive-procedural tasks was particularly affected. For instance, learning of logical puzzles, where symbols had to be manipulated according to arbitrary rules, was impaired by REM deprivation but memorising of paired lists of words was not.

A real-life investigation into the effects of sleep deprivation on learning is afforded by observations of junior doctors expected to work long hospital shifts without sleep. In casualty, doctors are required to listen to patients (who may be incoherent), extract medically relevant facts and memorise them in order to make accurate diagnoses. Deary and Tait (1987) studied medical house doctors who obtained an average of 1.5 hours sleep per night whilst on emergency admissions. When tested on memory tasks designed to measure the skills required for effective work, doctors on duty performed significantly worse than those off duty.

Experimental investigation with human participants also suggests that REM sleep is essential for learning. Herman and Roffwarg (1983) generated a novel task by asking participants to wear inverting goggles (which cause the world to appear upside down). Following this experience, the participants spent more time than usual in REM sleep. Tilley and Empson (1978) asked participants to memorise a ghost story before going to sleep. By detecting each participant's sleep stage with an EEG and waking them up when they entered the chosen stage, some participants were deprived of REM sleep, others of stage 4 sleep. The participants deprived of REM sleep had far poorer recall for the story in the morning.

for and against

reorganisational theory

+ Studies have confirmed that cognitive functioning is impaired when people are deprived of REM sleep.

− Crick and Mitchison's theory does not explain why dreams are such an intense subjective experience or why they hold so much personal meaning for dreamers.

where to now?

The following are good sources of further information about bodily rhythms, sleep and dreams:

▶ **Bentley, E. (1999)** *Awareness*. **London: Routledge** – an extremely clear and comprehensible introductory text, covering all the above areas in detail

▶ **McIlveen, R. and Gross, R. (1998)** *Biopsychology*. **London: Hodder & Stoughton** – a broader text, covering several areas of the biological approach to psychology.

real lives

The effects of shift work and jetlag

Shift work

When we are working 'out of phase' with our biological clocks our performance is reduced, we are less attentive and are slower to respond regardless of whether we have slept (Mitler, 1988). Moore-Ede (1993) reports that prior to the ill-fated decision to fly the Challenger, NASA officials had been awake for 20 hours after only two or three hours sleep the night before. Fatigue is a possible contributory factor in many disasters; consider those listed in Table 1.3, and the time of day when they occurred.

Place	Disaster	Time disaster occurred
Bhopal	Chemical plant explosion	12.40 a.m.
Chernobyl	Nuclear reactor disaster	1.23 a.m.
Three Mile Island	Nuclear reactor disaster	4.00 a.m.
Mexico City	Western Airlines crash	3.30 a.m.

Table 1.3 Some examples of disasters caused by human error by shiftworkers

Lorry drivers, like doctors, the police and many employees, have to work shifts. Two independent problems arise with shift work: the need to maintain a 24-hour cycle which is out-of-sync with the world and the demands of changing shift pattern. People working shifts are often sleep-deprived simply because it is difficult to sleep well when it is light and noisy outside. The social constraints of being awake when no one else is may tempt night shift workers to get up early or stay up late for company or facilities, depriving themselves of sleep. To solve the problem of being woken up by daylight, shift workers are recommended to use thick curtains or blackout blinds. These also help to solve the second problem of circadian disruption.

In order to work shifts, people have to reset their biological clock, so that they are awake during the late evening and/or early morning and sleep during the day. Unless workers succeed in resetting their biological clock, they experience sleepiness at work and insomnia when they go home. This is particularly severe if shifts change often, or if they move 'against' the body clock. After a shift change people take a week or more to adapt to the new regime, during which time they are less effective at work as they are operating during their body's 'night' and restless when they should be sleeping.

Many workers on night shift are performing passive tasks such as monitoring and are often provided with warm, dimly lit environments.

According to Czeisler *et al.* (1990) this is counterproductive to keeping them alert. They compared the rate of adaptation of two groups of participants to an imposed 'shift change' by asking them to report to the laboratory during the night and sleep at home during the day. The control group worked during the night in ordinary indoor lighting of about 150 lux. The experimental group worked under bright illumination of 7,000–12,000 lux, equivalent to early morning light. The experimental group were also asked to stay in complete darkness from 9 a.m. to 5 p.m., whilst the controls were given no specific instructions. The resetting of the participants' biological clocks was monitored by measuring body temperature, which varies rhythmically. After six days the experimental group had all shifted the low point of the circadian temperature rhythm by 10 hours, the controls had moved by only one hour. A similar pattern was observed in task performance. Bright lighting in the work environment seems to be a key to ensuring that workers adapt to new shifts so that they sleep well during the day and are alert during the night. Even in this situation adaptation can take up to four days, so people who change shift every week would spend most of their time desynchronised from their environment.

Jet lag

Air travel has introduced another problem for our internal clocks resulting in fatigue, gastrointestinal complaints and shortened attention span which cannot be explained by sleep loss alone. When we cross time zones we have to reset our biological clock to the local *zeitgeber* – sunrise and sunset. As with shift changes which extend the day, travelling east to west produces fewer problems, as we 'gain' time. The return journey however presents problems. Pilots can be severely affected by changing time zones repeatedly, due to frequent and erratic exposure to the bright light of sunrise. This causes them to sleep poorly when they can rest, resulting in tiredness when flying.

Harma *et al.* (1994a,b) and Suvanto *et al.* (1993) examined the effects of a four-day flight, which crossed 10 time zones, on the sleep, attentiveness, body temperature and salivary melatonin levels of flight attendants. Forty female participants logged their subjective sleepiness and sleep quality each day. Their alertness, visual task performance, melatonin level and body temperature were monitored every two hours. They found that the participants became increasingly sleepy over the four days and experienced poorer sleep quality, but pre-flight patterns resumed quickly after their return. Measures of attention indicated that their cognitive skills were also controlled by an endogenous rhythm, although these responses shifted rapidly to new time zones. The rhythm of melatonin secretion and body temperature had delayed by almost four hours after the westward flight out but after four days of travelling these two measures had desynchronised. Body temperature was faster to resynchronise than the melatonin secretion rhythm.

Recent research suggests that light may not be the most important *zeitgeber* in adjustment to new time zones. Amir and Stewart (1996) have shown that rats who receive a breeze before their light phase can reset their clocks by a change in the time of the breeze alone. For people there may be many contingent signals which help to maintain our circadian rhythm which are absent when we travel abroad, for example the sound of birds in the morning, the time we eat or TV programmes. Whereas light schedules exist everywhere, other aspects of our regulated lives are harder to transport, particularly if we are on holiday. These factors may contribute to the slow rate at which we adapt to new time zones. The simplest way to combat the effects of a long-haul eastbound flight is to start going to bed and getting up progressively earlier before you travel.

We all experience a minor version of jet lag each time the clocks change between Greenwich Mean Time (GMT) and British Summer Time (BST). In the spring the clocks are put forward to BST and we lose an hour. In the autumn (or 'fall') we gain an hour when the clocks are put back an hour to return to GMT (remember: spring forward, fall back). We find the autumn change easy because we gain an hour, simply allowing our body clocks to free-run for a day. In the spring the change produces poor sleep because we are trying to go to sleep early (Monk and Aplin, 1980).

where to now?

The following are good sources of further information on shift work and jet lag:

▶ **Bentley, E. (1999)** *Awareness*. **London: Routledge** – very useful for this part of the topic as well as for sleep, dreaming and bodily rhythms

▶ **Ayensu, E.S. and Whitfield, P. (eds). (1982)** *The Rhythms of Life*. **London: Book Club Associates** – an excellent book on bodily rhythms and practical applications such as understanding jet lag.

talking point

Seasonal affective disorder

Winter depression or *seasonal affective disorder* (SAD) is a condition experienced in the short days of winter by as much as 10 per cent of the population (Ferenczi, 1997). The symptoms of SAD include severe depression, craving for high carbohydrate foods and sleepiness. The prevelance of SAD among people in latitudes where winter nights are very long suggests that it may be related to day length. In Shetland, for instance, the shortest day lasts just 5 hours 53 minutes between sunrise and sunset, with no guarantee of any sunshine in between, with

December promising just 15 hours of sunshine all month. In the lighter, longer days of spring and early summer the symptoms of SAD disappear. During long winter nights secretion of melatonin reaches its peak then lowers as summer approaches. This pattern has tempted psychologists to search for a relationship between low exposure to light, high melatonin and SAD. This relationship is supported by the effectiveness of light therapy. SAD sufferers exposed to intense artificial lighting (1,000 lux or more) during the winter generally find relief from their depression. Even as little as half an hour a day is effective, lifting depression within a week. How this exposure to light affects mood is, however, unclear. Ferenczi (1997) has suggested that it may either reset the circadian cycle or increase the secretion of serotonin, which is also implicated in mood disorders. Light therapy is not effective in all cases, although failure may be attributable to mis-diagnosis rather than ineffectual treatment. The timing of light sessions has been the subject of much research, and certainly simulated 'early dawn' is effective but brightness and total exposure, rather than timing, appear to be the key factors.

research now

what sort of people suffer from SAD?

**Bagby, R.M., Schuller, D.R., Levitt, A.J., Joffe, R.T. and Harkness, K.L. (1996)
Seasonal and non-seasonal depression and the five factor model of personality.**
Journal of Affective Disorders, 38 (2–3), 89–95

Aim: It has long been established that many people feel a bit down in the winter but do not develop clinical depression. It has been suggested that the difference in people who do develop full-blown SAD is that they are of a particular personality type. The aim of this study was to investigate the personalities of a group of SAD sufferers and compare them to people who also suffered depression, but in whom it was not related to season.

Method: Participants were all out-patients of a university-affiliated clinic in Canada. One hundred participants were assessed during an episode of depression. Forty-three patients were classified as suffering SAD as they only got depressed in the winter. Fifty-seven were classified as non-seasonally depressed. All the participants were diagnosed as having a major depressive episode (*major* depression comes in waves of severe depression, unlike *dysthymic* depression which is usually milder but constant). The participants were given a personality test called the NEO-PI (which stands for neuroticism, extroversion, openness, personality inventory). This actually assesses people on five personality factors, neuroticism (anxiety and moodiness), extroversion (sociability and impulsiveness), openness, agreeableness and conscientiousness.

Results: On four of the five subscales of the NEO-PI – neuroticism, extraversion, agreeableness and conscientiousness – the seasonally depressed group and the non-seasonally depressed group did not differ significantly. However, there was a substantial difference in the scores of the two groups on the openness scale. The SAD group scored consistently higher than the non-seasonal group.

Conclusion: The SAD group emerged as considerable more *open* than other depressed people. *Openness* is known to be associated with strong imagination, great emotional sensitivity and tendency for unconventional ideas. The researchers suggested that one important factor in SAD may be a personality type that reacts strongly to and amplifies the normal depressing nature of winter.

If light therapy raised mood by affecting the pineal gland, reduced levels of melatonin would be expected following treatment. Illnerova *et al.* (1993) have demonstrated a shifting of the melatonin cycle using bright lights to extend the day. Non-SAD participants were exposed to three hours of bright light each morning and evening for five consecutive days during the winter. Their circadian clocks advanced by 1–3 hours and the new rhythm persisted for three days after the light schedule was returned to normal. This suggests that, for SAD sufferers, exposure to bright light may be affecting melatonin levels.

Stiles (1990) has suggested that SAD is merely the response of people to publicity. He suggests that people see psychiatrists less in summer because they are on holiday. If, however, they are asked to report problems as they arise, rather than retrospectively, a different pattern emerges. Depressed patients' ratings did not vary from month to month as would be expected with SAD, but they did exhibit a tendency for Tuesdays and Thursdays to be worse than Sundays!

Light therapy only seems to be effective in SAD characterised by sleepiness, carbohydrate craving and worsening of symptoms in the evening. For sufferers who are suicidal, insomniac and who experience more severe symptoms in the morning, light therapy is ineffective (Terman *et al.*, 1996).

After reading this many of you might feel that you have SAD, feeling miserable and hungry through the winter and losing weight in summer. This wider experience, a mild form of winter depression called season-ality, is experienced by a much larger percentage of people. Ennis (1997) has identified a correlation between *seasonality* and premenstrual syndrome. This relationship might imply a tendency for some people to respond more strongly in terms of emotions to cyclical changes in hormone levels.

where to now?

The following are good sources of further information on SAD:

▶ **Hammen, C. (1997)** *Depression*. **Hove: Psychology Press** – a good general text on depression with some useful information on SAD in particular

▶ **www.photothera.com** – a website devoted to information on SAD. Contains abstracts of a large number of recent studies of SAD. Will thus give you a very detailed and up-to-date understanding of the topic.

Conclusions

The biological approach to psychology looks at the ways in which our understanding of biology can be applied to helping us understand human psychology. One area of study in biology that is of growing importance in psychology is genetics, the study of inheritance. We have looked here at how genes are now believed to affect individual characteristics such as intelligence and susceptibility to mental disorder. We have also looked briefly at the human brain and the challenges involved in studying it, and gone on to look in some detail at the ways in which one aspect of biological functioning – bodily rhythms – affects our psychological functioning.

One particularly important rhythm is the sleep–wake cycle, and we have looked at the nature of sleep and dreams and at some theoretical explanations for sleep and dreaming. Our understanding of the importance of bodily rhythms has several practical applications, for example in understanding the effects of shift work and jet lag. We have also looked here at a further application, understanding and treating seasonal affective disorder, a form of depression associated with lack of daylight.

what do you know?

1 Briefly outline two key studies from the physiological approach to psychology. *(10)*

2 Outline one explanation for human dreaming. *(6)*

3 Describe and evaluate restorational theory as an explanation for sleep. *(10)*

4 Discuss one contemporary issue in physiological psychology. *(12)*

2

The Learning Approach

what's
ahead?

This chapter introduces the learning theory approach to psychology, sometimes also called *behavioural psychology* or *behaviour analysis*. This approach is based on the study of learning in non-human animals which, being generally less complex in their behaviour than humans, are easier to study. We look here at three particularly important types of learning: classical conditioning, operant conditioning and social learning. In our *real lives* section we look at behaviour therapy, an example of how learning theory can help us to alter people's behaviour deliberately in order to reduce maladaptive behaviour. In *what's new?* we look at the relatively new area of community behaviour analysis. In *talking point* we take a learning approach to an issue currently being debated in psychology – the risk of addiction to the Internet.

what's it
about?

The learning theory approach is based on the following ideas.

- Behaviour is influenced by the environment. We can best understand the ways in which the environment influences behaviour by the concept of *learning*.

- Animals differ from humans only in the complexity of their behaviour. The ways in which their behaviour is determined by the environment are the same as those in humans, therefore we can study the acquisition of behaviours in animals and apply the results to understanding human behaviour.

- The systematic study of learning can generate general laws about learning which can be applied to understanding, predicting and controlling behaviour in a variety of situations.

Classical conditioning

The work of Ivan Pavlov

Ivan Petrivitch Pavlov was born in Russia in 1849. He trained as a medical doctor and conducted research on the nervous system and digestion, for which he won the Nobel Prize in 1904. When Pavlov was appointed Director of the Department of Physiology at the Russian Institute of Medicine, he established the world's first clinic and operating theatre to be used exclusively for animals. He always took the same care in his operations on dogs as was taken with people. As he insisted on complete cleanliness, his dogs almost always made a complete recovery. Furthermore, he recognised that he could not expect to gain reliable results from his experiments if the animals were suffering pain, discomfort or fear. For tests on digestion, however, anaesthesia was impossible so Pavlov aimed to reduce the stress his subjects experienced by ensuring that each one received excellent care. He could not depend on his laboratory assistants for this so he took the animals home to be looked after. The importance of the mental health of research animals to the validity of experimental outcomes is only just beginning to resurface as a concern in modern psychology.

New behaviours for old: the paradigm of classical conditioning

Pavlov was insistent that his experimental animals were treated well. To this end, he often cared for them himself. As a physiologist he was interested, amongst other things, in digestion. To the detriment of his studies, the experimental dogs salivated to the sound of his footsteps, ahead of the arrival of their food. Pavlov deduced that the dogs' responses were in anticipation of the situation. The work on learning, for which Pavlov is now best remembered, explains how such associations are established.

The mechanism of classical conditioning relies upon the building of an association between a *neutral stimulus*, some aspect of the environment which does not elicit a response, and an existing unconditioned stimulus which does. These two stimuli are presented to the animal until the previously neutral stimulus acquires the same effect as the unconditioned stimulus, the ability to elicit a response. This behaviour, whilst not new, has developed a novel association to the neutral stimulus so is now called a *conditioned response* and the trigger a *conditioned stimulus*.

Pavlov (1927) demonstrated classical conditioning in his dogs using the sound of a metronome as the neutral stimulus (NS) and a bowl of meat powder as the unconditioned stimulus (UCS). Prior to the experiment, the dogs would salivate (the unconditioned response, UCR) in response to the meat powder but not to the sound. During the conditioning phase the meat powder was presented at the same time as the metronome. Repeated pairings of meat and metronome resulted in *conditioning* – the animal would subsequently salivate to the sound alone. As a result of the pairings, the NS (the sound) had become a *conditioned stimulus* (CS) capable of producing the behaviour (salivation) in a new situation. This behaviour, triggered by the CS, is called a *conditioned response* (CR). The diagram below summarises these learning processes. The experimental apparatus used by Pavlov is shown opposite.

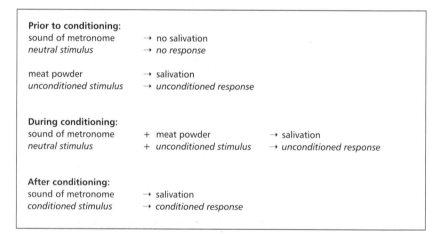

Prior to conditioning:
sound of metronome → no salivation
neutral stimulus → *no response*

meat powder → salivation
unconditioned stimulus → *unconditioned response*

During conditioning:
sound of metronome + meat powder → salivation
neutral stimulus + *unconditioned stimulus* → *unconditioned response*

After conditioning:
sound of metronome → salivation
conditioned stimulus → *conditioned response*

The process of classical conditioning in Pavlov's dogs

Just like Pavlov's dogs, you may have been classically conditioned to salivate. Visual stimuli such as chocolate wrappers (the NS) do not spontaneously cause salivation although eating chocolate (the UCS) will do so. As we open the wrapper before we eat the chocolate, we tend to have it in sight so it can become a conditioned stimulus. After many bars of chocolate the NS and UCS have had multiple pairings so salivation (the CR) becomes conditioned to the wrapper (the CS).

The acquisition of a conditioned response may take many pairings of the NS and UCS. Schneiderman *et al.* (1962) showed that a rabbit requires many trials to learn an eye blink response when exposed to pairings of a puff of compressed nitrogen directed towards its eye (UCS) and a tone (CS) (see Schneiderman's learning curve opposite).

This apparatus, used by Pavlov, enabled him to control the exposure of the dog to different stimuli and to accurately measure the response, in this case salivation

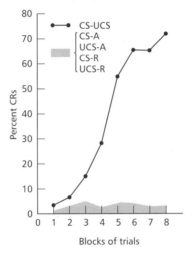

Schneiderman's learning curve (after Schneidermann *et al.*, 1962)

MEDIA WATCH

Q My boyfriend and I tried an experiment which I'd like to tell you about. For two months, we made love every night with Barry White on continuous play on our CD player. Now, whenever either of us hears that music we become sexually aroused.

A A long-dead foreigner called Pavlov did much the same sort of experiment but used dogs, bells and food. Your research project sounds far more interesting and I suggest that you apply for a grant to help you continue with your studies. You might like to see if your boyfriend's enthusiasm can be triggered by constant exposure to the sound of the Abergwili Male Voice Choir airing their tonsils.

Alternatively, try Seth Pitt and Eva Legova singing Tonight's The Night. Meanwhile, a warning: You could find yourself in a tricky situation if a Barry White track is played when you're in your local pub.

(*News of the World*, January 2000)

Higher order conditioning

As Pavlov demonstrated, for a strong CS (that is, one producing a strong CR) there appears to be little difference between the UCR and CR; they are the same response to different stimuli. Pavlov (1927) demonstrated that after a dog had learned to respond to one stimulus, this CS could be used to condition the same response to another neutral stimulus, as shown below. This is *higher order conditioning*. The only way in which the new response differs is that it is weaker.

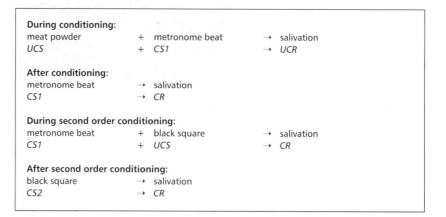

```
During conditioning:
meat powder          +  metronome beat    →  salivation
UCS                  +  CS1               →  UCR

After conditioning:
metronome beat       →  salivation
CS1                  →  CR

During second order conditioning:
metronome beat       +  black square      →  salivation
CS1                  +  UCS               →  CR

After second order conditioning:
black square         →  salivation
CS2                  →  CR
```

Higher order conditioning

Does timing matter?

It is usually assumed that the UCS and CS must be presented simultaneously and although this is the most effective arrangement, it is not the only one. *Forward* or *delayed conditioning* appears to 'prepare' the animal for the arrival of the UCS, which follows the CS in time. As a consequence it may be as effective as simultaneous presentation of the CS and UCS. *Trace conditioning* introduces a time delay between the appearance and disappearance of the CS and the arrival of the UCS. As such, the UCS can still be of some use in predicting the CS. In *backward conditioning*, the UCS appears before the CS and this is generally the least effective.

Consider these in terms of utilising the information provided by an aircraft seat-belt light. A sign (CS) which is illuminated before the flight becomes bumpy (UCS) will be a highly effective warning (equivalent to forward conditioning). Signs which appear a long time before the bumps (trace conditioning) may be of some use but one which only lights up after the bumps (backward conditioning) is of no value; we would learn nothing new about dangers of the journey.

Russell *et al.* (1984) tested the simultaneous presentation of an odour of fish or sulphur (CS) and the injection of an allergen (UCS) in guinea pigs. The animals were conditioned to produce an allergic reaction (CR) to the associated odours. If you suffer from hay fever and have ever sneezed at the sight of a combine harvester or a vase of plastic flowers, classical conditioning could be the reason!

One-trial learning: is once enough?

Whilst the rabbit response referred to on page 38 takes hundreds of trials to become conditioned, not all conditioning is this slow. In some instances an animal can acquire a new behaviour in a single pairing of the NS and UCS. This is called *one-trial learning*, and it tends to happen when the consequences of failing to learn are fatal.

Garcia *et al.* (1974) demonstrated one-trial learning by rats in a taste aversion task (see the diagram below). Rats tend to taste a little food, wait to see if it makes them ill, then consume more if it doesn't. Their survival therefore depends on being able to remember unwholesome foods they have consumed only once. When tested with poisoned bait, Garcia *et al.*'s wild rats learned to avoid the food with a single vomit-inducing incident. It seems that consuming excessive alcohol can have a similar effect in humans! If you have ever had the experience of drinking slightly too much of a distinctively flavoured drink, such as gin or cider, and feeling ill, you may be unable to face that taste or smell for some time.

During conditioning:			
smell and taste of novel food	+ vomit-inducing substance	→	unpleasantness of sickness
NS	+ *UCS*	→	*UCR*
After conditioning:			
smell of novel food	→ unpleasantness (aversion)		
CS	→ *CR*		

One-trial learning

Ferguson and Cassidy (1999) have suggested that *Gulf War syndrome* (GWS) can be explained by a similar process. Gulf War syndrome is a set of symptoms including memory, sexual and sleep problems, nausea, headaches, depression, rashes and increased sensitivity to pain. Typically, each individual suffers only some of these symptoms. Medical explanations for GWS, such as exposure to organo-phosphates or the cocktail of drugs administered to soldiers to protect them, cannot easily explain this wide range of symptoms in sufferers. Ferguson and Cassidy have proposed a classical conditioning model which suggests that a sickness response has been acquired by association with a range of stimuli including oil fire fumes (present throughout the fighting) and stressful events such as witnessing injuries during the war. The symptoms of GWS can be explained as the body's conditioned responses (CRs) to these. After the war exposure to any of these conditioned stimuli would produce the conditioned sickness response. An example of one case which can probably be best explained by classical conditioning comes from Ferguson and Cassidy, who described an army mechanic who, following the war, could no longer tolerate the smell of petrol without acute nausea. Presumably, the smell of petrol had become associated with other noxious stimuli from the war.

The symptoms of Gulf War syndrome may be conditional responses to stimuli like the smell of burning oil

Extinction and spontaneous recovery

What happens if the CS is repeatedly presented in the absence of the UCS? Over time the strength of the CR declines and eventually disappears, an effect called *extinction*. Thus if a dog was conditioned to salivate to a bell, then the bell was rung many times in the absence of food, salivation to the bell would eventually cease. However, if the bell is silent for a while, then subsequently rung again, the response may reappear. This is called *spontaneous recovery*.

Generalisation

How does an animal respond to stimuli which are similar to the CS? If they are sufficiently alike, the new stimulus can also trigger the CR; this is called *generalisation*. These responses may, however, be slower to appear after the presentation of the CS or they may be weaker. For example, a rabbit which has been conditioned to blink to a certain tone may also do so to a tone of a higher frequency but its response may be a fraction of a second slower. Similarly, a dog that has been conditioned to salivate to a particular shaped stimulus may salivate less to a slightly different shape.

Preparedness: do we learn some responses more easily than others?

In much the way that evolution has shaped rats to learn taste aversions to foods, people seem to learn some responses more readily than others. *Phobias* are a case in point. There are millions of objects and situations in life which could be the focus of fear, but only about 130 common enough to have been given a technical term of their own. Furthermore, we are only likely to develop a phobic response to objects and situations which, in our evolutionary history, may have presented a threat. Snakes, spiders, rats, heights, small spaces and the dark are all common targets for fear, why not trees, electrical sockets, guns, knives or garden strimmers?

Thousands of years of human evolution have favoured the survival of individuals with a readiness to become afraid of threats to health and life. Snakes and spiders may be poisonous, rats carry disease, confined spaces are unsafe and darkness exposes us to dangers we cannot see. Trees, however, have never posed a threat. In contrast, electricity and the like, whilst being potentially dangerous, are too recent in terms of evolution for any benefit to have accrued from a tendency to fear them. For such benefits to evolve, deaths from these situations would have to limit the survival of those who failed to respect the risks they impose.

The tendency to learn more readily about ancient dangers has been termed *preparedness*. Ohman *et al.* (1976) provided evidence to support this notion by conditioning student volunteers to fear pictures of snakes and spiders (prepared stimuli) or houses, faces and flowers (unprepared stimuli). The pictures acted as the CS and preceded a brief, painful electric shock (UCS) by 10 seconds, the fear associated with this caused sweating, detected as a decrease in GSR (galvanic skin resistance). This forward conditioning resulted in the acquisition of a CR to all pictures. However, conditioning to the prepared stimuli was both quicker, taking only one trial to establish (compared to four or five for the unprepared stimuli) and more resistant to extinction.

Chainsaws, recent inventions in terms of our evolutionary history, are unlikely to elicit phobic responses

for and against

classical conditioning as an explanation of human behaviour

+ It can explain the acquisition of some aspects of behaviour, where a specific response is associated with a particular stimulus, for example, in taste aversion. Complex sets of responses, possibly including Gulf War syndrome, can be explained in this way.

+ Classical conditioning has a range of practical applications. Later in this chapter we shall look at how the principles of classical conditioning are used in behavioural therapies.

– It can only account for the appearance of existing responses in new situations, not the acquisition of entirely new behaviours.

– It is insufficient as an explanation of all human learning. Early learning theorists believed that all learning could be accounted for by classical conditioning, but nowadays we believe that there are other important mechanisms of learning.

Operant conditioning

Observe the random behaviour of a cat in a kitchen and it won't be long before it has located a source of food; not by smell but by hanging off cupboard doors and making them swing open or pushing its paw into a swing top bin. It seems that the cat is not systematically investigating the room but is rather experimenting with exploratory behaviours until it chances upon food. Some of the earliest experiments into such behaviours were conducted by E.L. Thorndike. To Thorndike, animals did not work out things like the whereabouts of food by any logical process; they simply engaged in behaviours which, by trial and error, led to the discovery of a useful response. Even then they were not always quick to benefit from the experience, often taking many rewarded repetitions to learn.

The work of E.L. Thorndike

Thorndike (1911) studied the acquisition of novel behaviours in cats using a range of specially built puzzle boxes (see below). A typical experiment involved a cat confined to a box containing little but a paddle on the floor, with food outside which it could see and smell. Pushing the paddle opened the door of the box via a series of pulleys. A hungry cat would engage in various behaviours – biting, clawing, moving around the box or trying to squeeze out between the bars before eventually operating the mechanism to open the door by accident, thus leading to the food. Such a procedure differs from Pavlov's classical conditioning because the cat only received the food as a consequence of performing the appropriate behaviour. After feeding, the cat was returned to the box and would repeat its array of behaviours, again stumbling by chance on the one resulting in escape. After several repetitions, the cat performed the response necessary to open the door more quickly. This reduction in

Thorndike's puzzle box

latency from about five minutes to as little as five seconds over ten trials indicated that the cats were learning the puzzle.

The law of effect

Thorndike, unlike many contemporary observers of animal behaviour, did not assume that the cats improved their performance because they understood the situation. Instead, he suggested that their change in latency depended upon the strengthening of a response which had arisen by trial and error. The consequence of enhancing such links between the stimulus and the response is expressed by Thorndike (1911) as the *Law of Effect*:

> 'Of several responses made to the same situation, those which are accompanied or closely followed by satisfaction to the animal will, all other things being equal, be more firmly connected with the situation.'

In sum, Thorndike demonstrated that an animal learns a response not through reasoning but because favourable consequences increase the probability that the behaviour which immediately precede them will be repeated.

The work of B.F. Skinner

The kind of learning studied by Thorndike became known as *instrumental* or *operant conditioning* and was studied in detail by B.F. Skinner (1874–1949). To maximise the objectivity, accuracy and ease of recording behaviour in his experiments, Skinner developed a chamber in which an animal, such as a rat or pigeon, could learn a specific response. The apparatus could present stimuli (called *antecedents*) and allowed responses (called *behaviours*) to be measured and recorded. *Consequences* followed the performance of a particular behaviour. The antecedents (A) included lights and noises, the behaviours (B) were bar presses or pecks directed at a disc and the consequences (C) were food or electric shocks (see the diagram below). These chambers, later known as *Skinner boxes*, offered precise control over the animal's experience so that the factors affecting learning could be rigorously investigated.

The process of operant conditioning

The learning sequence can be represented as:		
A →	B →	C
bar →	press →	food
A elicits B which results in C.		

A rat placed in a Skinner box will perform a range of behaviours, the majority of which are irrelevant to the situation. When it chances to strike the bar, perhaps by stretching up against the wall, the mechanism will release a food pellet into the hopper. As this makes a 'click' the rat may investigate and find the food immediately or may only do so later. Each time the rat hits the bar another pellet is released and as it discovers food in the

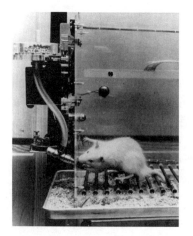

A Skinner box

hopper, it checks more often. The rat is thus likely to encounter the food soon after pressing the bar. As food is found only after the bar (A) is pressed and not following any other behaviour, it is this response which is *reinforced*, that is the frequency of the bar-pressing (B) is increased because it immediately precedes the arrival of the food (C). This is a reiteration of Thorndike's Law of Effect and was expressed by Skinner (1938) as 'behaviour is shaped and maintained by its consequences'.

Reinforcement: the effect of rewards

Skinner proposed that the consequences of a behaviour could serve to strengthen or weaken a response. How can this occur? Reinforcement, the process by which an animal is rewarded for a behaviour, can occur in two ways, each of which acts to increase the frequency of the immediately preceding behaviour.

- *Positive reinforcers* are things which can happen to an animal which are good, such as receiving food, water, the opportunity to play with a companion or access to a mate. When a behaviour is followed by a positive reinforcer, its frequency increases; an animal is more likely to perform a behaviour which has pleasant consequences. A rat will press a bar to receive food; children will tidy their bedrooms for the opportunity to watch TV.

- *Negative reinforcers* are things which are good when they *stop* happening, such as the reduction of pain when an electric shock is switched off or the relief when the sound of a pneumatic drill outside your house stops. When a behaviour is followed by a negative reinforcer, as with a positive reinforcer, its frequency increases because the situation is more pleasant than before. A rat will press a bar to turn an electric current off and I will repeatedly walk across the room to bang the TV to stop it buzzing.

Punishment: learning what not to do

Unlike reinforcement, which always has pleasant effects, *punishment* imposes an unpleasant consequence. This may be the arrival of something nasty (such as a shock) or the removal of something nice (such as pocket money). Punishment serves to reduce the frequency of the behaviour which precedes it. If it rains each time I leave the house and I find this unpleasant, I will be disinclined towards excursions – the effect of the rain is to reduce the likelihood of my going out. In this case rain is a punisher.

Shaping: reinforcing successive approximations

Skinner proposed that a particular action could be conditioned by reinforcing behaviours which more closely resembled the desired response on each occasion, that is, *successive approximations*. To make children keep their rooms tidy, parents might initially reward them for picking up their dirty clothes, later for putting their books away as well and subsequently only when the entire floor is visible. On each occasion the child is only rewarded if its attempts at tidying are better than the last.

A squirrel can be shaped to run along a rope by placing food successively further along it

Our belief that walking under ladders is dangerous is perpetuated every time we walk safely around them

Uncontrollable reinforcers and learning to be superstitious

When a positive consequence follows a behaviour we tend to repeat that behaviour even when it was not the cause of the reward. Positive consequences that occur regardless of our behaviour are called *uncontrollable reinforcers* – 'uncontrollable' because they occur regardless of our behaviour and 'reinforcers' because they increase the probability of the behaviour being performed at the time being repeated. The power of uncontrollable reinforcers was first demonstrated by Skinner (1948). We look at this study in some depth on page 48.

More recently, Helena Matute has examined the role of uncontrollable reinforcers in human behaviour. In one study, Matute (1996) looked at the how uncontrollable reinforcers affect our behaviour in relation to computers. We look at this study in detail on page 49.

Schedules of reinforcement

Skinner investigated the effects of different reinforcement regimes. Do animals learn better when they are reinforced on every performance of the required behaviour or not? The answer to this question depends on what is meant by *better*. In some respects, frequent, predictable reinforcement is better, in others infrequent, unpredictable reinforcement is more effective.

An animal which receives a reward for every performance of a behaviour is on a *continuous reinforcement* schedule. This is like getting a treat every time you go to the dentist. Continuous reinforcement results in a low but steady response rate and the behaviour will extinguish very readily if reinforcement is withheld. All other patterns of reinforcement offer rewards for only *some* instances of the behaviour, this is called *partial reinforcement*. A *fixed interval* schedule provides reinforcement at regular times, for instance receiving pocket money every Saturday if your room has been tidy. This results in an uneven pattern of response; you suddenly start to clear up on Thursdays and Fridays. The response extinguishes quite quickly; you are unlikely to bother at all if no money is forthcoming.

On a *fixed ratio* schedule, reinforcement is related to the number of behaviours performed, for example, a person working on a production line might be paid per 100 items they process. Immediately after each batch is completed their work rate would fall, then rise again towards the end of the next 100. As with fixed interval schedules, this produces an uneven response rate and extinction is quite rapid in both cases. *Variable interval* schedules provide reinforcement at timed intervals but the gap

classic
research

pigeons are superstitious!

Skinner, B.F. (1948) Superstition in the pigeon. *Journal of Experimental Psychology,* 38, 168–72

Aim: Skinner held the extreme viewpoint that all human behaviour could be understood within the framework of learning and that failure to do so was simply an inability to identify the reinforcers which shape and maintain the response. Superstition, a belief in some presumed relationship which does not in fact exist, appears to be uniquely human as we assume that animals do not have beliefs. Skinner designed this experiment to demonstrate that superstitious behaviours could be acquired by animals. He proposed that superstitious behaviours simply arise because they are accidentally reinforced by some consequence which is *not* dependent upon that response.

Method: Eight hungry pigeons were placed in individual conditioning chambers (Skinner boxes) for a few minutes a day and received a food pellet every 15 seconds regardless of their behaviour. After several days of conditioning, two independent observers recorded the birds' behaviour. Finally, the time interval between pellets was increased.

Results: Of the eight pigeons, six developed repetitive behaviours which they performed between the arrival of pellets. These included turning anti-clockwise, hopping, head tossing and pendulum swings of the head. None of these behaviours had been exhibited before the experiment nor did they have anything to do with the appearance of food. When the time between reinforcers (food pellets) was increased to one minute the pigeons' behaviour increased until they became frantic.

Conclusions: The pigeons behaved as though they believed that the delivery of food pellets depended upon their response even though it did not. This is exactly what people are doing when they hold superstitions. Since reinforcement was intermittent, the pigeons' behaviour, like that of superstitious humans, was difficult to extinguish.

between each reinforcement varies around an average. For example, a variable interval schedule of one minute would provide rewards on average every 60 seconds but these may in fact arrive at 20, 80, 90, 40, 30 and 100 second intervals. The response rate is high and steady and extinction occurs only very gradually. You are most likely to keep working

research
now

learning to be superstitious about computers

Matute, H. (1996) Illusion of control: detecting response–outcome independence in analytic but not in naturalistic conditions. *Psychological Science, 7,* 289–93

Aim: From a learning perspective, superstitious behaviours can arise because we fail to test the possibility that a positive outcome can occur irrespective of our behaviour. The idea of this study was to see whether computer users whose computer periodically emitted a loud, unpleasant noise would come to believe that the noise only ceased because of their attempts to stop it by pushing buttons. Computer users were also tested to see whether they would come to believe that beeps were only emitted from their computers because they were pressing buttons in an attempt to elicit a beep.

Method: A total of 32 participants, university students, worked on computers in a psychology laboratory. There were four conditions. The computers of two groups were programmed to emit loud, unpleasant noises from time to time. One of these groups was given instructions to stop the noise by pressing the space bar within one second (the control group), whilst the other group was instructed to vary their responses. In the other two conditions, the computers would emit a more mild beeping sound. Both of these groups were instructed to respond to each beep by making a further beep. One group was instructed to vary their responses. In fact, the unpleasant noise would cease and the beep would be repeated regardless of whether the participants responded by pressing buttons on the computer. The rationale for the study was that the students in the control group would always experience the cessation of the noise after their efforts to stop it, and the 'beep' group would always experience a further beep after pressing buttons in order to create the sound. This would mean that the behaviours they used in order to affect the noise would be reinforced. The informed groups would however learn that the result (cessation of noise or a further beep) did not result from their actions and so would not be reinforced.

Results: After several instances of computer noise, the participants were assessed on the basis of how often they responded to the computer when it emitted a noise or beep. As expected, the students who received no explicit instructions to pause in their responses tended to respond every time the computer emitted a noise, either by trying to stop the noise or repeat the beep. The informed groups however ceased to respond at every opportunity.

Conclusions: As the uncontrollable reinforcers occurred with the same probability regardless of whether the participants responded or not, the uninformed participants always responded. Without the benefit of 'doing nothing' in response to a noise, they failed to learn that the noises were actually controlled by the computer rather than themselves. For these participants, the reinforcer (the termination of the noise or the repeat beep) became associated with their own behaviour rather than other causes, i.e. they learned to behave superstitiously. The informed group, in contrast, learned that they had no control over the noises.

hard if you are unsure when an inspector is going to arrive to judge the quality of your output.

Finally, on *variable ratio* schedules animals are reinforced only after several responses have been made, the exact number varying around an average. A variable ratio of five, for instance, would reward every fifth behaviour *on average*, in reality the first, tenth, 13th, 17th and 25th response may be reinforced. This pattern of reinforcement produces the fastest response rate and the greatest resistance to extinction. Gamblers receive pay-outs after variable numbers of attempts; their behaviour is persistent even in the face of nil returns.

Partial reinforcement clearly affects both response rate and resistance to extinction. Gambling seems to fulfil the criteria of a variable ratio schedule, producing both high response rates and resistance to extinction, in fact gambling shows many properties of addiction. However, Delfabbro and Winefield (1999) have shown that the response rates of gamblers do not exactly replicate the high, steady response rates predicted for a variable ratio schedule of reinforcement. Rather, the response rate of players on poker machines (the Australian equivalent of fruit machines or slot machines) dipped after a pay-out. These post-reinforcement pauses were dependent on the size of the reward and the experience of the players (experienced players taking longer pauses after a big win). These findings suggest that gamblers, unlike rats, are sensitive to machine events.

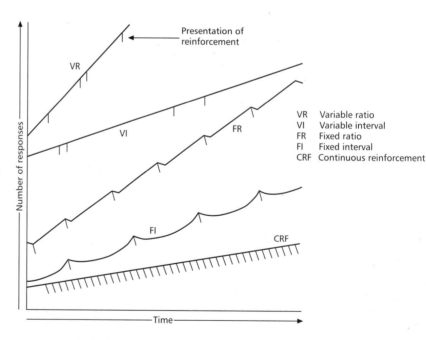

The different schedules of reinforcement produce differing response patterns

Operant conditioning and language acquisition

Skinner (1957) proposed that children acquired language through imitation and shaping. Imitation must clearly play a part in language acquisition as our speech resembles that of those around us. It can, for instance, account for why we develop a regional accent. The acquisition of speech sounds or phonemes can also be explained by imitation. Infants initially generate an international range of phonemes before limiting their scope to those of the language they hear (Oller, 1981). Deaf babies fail to do this and eventually stop babbling altogether although those exposed to sign language imitate signs on schedule (Pinker, 1994). The learning of whole words also depends on imitation, children who imitate the most expand their vocabulary the fastest (Masur, 1995).

Shaping also plays a part in language acquisition. A child's first utterances will be met with enthusiasm, a positive reinforcer and subsequent attempts at words are praised and further reinforced. For infants learning their first words, it is easy to see how shaping could operate. A child hears the sound of the word *granddad* and goes *g-g-g* to the delight of the grandparents; their excitement is rewarding. Subsequently the child may be praised for saying *gagad* long before the whole word can be articulated. This progressive reinforcement could shape the child's utterances.

Consider why older children start to swear; they copy words they hear, repeating them to their friends from whom they receive respect – a positive reinforcer. They then say them to their parents and are reprimanded. This may serve as a genuine punisher, reducing the probability of such language being used (at least in the home) or the consequence may act as a positive reinforcer via attention or a sense of revenge.

One might expect the greatest reinforcement to come from being understood. Children with accurate speech should be more likely to achieve their aim, to obtain an ice-cream for instance. This is not, however, the case: *i-keem, i-keem* is very likely to be effective. Adults (and siblings) are adept at deciphering attempts at language, thus reinforcing incorrect speech. Truth and intelligibility are more important than grammatical correctness; parents are likely to reinforce a child who says 'nice brown doggy' to a golden labrador but not one who says 'That's a nice brown dog' to a white cat (Brown *et al.*, 1969).

'Nice doggy' is more likely to be reinforced than the grammatically correct 'That is a nice black cat'

In fact, attempts to correct speech are usually fruitless. Take this example from Kuczaj (1982):

Ben:	*I like these candy. I like they.*
Adult:	*You like them?*
Ben:	*Yes, I like they.*
Adult:	*Say them.*
Ben:	*Them.*
Adult:	*Say 'I like them'*
Ben:	*I like them.*
Adult:	*Good.*
Ben:	*I'm good. These candy good too.*
Adult:	*Are they good?*
Ben:	*Yes. I like they. You like they?*

This shows that, whilst children can imitate and are reinforced for doing so, their capacity to extract rules from the language they hear and reapply them is also important. Eventually, however, exceptions to the rules must be learned by example. Nelson (1973) found that correcting grammatical errors may in fact be detrimental. She observed mothers' responses to incorrect speech and found that children who were systematically corrected expanded their vocabulary more slowly than children of more forgiving parents.

The greatest problems for the learning theory approach to language acquisition are, however, the speed at which it is acquired and the systematic nature of children's linguistic understanding. At our peak, we learn words at nine per day (Carey, 1978), too many for each to be individually reinforced. From the speech we hear, we seem to extract and re-apply rules of language (syntax) allowing us enormous linguistic

for and against

operant conditioning as an explanation of human behaviour

+ Children and adults can learn by 'trying for themselves'.

+ Children learn the sounds and words of their language through operant conditioning.

– Studies of operant conditioning focus on generalisations, thus ignoring the differences between individuals' experiences.

– Many human behaviours, such as language, are too complex to be acquired solely through conditioning.

– Humans are capable of insightful learning where no trial and error process is evident – the solution is achieved through reasoning.

flexibility; even the very young generate novel utterances. As this process is rule-governed, we cannot be exposed to examples of every combination so imitation and shaping are insufficient as explanations. This approach cannot account for the similarity of the sequence of language learning between individuals and across cultures nor the tendency of children to make over-generalisation errors, such as *I runned* and *we goed*.

where to now?

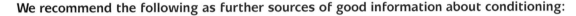

We recommend the following as further sources of good information about conditioning:

▶ **Gross, R. (1998)** *Key Studies in Psychology*. **London: Hodder & Stoughton** – contains detailed accounts of a number of major studies of learning

▶ **Clamp, A. and Russell, J. (1998)** *Comparative Psychology*. **London: Hodder & Stoughton** – a rigorous but user-friendly account of conditioning with an emphasis on animal studies.

Social learning theory

Learning by example

Social learning, by definition, depends on the presence of other individuals and the role they play must be more than merely incidental. Being surrounded by others may enhance learning by increasing competition or reducing fear, but this is not *social*. For social learning to occur, one individual must acquire a new behaviour by imitating another, the *model*. This model need not be aware of their role, although in tutoring the model alters their behaviour to maximise learning opportunities. So a hunting lioness may act as a model for cubs to imitate, whereas a mother cheetah which repeatedly catches and releases her prey for the young to observe is tutoring them.

Monkeys in the wild are afraid of snakes. An adult monkey encountering a snake will indicate fear with its facial expression, make an alarm call and flee. These reactions are notably absent from the response of a laboratory reared monkey in the same situation. Mineka and Cook (1988) studied how rhesus monkeys (*Macaca mulatta*) learn this response. When laboratory-reared subjects observed the agitation displayed by a wild-reared monkey in response to a snake, they modified their behaviour to match the model. On subsequent exposure to snakes, the previously naïve monkeys displayed fear; they appeared to have learned to be afraid by watching the behaviour of other individuals. Observing an unafraid model which failed to respond to a snake appeared to immunise the naïve monkeys against developing a fear. When later exposed to models behaving appropriately, these monkeys failed to learn to be afraid of snakes.

Animals can also learn behaviours for which they have not been 'prepared' by evolution. Herbert and Harsh (1944) found that cats would learn to escape from a box more quickly if they observed the trials of a demonstrator learning to get out of the box. The cats did, however, learn faster if they watched the whole learning process than if they just saw a skilled performer at work.

When will observational learning occur?

According to Bandura (1977) there are four requirements for observational learning to occur. These are:

- *attention* – the observer must be paying attention to the model

- *retention* – the observer must be capable of retaining a memory of the observed behaviour

- *reproduction* – the observer must be capable of performing the observed action

- *motivation* – the observer must be motivated to generate the learned behaviour either in return for an external reward or because of some intrinsic motivation generated by the model (hence individuals differ in their power as models).

For humans, we must be watching or listening to the model to attend. As school children we may remember the plaintive cry of 'pay attention or you won't learn anything' and even earlier than that we may have heard 'watch how mummy does it'. Having seen the model in action, we must then be able to remember their behaviour. This is sometimes more difficult than it sounds. I may have carefully watched the way the mechanic at the garage assembled my new windscreen wipers and be perfectly capable of the actions myself but completely unable to remember what to do.

Unlike classical or operant conditioning where the animal's learning is indicated immediately by its performance, in social learning an animal may acquire but not necessarily demonstrate the new behaviour. A young child may observe his parents in the evening having a 'G and T' or a lager, but it is not until he is sitting in the trolley at the supermarket pointing at the goods on the conveyor belt that it becomes apparent that he has learned 'Gin for mummy, beer for daddy'. Such examples do, however, serve to illustrate another difference between conditioning and social learning. In the latter there is no requirement for reinforcement, at least not to learn. Reinforcement may play a part in the expression of the behaviour. Children who imitate the offensive language of others may learn to demonstrate their behaviour only in situations where it will be rewarded.

MEDIA WATCH

Call to turn off South Park

Parents at a North Yorkshire primary school have been urged to stop their children watching the cult TV cartoon *South Park* after an increase in swearing and bad behaviour in the playground.

Glyn Hopper, head of Sowerby County Primary School, near Thirsk, wrote to parents after children raised the issue in her school council.

(*Times Educational Supplement*, 11 February 2000)

Duck (1990) suggests that the extent to which the characteristics of the model are reflected in the observer's characteristics may determine their effectiveness as a model. What features might affect the modelling process? As indicated by the findings of Bandura *et al.* (1961) (see page 56), same-sex models are more effective than opposite-sex models for increasing aggressive behaviour in children. Other key attributes of effective models include power and likeability, hence pop stars and sports personalities as well as parents are potent models. In animals, as well as in people, status affects the likelihood of being copied. In a recent study, Nicol and Pope (1999) found that when exposed to different demonstrators, chickens tended to imitate the feeding locations of dominant hens rather than submissive ones or cockerels.

research now

how do chickens choose their role models?

Nicol, C.J. and Pope, S.J. (1999) The effects of demonstrator social status and prior foraging success in observational learning in laying hens. *Animal Behaviour*, 57, 163–71

Aim: Hens, which live in flocks, have complex social relationships and each flock comprises birds of different social status. It has long been established in humans that children do not imitate all adults equally but tend to favour same-sex role models. The aims of this study were to see whether hens would have a greater tendency to imitate same sex models than opposite sex models and to see whether they would be more likely to imitate members of the flock with high social status. A secondary aim was to see whether the observers' status would affect their likelihood of imitating modelled behaviour.

Method: From each of 24 flocks, a dominant cockerel, a dominant hen and a mid-ranking or subordinate hen were selected and trained to perform a particular task to obtain food – pecking in a particular place. Six 'observer' hens from each flock watched the 'model' birds perform the task for four five-minute sessions on consecutive days. Each 'observer' was then tested individually to see whether they would imitate the modelled behaviour in order to obtain food. Comparisons were made between the extent to which chickens imitated high- and low-status hens and cockerels. Comparisons were also made between the tendency of high- and low-status hens to imitate the pecking task.

Results: Results from 19 flocks were analysed. High-status observers tended to imitate the pecking task more frequently than did low-status observers. High-status models were also imitated more frequently than lower-status models. Same-sex models were imitated more frequently than opposite-sex models.

Conclusion: Social status and sex both appear to have an impact on the imitation of modelled behaviour in hens, observers showing a preference for same-sex and high-status models.

Pennington (1986) identifies three categories of variable that affect imitation: characteristics of the observer and of the model and the consequences of the behaviour for the model. These features include the age and status of the model and the observer's level of self-esteem. Models who are of similar age and who are high in status are more likely to be imitated. For example, young people who perceive drug-users as high in status may be drawn into drug-taking because the sight of high-status people taking drugs is more influential than their parents' threats.

classic
research

will children copy violent behaviour?

Bandura, A., Ross, D. and Ross, S.A. (1961) Transmission of aggression through imitation of aggressive models. *Journal of Abnormal and Social Psychology,* 63, 575–82

Aim: To investigate whether aggression learned through observation of the aggressive acts of others would generalise to new settings where the model was not present and to investigate the effect of gender on such modelling.

Method: Children aged three to six years (36 boys and 36 girls) were first scored for initial level of aggressiveness, being rated by a teacher and an experimenter for physical aggression, verbal aggression and aggression towards objects. The children were divided into groups matched for initial behaviour: a control group who did not see a model and two groups which were exposed to adult models who behaved in either aggressive or non-aggressive ways. Half of each group saw a same-sex model, the others an opposite-sex model. The children were then tested in different situations to ascertain the extent to which they would imitate the aggressive acts of the model. The experimenter took each child to a playroom, meeting an adult (the model) who was invited to 'join in the game'. The child sat at a table offering potato printing and coloured stickers to play with whilst the model sat at another with Tinker toys, a mallet and a five-foot high inflated Bobo doll. In the non-aggressive condition, the model assembled the Tinker toys for 10 minutes, in the aggressive condition this lasted only one minute after which the model attacked the Bobo doll. The sequence of behaviour was identical each time, Bobo was lain on its side, sat upon, punched on the nose, picked up and hit on the head with the mallet. It was then thrown up in the air and kicked about the room. This sequence was performed three times over nine minutes accompanied by aggressive comments such as 'kick him' and 'pow'.

After exposure to the model, all participants were put in a situation designed to frustrate them, to increase the likelihood of aggression being displayed. They were taken to a room containing attractive toys such as a fire engine and a doll with a wardrobe (remember, this is the 1960s). After a short opportunity to play the children were told that these toys were for other children and were moved to another room. This final stage offered non-aggressive toys such as crayons, dolls, a ball, cars, a tea set and plastic farm animals and aggressive toys including a Bobo doll, a mallet and dart guns. The children were allowed to play here for 20 minutes and were observed by the experimenters using a one-way mirror. Records were made of aggressive acts which replicated the model's behaviour (both physical and verbal), other aggression with the mallet and non-aggressive behaviour. These were then compared.

Results: Children exposed to violent models imitated their exact behaviours and were significantly more aggressive than those children who did not receive aggressive modelling. This effect applied to both physical and verbal aggression. The increase in aggression for boys was greater than for girls, although girls were more likely to imitate verbal aggression and boys physical acts. Boys were also more likely to imitate a same-sex model as, to a lesser extent, were girls. The effects of non-aggressive modelling, however, were inconsistent with some behaviours being reduced compared to the control group but others not.

Conclusion: The findings demonstrated that observation and imitation can account for the learning of specific acts without reinforcement of either the models or observers. In this case it is possible that seeing an adult's aggression suggests to the child that such behaviour is permissible, reducing their inhibitions against it and increasing the probability that they will perform aggressive acts in the future. Same-sex modelling may have been more effective for boys than for girls because male aggression is more culturally typical so carries the weight of social acceptability.

for and against

social learning theory as an explanation of human behaviour

+ It can explain the acquisition of behaviours, such as aggression, through observation.

+ It can explain why children may appear to have spontaneously acquired a new behaviour because social learning can occur without immediate demonstration.

— It cannot account for the acquisition of new behaviours which have not been observed in a model.

where to now?

We recommend the following as a further source of good information about social learning:

▶ **Pearce, J.M. (1998)** *Animal Learning and Cognition: An Introduction*. **Hove: Psychology Press** – an excellent account of animal learning.

real lives

Behaviour therapy

Learning theory can be used in clinical settings to deliberately alter people's behaviour. The clinical application of classical conditioning is called behaviour *therapy*, whilst operant conditioning has given rise to behaviour *modification*. In this chapter we shall just be looking at behaviour therapy – the use of classical conditioning principles to alter maladaptive behaviour. Behaviour therapy techniques include treatment of phobias using systematic desensitisation and flooding and the use of aversion therapy to eliminate behaviours.

Systematic desensitisation

Systematic desensitisation relies on the therapist being able to induce a state of relaxation in the client. This may be achieved by progressive muscle relaxation, hypnosis or the use of anti-anxiety drugs. This relaxed state is the UCR. During conditioning, relaxation is paired with items relating to the feared stimulus, working through a graduated sequence called an anxiety hierarchy. This is a list of stimuli, agreed between the client and therapist, of increasingly more feared items leading to the phobic stimulus itself. During desensitisation the UCR is maintained throughout exposure to the hierarchy of increasingly more frightening CSs. *Reciprocal inhibition* prevents the client from feeling two opposite emotions at once thus, as the state of relaxation is maintained, they cannot become afraid. Each pairing results in the new CS becoming associated with the CR of relaxation rather than fear.

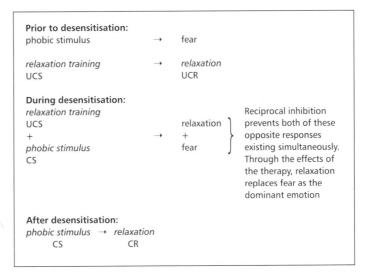

The process of desensitisation

Freeling and Shemberg (1970) used systematic desensitisation for exam nerves in a group of students. They first developed an anxiety hierarchy of 15 items ranging from 'you are sitting in a classroom of 100 students listening to a lecture' to 'the test papers are being handed out'. The students were then taught how to achieve deep muscle relaxation and asked to practise the technique every day at home. During desensitisation sessions, the students relaxed with the help of suggestions from the experimenter and were asked to imagine each scene from the hierarchy in turn. They moved on to the next item only when they felt relaxed with the image, up to four items being introduced during each weekly meeting. After six weeks the students were less anxious, indicated by both questionnaire responses and exam performance.

The following example from Wolpe (1969), who first developed systematic desensitisation, illustrates an anxiety hierarchy for a phobia of physical deformity. As you can see, it begins with mildly fear-evoking stimuli and culminates in the most severely fear-inducing situation for the client. As desensitisation proceeds, the relaxation associated with one situation may generalise to the next, paving the way for progression through the stages.

1 Ambulances
2 Hospitals
3 Wheelchairs
4 Nurses in uniform
5 Automobile accidents
6 The sight of someone who is seriously ill
7 Someone in pain
8 The sight of physical deformity

An anxiety hierarchy for a phobia of physical deformity (Wolpe, 1969)

In research involving long-term follow-up of clients with phobias, Zinbarg *et al.* (1992) report that systematic desensitisation is more effective than any other form of therapy for most clients with phobias. It is also effective across a range of phobias including post-traumatic stress disorder, sexual dysfunction and asthma attacks (Emmelkamp, 1994).

Nyctophobics don't go out at night and zoophobics steer clear of pet shops. People with phobias tend to avoid the source of their fear, thus are never in a position to test whether the feared situation is actually as unpleasant as they believe. It could be argued that the reason systematic desensitisation works is because it places the client in a situation where they are forced to test reality. On discovering that the feared situation is not, in fact, as horrific as imagined, the phobia is dispelled.

Flooding

In contrast to the progressive approach of systematic desensitisation, *flooding* achieves reality testing in a single step. The client is placed in a safe, supportive environment and confronts the feared situation head-on, effectively stepping straight up to the top of their hierarchy. They are immersed in this situation until their fear subsides. As with the final stage of a desensitisation hierarchy, the flooding procedure may be *in vivo*, a 'live' situation or covert, a described, illustrated or imagined scene. The latter is termed *implosion therapy* as the fear *implodes*, that is it is destroyed inwardly. The example of implosion opposite was used by a therapist for a client with a fear of snakes. Covert procedures tend to be used when the feared stimulus would be impractical to introduce into the therapist's consulting room; snakes, water, fire or heights for example. Virtual reality simulators can offer very effective covert procedures in these instances.

Studies with animals support the effectiveness of the flooding paradigm. Rats that have learned a signalled shock-avoidance response to a tone are subjected to repeated tones *without* receiving a shock. This forces reality-testing and exposes the rats to a situation which eliminates their fear of the tone (Baum, 1969).

Ophidiophobics, who fear snakes, benefit from systematic desensitisation

Success with flooding therapy appears to be even better than with systematic desensitisation (Marks, 1987). In work with agoraphobics, who fear being helpless and unaided when they are away from their place of security, flooding has been particularly successful. Agoraphobia, which literally means 'fear of the market place' (the *agora* of ancient Greece), is often triggered in crowded places such as shopping centres where the sufferer feels alone and at risk. Therefore, flooding often requires the client to agree (with great trepidation) to spend a prolonged period of time alone in a busy public place. This may be preceded by exposure to a graphic description of their worst fears, for example being knocked down, trampled on and laughed at. After several hours of horrifying immersion during which nothing terrible happens, the client should find that their anxiety has subsided. The improvement achieved through flooding persists; after four years Emmelkamp and Kuipers (1979) found that 75 per cent of a group of 70 agoraphobics were still benefiting from the effects of their treatment. Similar gains are found with flooding therapy for obsessive-compulsive disorders such as repetitive washing in response to fears of contamination (Marks and Rachman, 1978). Whilst more effective, flooding is of course, more immediately distressing for the client.

Implosion confronts the phobia directly, as is evident in the example below.

Close your eyes again. Picture the snake out in front of you. Now make yourself pick it up. Reach down, pick it up, put it in your lap, feel it wiggling around in your lap, leave your hand on it, put your hand out and feel it wiggling around. Kind of explore its body with your fingers and hand. You don't like to do it, make yourself do it. Make yourself do it. Really grab onto the snake. Squeeze it a little bit, feel it. Feel it kind of start to wind around your hand. Let it. Leave your hand there, feel it touching your hand there, feel it touching your hand and winding around it, curling around your wrist.

Okay, now put you finger out towards the snake and feel his head coming up. Its head is towards your finger and it is starting to bite your finger. Let it, let it bite at your finger. Put your finger out, let it bite, let it bite at your finger, feel its fangs go right down into your finger. Ooooh, feel the pain going right up your arm and into your shoulder.

Okay, feel him coiling around your hand again, touching you, slimy, now he is going up on your shoulder and he crawls there and he is sitting on your chest and he is looking you right in the eye. He is black and he is big and he is ugly and he's coiled up and he is ready to strike and he is looking at you. Picture his face, look at his eyes, look at those long sharp fangs.... He strikes out at you. [Therapist slaps hand.] Feel him bite at your face. Feel him bite at your face, let him bite; let him bite; just relax and let him bite; let him bite at your face; let him bite; let him bite at your face; feel his fangs go right into your cheeks; and the blood is coming out on your face now... feel it biting your eye and it is going to pull your eye right out and down on your cheek. It is kind of gnawing on it and eating it, eating at your eye. Your little eye is down on your cheek and it is gnawing and biting at your eye. Picture it. Now it is crawling into your eye socket and wiggling around in there, feel it wiggling and wiggling up into your head.

An example of implosion (from Hogan, 1968)

for and against

behavioural therapies

+ These techniques can be extremely effective in treating conditions such as phobias.

+ Behavioural techniques can also reduce symptoms in more complex conditions.

− In cases where genes (see Chapter 1) or family relationships (see Chapter 5) have played a role in the development of symptoms, behavioural treatments which just alleviate symptoms cannot be considered cures.

− Sometimes (as we have seen!) behavioural treatments can be, to say the least, traumatic for patients.

where to now?

The following are good sources of information about behavioural therapies:

 Cave, S. (1999) *Therapeutic Approaches*. **London: Routledge** – a simple and user-friendly introduction to therapies including behavioural approaches

Bergin, A.E. and Garfield, S.L. (1994) *Handbook of Psychotherapy and Behaviour Change*. **New York: Wiley** – a very advanced and detailed text with numerous examples of studies of behavioural therapies and their applications and effectiveness.

Community behaviour analysis

We have looked at how behavioural therapies can help people eliminate unwanted behaviours. The aim of community behaviour analysis is to tackle *social problems* using the same principles. Social problems can stem from individuals but they also come from communities (for example, in the form of vandalism), from the state (for example, unemployment) or from an entire culture (for example, in the acceptance of sexual discrimination and harassment). Modern behavioural psychologists have used the principles of learning theory to intervene on all these levels in an attempt to tackle social problems. The failure of some conventional methods for tackling social problems can be understood in terms of learning theory. Fawcett (1991) has suggested that our failure to reduce illicit drug-taking is in part due to the lack of provision of alternative forms of reinforcement. Law and order relies on punishing inappropriate behaviour, but the study of punishment has shown us that *punishers* only tend to eliminate behaviour when they are immediate, severe and inevitable; clearly the legal system does not always allow this. *Reinforcement*, which has been demonstrated to be more effective than punishment in modifying behaviour, is not normally available in the legal system.

An example of successful community behaviour analysis using punishment with individuals comes from Sherman (1992), who reported a project by Minneapolis Police Department to tackle domestic violence. It was proposed that if punishment were sufficiently immediate, severe and inevitable, violent men could be dissuaded from re-offending. A programme was instituted such that, instead of telling the offender to leave the scene or counselling the couple jointly (standard practice at the time), the police arrested the man immediately and kept him in jail overnight. The programme was highly successful and only around 10 per cent of the men were recorded as re-offending.

Fox *et al.* (1987) has provided another example of successful community behaviour analysis, this time involving *reinforcement* and a whole community. A *token economy* system was used to improve safety at two open mines over ten years. Token economies are a way of applying operant conditioning to large numbers of people. Appropriate behaviour is rewarded with tokens, which can then be exchanged for reinforcers, in this case goods from local shops. Tokens were given to miners at the end of each month in which they had no involvement in any accident. Additional tokens were given to work groups in which no worker had been injured, thus encouraging a sense of shared responsibility. The programme was highly successful – over the ten years accidents were reduced by more than 75 per cent.

As we have seen, behavioural principles can be applied to community settings although there is a certain tension between pure learning theory specialists and community behaviour analysts, due to the lack of experimental control outside the psychology laboratory. Remember that of all the major approaches to psychology, behavioural psychologists place the greatest value on conducting very tightly controlled research in the laboratory. To those traditional behavioural psychologists, the studies by Fox *et al.* and Sherman are flawed because the real-life settings in which they were performed may introduce any number of other factors that might have interfered with the results. Despite these difficulties, community behaviour analysis is a growing area and a promising approach to tackling social problems.

where to now?

The following is a good source of further information on community behaviour analysis:

▶ **Leslie, J.C. and O'Reilly, M.F. (1999)** *Behaviour Analysis: Foundations and Applications to Psychology*. **Amsterdam: Harwood Academic Publishers** – contains a very well explained section on community behaviour analysis as part of an excellent chapter on future directions in behaviour analysis.

talking point

Internet addiction disorder

In the 1990s the concept of Internet addiction was treated as a joke. But now, in the twenty-first century, is it becoming a reality? Chat rooms and MUDs are developing a following of Internet users who are showing the characteristics of addiction demonstrated by compulsive gamblers. MUD actually stands for *multi user dungeon* because MUDs were originally used for playing the game *Dungeons and Dragons*. However, the term MUD is now used to mean *multi user domain* – any shared environment in virtual reality. Can learning theory shed any light on how these behaviours develop? As we saw on page 48, a variable ratio schedule of reinforcement, one where rewards are infrequent and unpredictable, produces both the highest response rate and the greatest resistance to extinction. Once a behaviour has been learned in this way it is frequently repeated and hard to stop.

Young (1998) investigated the habits of Internet users with a questionnaire based on one designed to assess pathological gambling. The questionnaire included, for example:

- Do you feel preoccupied with the Internet (think about previous on-line activity or anticipate the next on-line session)?

- Do you feel the need to use the Internet with increasing amounts of time in order to achieve satisfaction?

- Have you repeatedly made unsuccessful efforts to control, cut back, or stop Internet use?

- Do you feel restless, moody, depressed or irritable when attempting to cut down or stop Internet use?

- Do you stay on-line longer than originally intended?

- Have you jeopardised or risked the loss of a significant relationship, job, educational or career opportunity because of the Internet?

- Do you use the Internet as a way of escaping from problems or relieving a dysphoric mood (for example, feelings of helplessness, guilt, anxiety, depression)?

Young sought participants through various routes including newspaper advertisements, posters and ironically, electronic support groups dedicated to Internet addiction. 'Dependent users' were defined as those participants answering 'yes' to five or more of the questions.

Of approximately 600 respondents, almost two-thirds were rated as dependent. Whilst this figure is high, it is unsurprising given the sample taken. A typical dependent user was not, as the stereotype might suggest, a young male but a woman in her forties. The non-dependent users in contrast were males in their twenties. Other studies, with less biased samples, have produced lower estimates of addiction (for example, Brenner, 1996).

In Young's study there was a key difference in the way dependent and non-dependent users spent their time on-line. The non-dependent users spent an average of 4.9 hours per week on-line, 79 per cent of which was on e-mail, the Web and information gathering (doing searches and downloading software). Dependent users, in contrast, spent 63 per cent of their time in synchronous communication environments, including chat rooms and MUDs. How do such differences in use arise?

According to Wallace (1999) synchronous spaces are one of the most compelling Internet environments in part because they offer the same powerful attractions as gambling. Your 'behaviour', perhaps the message you send to a chat room, may generate an immediate consequence (a reply) or may not. This combination of a short time delay when a reward is forthcoming and its unpredictability, create a powerful variable ratio schedule of positive reinforcement. For a rat in a Skinner box or a gambler at a slot machine there are few possible changes they can make to their behaviour in a search for a more profitable response. On the Internet, however, the personality one portrays can be endlessly varied to test the probability of success. Trial and error has far more scope when there are limitless possibilities.

Game-oriented MUDs and chat rooms also construct variable ratio schedules of reinforcement. In the Trivbot chat room users join a team playing a 'trivial pursuit' style game. The first player to enter a correct answer is both congratulated and earns a point for their team – the rewards are immediate if infrequent. Similarly, adventure MUDs provide unpredictable reinforcement when the player slays an opponent. Apart from the intrinsic reward of success, there may be on-screen reinforcement and the respect of lower level players. Therefore, there is a significant motive to spend more time engaged in play as this is the only route to higher levels.

Compulsion to return to a particular Internet location was studied by Suler (1996). He has observed the behaviour of visitors to the 'Palace', where paying users develop a character and wend there way through its graphical *metaworld* appreciating their surroundings and chatting to other subscribers. Virtual communities such as the Palace owe their appeal to the sense of membership they develop; individuals are known and feel welcome, thus providing positive reinforcement. Developing a 'popular' persona, however, demands an investment of time; if you aren't 'seen' you'll be forgotten.

where to now?

The following are good sources of further information about Internet addiction:

▶ **Wallace, P. (1999)** *The Psychology of the Internet*. **Cambridge: Cambridge University Press** – a generally excellent text on all aspects of internet use

▶ **Griffiths, M. (1999) Internet addiction: fact or fiction.** *The Psychologist*, **12, 246–50** – a state-of-the-art review of recent research into the phenomenon of Internet addiction.

Conclusions

The learning theory approach to psychology is based on the importance of learning behaviour by the processes of classical and operant conditioning and by social learning. Because the learning approach sees humans and other animals as learning by similar processes, it is often easier to study animals and then apply the results to humans. We have looked here at both human and animal studies of conditioning and social learning. Early behavioural psychologists believed that all behaviour could be accounted for by conditioning, but more recent research has revealed that both humans and other animals seem to be predisposed to learning biologically useful behaviours rather than unhelpful behaviours.

The learning approach has given rise to behavioural therapies, which are designed to help people learn new and healthier behaviours in place of maladaptive behaviours. We have looked in particular at behaviour therapy, which is based on classical conditioning and is particularly useful for treating phobias. A more recent application of learning theory is in community behaviour analysis, in which the principles of conditioning and social learning are applied to changing the behaviour of communities and society as a whole as well as individuals. Finally we have used a learning perspective to look at a growing problem – Internet addiction.

what do you know?

1 Describe how a behaviour may be learned by classical conditioning. *(6)*

2 Outline the mechanisms of operant conditioning. *(10)*

3 Describe and evaluate one study which explores the learning theory approach. *(10)*

4 Discuss one contemporary issue relating to learning theory. *(10)*

3

The Cognitive Approach

what's **ahead?**

This chapter concerns the cognitive approach to psychology. This approach has become increasingly popular since the 1950s, focusing on mental processes, including perception, memory, language and thinking. In this chapter, we will focus on research and theory on memory. We will look at two traditional models of memory, the multi-store approach and levels of processing theory. In our *what's new* section we also have a brief look at a more recent area of research, that of autobiographical memory. We will discuss theories of forgetting (repression, decay and cue-dependent forgetting). In our *real lives* section we see how research on memory has helped us to understand the sometimes fallible nature of eye-witness testimony. In *talking point* we look at an issue that is currently hotly debated in psychology – the accuracy of recovered memories and false memory syndrome.

what's it **about?**

The cognitive approach is based on the following ideas.

- Like behaviourists and biological psychologists, cognitive psychologists see psychology as a pure science. Research is thus highly scientific in nature.

- Whereas behaviourists are interested primarily in observable behaviour and psychodynamic psychologists (see Chapter 5) are interested primarily in emotion, cognitive psychologists are primarily interested in thinking and related mental processes, such as memory.

- The major influence on human behaviour and emotion is how the mind processes information.

- Like a computer we are influenced by the ways in which our brains are 'hard-wired' and by the ways in which we have been 'programmed' by experience.

The brain as an information-processing system

Your brain is a lump of grey matter sitting in a dark cavern of a skull. Somehow, it can detect and interpret events in the environment surrounding it. It (you) can predict, plan, recognise friends and enemies, tell cats from cars, solve problems and make decisions. You are, now, able to focus your attention on this book, perceive the squiggles of ink on the page, and give meaning to those squiggles in the form of words and sentences. Cognitive psychologists want to know *how* it is that you (and they) can *do* these things.

Currently, the dominant approach in cognitive psychology is the *information processing approach*. This approach looks at the flow of information through the system of the mind. Information comes in, is processed somehow and then the system responds with appropriate thought, emotions and behaviour. Cognitive psychologists compare the way the human mind processes information with the working of a computer. Information comes in to a computer through a keyboard or software disk. Humans receive information through their senses. The computer then runs programs that do something with this information (for example, it applies rules that let you play a game). Humans process information (via the central nervous system and the brain), so that they can see, hear, recognise, etc. The computer gives output in terms of a printout on paper or images on a screen, and humans give a wide variety of outputs as behaviour.

Be clear that this approach is not saying that the mind is a computer. Rather, it is saying that both humans and computers process information, and there are abstract principles that apply to all information processors. For example, the system must have input and output mechanisms so that information can be received and responded to. The system must have memory, so that information can be stored as data and used in performing operations. The system must have a processor, which can take the information in memory or from the environment and perform operations on it by following particular rules or programs. Computer specialists are concerned with the ways in which computers deal with information that lets us use them to do things like calculate, play games, write letters, etc.

Cognitive psychologists are concerned with the ways in which humans use information that lets us see, remember, solve problems, etc. The chapter focuses on the memory system.

Memory

Memory holds all the information that tells us who we are, what the world is like and what we should be doing next. Without memory, all learning is impossible and so is human life as we know it. In studying memory, psychologists have tended to focus on three processes:

- *coding*, or how information is put into the system. Quite how it is done is still mysterious, but psychologists recognise that information may enter the system in different forms (for example, according to how it looks, or sounds or what it means)

- *storage*, which refers to holding information in the system. We can ask questions here such as, how much information can the system hold, and how long does it hold it for?

- *retrieval*, which refers to getting information in storage back out again so that we can use it when we want to. We can ask questions here such as, how do we go about finding the information we want, and what might prevent us from succeeding?

In the light of these processes, psychologists have developed theories about the general ways in which the memory system operates. They have proposed different models of memory in an attempt to provide a framework by which memory can be studied and understood. We shall turn now to consider some of these models.

As you read, bear in mind that cognitive processes are not directly observable. Psychologists are forced to infer the nature of underlying processes from the research findings. Some psychologists prefer to bring research into the laboratory to gain better control and more careful measurement. This has often resulted in testing participants' recall for lists of words and nonsense syllables. Even so, it is sometimes possible to offer more than one explanation for the same set of results. Others question the ecological validity of laboratory based research altogether (see page 232 for a discussion of ecological validity). They argue that our memory system did not evolve for learning meaningless lists in the laboratory. These psychologists are willing to accept the loss of control associated with field research in the belief that this is the only way to understand properly how memory operates in the real world. In general, it is probably fair to say that most psychologists favour a mixture of approaches to improve our understanding of what is a complex topic.

Theories of memory

The multi-store model

A major consideration in devising a model of memory is to decide just how many different systems or stores we possess. Multi-store models assume that we can distinguish distinct and separate stores, each of which have their own unique characteristics. One of the most influential models of memory is the two-process model by Atkinson and Shiffrin (1968, 1971). This suggested that incoming information is automatically stored very briefly in a sensory register. Thereafter, control processes like coding and rehearsal determine the fate of this information. Material in the sensory register that is attended to is coded in short-term memory (STM), and information in STM that is sufficiently rehearsed is coded in long-term memory (LTM). Note that these different kinds of memory should not be considered as separate regions or boxes in the brain, but as descriptions of different mental processes.

Atkinson and Shiffrin's multi-store model

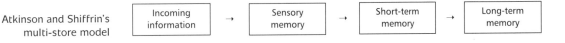

Incoming information → Sensory memory → Short-term memory → Long-term memory

Sensory memory

If you wave your fingers quickly from side to side before your eyes, you will see a blur between your fingers. This is because of a very short-lived memory trace in the visual system. It needs to be short-lived for an obvious reason (all moving objects would appear blurred). This form of sensory memory is known as *iconic memory*, and it is thought to last for less than a second. Sensory memory for sounds is called *echoic memory*. Echoic memory is thought to last for around two seconds. Sensory memory explains the irritating phenomenon that takes place when someone asks you a question and you respond 'What?' and then you answer the question before you are asked a second time. This is because the sound of the question hung around in echoic storage long enough for you to figure out what was asked.

Short-term and long-term memory

If someone gives us their telephone number, then we know that if we aren't careful we will quickly forget it. If we can't write this information down (or otherwise record it) we can repeat (rehearse) it to help us remember. Of course we can usually remember our own telephone number and don't seem to need to keep rehearsing this information. This distinction between information that is quickly forgotten and information that is relatively permanent is what underpins the STM/LTM distinction in the two-process model.

Short-term memory is believed to hold about seven 'bits' or chunks of information for about 20 seconds without rehearsal. The size of a 'bit' can vary, and information is often coded acoustically (by sound). The life of the store can be prolonged through rehearsal. If information is sufficiently rehearsed it will be transferred to long-term storage. Long-term memory has an unlimited capacity, information within it is often coded semantically, and it can last from a few minutes to a lifetime. Let us examine the evidence for these beliefs in terms of encoding, storage and retrieval mentioned above.

Coding

Evidence suggests that in general, information is coded differently in STM and LTM. In rehearsing a list one thing we commonly do is repeat the information to ourselves, over and over. We don't often try to give meaning to a telephone number we've just looked up before we dial it or picture the numbers – the *sound* of it is what seems important for short-term recall. This is called *acoustic coding*. On the other hand, in trying to remember a lecture on memory, the exact words are less important than what they mean. Meaning is important for long-term recall, and this involves semantic coding, i.e. coding according to the meaning of words. There is also considerable evidence to support the view that visual imagery is often important in LTM too. Information *can* be coded in STM and LTM in a variety of ways (for example, the sound of your telephone ringing is stored in LTM), it is just that *usually* coding is different.

Storage

The *capacity* of LTM is thought to be unlimited. We don't know of anyone whose memory was so full they couldn't learn anything new. STM, on the other hand, is limited in the amount of information that it can store. Remembering 8361 is easy. Remembering 5927482103839 is hard, precisely because the number is so long. You can test the limits of STM quite simply by asking a friend to remember number strings of increasing length. Miller (1956) suggests that most of us can hold between five and nine chunks of information in STM. In other words, we have about seven 'slots' available in STM in which to store information. Just how much information we fit into a slot varies according to how well we are able to organise the information into a meaningful unit or 'chunk'. Consider this:

E	N	L	E	S	W
R	O	I	B	T	O
I	I	M	O	N	H
A	L	A	T	A	W

This grid is hard to recall as 24 separate letters, but easy to recall if chunked into a meaningful unit. You can do this by starting at the bottom right-hand corner and working backwards from there. Miller believed that some people who are able to remember very long strings of numbers do this by organising them into meaningful mathematical units. In this way we can fit a lot of information into STM, although we can still only recall about seven chunks. A meaningful chunk can be very large. An experienced chess player can take a quick look at a game and remember where the pieces are because they can chunk the pieces into recognisable configurations and strategies, something an inexperienced player can't do.

Retrieval

Information in STM is usually retrieved very rapidly or not at all. You can either remember the telephone number you just looked up, or you've forgotten it and have to look it up again. It doesn't usually help to sit and think. Sternberg (1966) measured how long it took people to say whether or not a particular number was in a list of numbers that they had just heard. Although a complete search of a full store would typically take only a few hundred milliseconds, he found people did take a bit longer to answer the longer the list was that they were initially presented with. This suggests that STM recall does involve a very rapid search process.

Searches of LTM may be longer and more involved. To be sure, items are sometimes retrieved immediately (like your phone number), which indicates a high level of organisation in such a massive store. But sometimes we have to take time to work our way to a memory. For example, in trying to recall where you left your keys last night you may reconstruct events: What state were you in? Who (if anyone) were you with? What rooms did you visit? etc. This ability to access hard-to-find memories using cues and other memory 'joggers' seems different to the all or nothing recall that is often a feature of STM. The section on forgetting in this chapter will discuss some of the reasons why we may fail to retrieve information.

Evidence for separate STM and LTM

The model provides a conceptual framework that is useful and has support from a number of sources. A major attraction of the model is that it can help to explain a finding that is known as the serial position effect. This refers to the fact that, in tests of *free recall*, where people are asked to recall lists of words in any order they like, they typically recall more words from the end of the list (the recency effect) and from the beginning of the list (the primacy effect) than they do from the middle. Plotted graphically the findings give what is known as a serial position curve.

It is suggested that this finding can be explained by reference to STM and LTM. The information at the beginning enters an empty store and has more time for rehearsal. Consequently it may be passed to LTM. As more information comes in there is less time for rehearsal and so STM is used, but this rapidly fills up so that the later items in the list push out or displace the earlier items in the store. The last items are well remembered, therefore, because they are freshly arrived and have not been

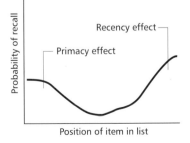

The serial position curve

displaced from STM, and the earliest items are able to be recalled from LTM. Furthermore, Glanzer and Cunitz (1966) found that delaying recall of the list by 30 seconds destroys the recency effect, the end items being recalled no better than those in the middle, but it does not damage the primacy effect. The ability to selectively damage recall and explain these findings by reference to distinct memory stores is support for the model.

Further support for separate STM and LTM comes from studies of patients with brain damage causing anterograde amnesia. This form of memory loss is especially likely if a region of the brain called the hippocampus is damaged through accident or illness, and results in people effectively being unable to recall new learning from LTM. Old memories accrued before the injury are still intact, and STM still functions (for example, conversations are possible), but new people are never remembered, nor are recent visits from known friends or family, newspaper articles may be constantly reread without realising it, etc. Patients also demonstrate the recency effect in free recall but not the primacy effect (Baddeley and Warrington, 1970). Once again, then, we have evidence of distinct memory stores, a functioning STM but impaired LTM. Whether this reflects an inability to form new long-term memories, or an inability to consciously retrieve these memories once formed, is still not clear.

for and against

the multi-store model

+ The distinction between STM and LTM provides a framework many psychologists still find useful for thinking about memory.

+ It explains findings from research into the serial position effect.

+ It helps explain some kinds of memory problems like anterograde amnesia.

− The model in its original form is too simplistic. We now believe that both STM and LTM have several separate storage systems.

− Some psychologists believe that memory is better understood as a byproduct of information processing (see the levels of processing approach) rather than as a series of stores.

Different kinds of LTM

LTM as characterised in the two-process model has been criticised as inadequate since it fails to distinguish between different kinds of long-term memory that we possess. We know, for example, that some memories (like memory for some details of psychology perhaps) are more readily forgotten than others (like memory for how to ride a bike). Indeed memory for motor skills seems to use a particular region of the brain towards the back of the head, the cerebellum, whereas memories for events and concepts may involve patterns of neurons spread across the cortex. Brain damaged sufferers of anterograde amnesia can often still learn new motor skills, for example playing the piano, though they may not be able to recall that they have learned them.

Cohen and Squire (1980) suggest we can distinguish between *declarative* memories, and *procedural* memories. Declarative memory is to do with knowing 'that...'. It includes the vast range of information of things that we know and can easily tell other people about (declare). Procedural knowledge is knowledge of *how to do* things, like how to ride a bike. This is not knowledge that is easy to impart verbally since it is not open to conscious introspection. You can tell someone who wants to know how to ride to sit on the saddle and pedal, but that doesn't capture it. They are still likely to fall off, and it is only through repeated practice that they will come to know how to ride a bike.

Tulving (1972; 1985) also distinguishes procedural memory and *two* broad types of declarative memory: *episodic* and *semantic* memory. Episodic memories are memories for particular life events (things that you have done or had happen to you). Semantic memories are memories for concepts, rules (including the rules of language), and general knowledge of the world. Both kinds of memories are closely interlinked in everyday remembering. Clearly much semantic memory is acquired through personal experience, and personal experiences are interpreted and understood in the light of knowledge stored in semantic memory. Broadly, knowing how to catch a bus involves semantic memory (there are rules about queuing, signalling, paying, etc.). How we learned these rules we may not be precisely able to recall, but if we remember catching the bus this morning then that involves episodic memory. This distinction between episodic and semantic memory can help to explain some cases of amnesia where people may lose personal information about themselves, their address, job or name, but still know how to speak or read or get dressed.

The levels of processing approach (LOP)

This approach was put forward by Craik and Lockhart (1972). They argued that it is useful to think of memory as a *byproduct* of information processing. Whether we remember something depends on how we process it (i.e. what we *do* with the information). Many of the day-to-day events in our lives are trivial and so we are not predisposed to think about them much and they are forgotten. Important events are better remembered simply because of the extra consideration or "work" that we put into processing the information. Deep processing produces more elaborate, longer lasting memory traces. Craik and Lockhart identified three levels of processing:

- *structural* – what something looks like

- *phonetic* – what something sounds like

- *semantic* – what something means.

The deepest level is semantic processing, and the shallowest is structural processing. Two basic ideas of this approach are simply that:

- semantic analysis results in deeper processing

- deeper processing results in a more durable memory (Craik, 1979).

Support for this approach comes from a classic study by Craik and Tulving (1975).

classic
research

do we remember deeply encoded material better?

Craik, F.I.M. and Tulving, E. (1975) Depth of processing and retention of words in episodic memory. *Journal of Experimental Psychology: General*, 104, 268–94

Aim: Researchers were interested in the ways in which different forms of processing of verbal information might affect recall. Specifically they aimed to see whether there would be a difference in the extent to which participants would recall words that had been processed structurally, phonetically or semantically.

Method: Participants were presented with lists of words via a tachistoscope, a device which presents items for a very brief period of time. After each word was presented the participants were asked one of four different questions:

a) Is it in capital letters? (requiring structural processing)
b) Does it rhyme with …? (some other word, for example, frog – requiring phonetic processing)
c) Is it a …? (some category, for example, vegetable – requiring semantic processing)
d) Can you fit it in this sentence …? (insert some sentence with a word missing – also requiring semantic processing).

Participants had to respond 'yes' or 'no' to these questions. At this point they were not aware that they were going to be tested on their memory for the words. Later, however, they were given an unexpected *recognition* test. They were shown the words they had seen and answered questions on, mixed in with an equal number of new words. The participants' task was to identify the words they had seen before.

Results: The researchers found, as expected, that participants recognised around 70 per cent of the semantically-processed words, around 35 per cent of the phonetically-processed words, and around 15 per cent of the structurally-processed words. Also, recall was better if the answer to the initial questions was 'yes' rather than 'no'.

Conclusion: Craik and Lockhart believed that simply deciding what letters look like does not require a person to do much mental work. There is relatively little cognitive processing involved. To imagine what a word would sound like if spoken requires that you process a visual image in terms of an auditory one, so rather more cognitive processing is required. To extract meaning from a word, and to consider it in the light of other words in a sentence requires still more processing. The results of this study support the principle that deeply processed material will be better remembered.

Discussion of the LOP approach

Craik and Lockhart argued that the LOP approach is not meant to be a complete theory of memory so much as a framework to guide research. It is useful in that it focuses attention on the different ways in which information can be manipulated. For example, the approach can help explain a finding by Morris *et al.* (1981) that keen football supporters were better at remembering football scores than those disinterested in football. Quite simply, the enthusiasts related the scores to other information they have about the teams, the players, their league positions, etc. and so processed the information more deeply. The approach can also be applied to other information than purely verbal information. For example, Bower and Karlin (1974) asked participants to judge whether faces were male or female (shallow processing), or to judge from the faces how honest or how likeable the person was (this was assumed to require a bit more thought and so deeper processing). They found the deep processing condition resulted in better recognition than the shallow condition in a later test.

for and against

levels of processing

+ It provides an alternative explanation for anterograde amnesia (processing too shallow to enable retrieval).

+ In the two-process model information that is held for a few minutes is considered to have entered LTM, but then so is information that is stored for years. This is too crude a way of representing all the different types of memory that we have or their differences in durability. The LOP approach encourages us to recognise that we should expect wide variety in memory because there is a wide variety of ways in which information is dealt with.

— Baddeley (1990) believed that one of the greatest weaknesses of the LOP approach is that the definition of depth is circular. The approach seems to argue that well remembered material has been deeply processed and deeply processed material is that which is well remembered. There is no independent way to verify how 'deep' processing actually is.

— Much research has shown that making a memory stand out and be *distinctive* somehow is often a useful way of improving recall. There are ways of adding distinctiveness apart from simply imparting meaning (for example, forming distinctive mental images), and so imposing meaning is not the only way of improving recall.

where to now?

The following are good sources of further information on theories of memory:

▶ **Eysenck, M. (1994) How many memory stores?** *Psychology Review*, **1, 1–4** – an article specifically written for pre-degree students by one of the most eminent cognitive psychologists in the world. Looks at experimental and neuropsychological evidence for separate short- and long-term memory

▶ **Baddeley, A. (1995)** *Your Memory: A User's Guide*. **London: Penguin** – a popular rather than academic book, but contains enough detail in a user-friendly format to be extremely useful to students at A-level

▶ **Baddeley, A. (1996)** *Human Memory*, **2nd edition. Hove: Lawrence Erlbaum Associates Ltd** – a more detailed and academic text, aimed at undergraduates. Sufficiently clear however to be of use to those studying introductory psychology who want a little more detail to get their teeth into.

what's new?

autobiographical memory

Over the last 20 years, a major development in memory research has been the everyday memory movement. The central idea of everyday memory is that, as well as studying memory in the laboratory, we should also look at how memory functions in people's everyday lives. One area of research that has flourished in the area of everyday memory is the study of people's autobiographical memory, i.e. memories for events from their own lives.

We want to know for example what kinds of autobiographical memories are likely to be well remembered (an 'unforgettable' experience), and which are likely to be forgotten. In general, it seems that events that are unique, personally important, surprising or emotional are likely to be well remembered. Again, in general, the accuracy and quality of our memories decline with time (Cohen, 1991). Since we know that time leads to the fading of memories, this can result in a distortion of our memory for when things happened. The *less* that people can remember about an event, then often the *older* the memory is thought to be. Brown *et al.* (1985) asked people to date 50 news events (relating to the period 1977–82) that they would likely either know a lot about (for example, the shooting of President Reagan), or else have little knowledge of (for example, 25 killed in mudslides). They found, as expected, that the events which people knew a lot about were dated as too recent by over three months, whereas low-knowledge events were dated as too old by about two months. Accuracy of dating is improved if we can associate the event with some landmark date to help us, for example the event happened on the same day as the day we got married (Loftus and Marburger, 1983).

Rubin *et al.* (1986), in an analysis of a number of studies, found that when elderly people look back over their lives, there is a *reminiscence bump*. That is, people tend to recall a surprisingly high number of events for when they were between ten and 30 years old, and especially between 15 and 25. Eysenck and Keane (1997) suggested that it may reflect the fact that most people develop a stable self-concept around adolescence. As a consequence, their general approach and outlook on life as, say, a 70-year-old, may in many ways be similar to that in early adulthood, and these similarities help in the retrieval of memories. The lack of a stable self-concept before adolescence hinders later recall. Additionally, adolescence and early adulthood are a time associated with much change. There are many new and personally relevant events, first dates, jobs, marriage, etc., and so these events are especially memorable.

Some events in life seem to stand out in memory with particular vividness and clarity. People sometimes report a wealth of details (who they were with, where they were, what they were doing, and other, peripheral details) at the time of some dramatic event (such as the assassination of President Kennedy, or the death of Princess Diana). Brown and Kulik (1977) gave the name *flashbulb memories* to memories of this sort. They proposed that emotional and surprising events which are personally important may automatically become fixed in memory by some special, neural mechanism. Brown and Kulik suggested that flashbulb memories are different from other memories in that they are so clear, long-lasting, detailed and accurate. Clearly, the ability to remember profound or important events could have survival value, although whether we do always remember accurately is in dispute (Neisser and Harsch, 1992). It is possible that improved recall may simply be a product of thinking more about a memorable event rather than a special neurological mechanism.

One way to study the accuracy of autobiographical memory is to conduct a diary study. This approach was adopted by Linton (1982). Over a six-year period, every day, Linton wrote on a 6 x 4 inch card a short description of at least two events that had happened that day. Every month she selected two descriptions at random from the accumulating pool and attempted to remember as much as she could about the events mentioned, and date them. Linton noted two types of forgetting. One type was associated with repeated events. For example, she regularly attended a committee meeting in another town, and found that, over time, memories for particular meetings became indistinguishable, blurring together into a general, composite memory. This is in line with most people's everyday experience. For example, a unique event (such as a birthday dinner) may stand out in memory, but repeated events (such as Sunday lunches over the past year) blend together into a somewhat indistinguishable lump. Linton also found that some events she simply could not recall at all. Forgetting of this sort was quite steady (about 6 per cent of events were forgotten each year, so that by year six, 30 per cent of events recorded in year one were totally forgotten).

A surprising finding was that events rated as important or emotional at the time they were recorded were no more likely to be remembered than those which weren't. However, the importance and emotionality ratings she gave to events with hindsight often differed from those given initially. It may be that an event rated emotional at the time is more likely to be remembered later only if it is still rated as emotional at the time of recall. A similar study by Wagenaar (1986), however, in which he recorded 2,400 events over a six-year period, found that events rated as emotional and important *were* more likely to be recalled. Interestingly, if other witnesses were able to provide extra information about an event that he could not remember, this nearly always enabled Wagenaar to recall the event. This suggests that much forgetting in autobiographical memory is cue dependent, and in fact most of the events in our lives may be stored in long-term memory.

Forgetting

Although forgetting is often a nuisance, it may well be a necessary feature of the memory system. If we were unable to forget things, and all past events were constantly competing in our minds for conscious attention, life would be intolerable. Luria (1968) reported the case of S who was able to recall minute details of events, or lists of numbers or words even 30 years after first learning them. This was linked to S's ability to form intense mental imagery. He suffered from a condition known as synaesthasia in which information entering one sense modality may produce sensations in another, so words and sounds can evoke images (for example, a particular word might evoke the image of a green square). Although it might seem pleasant to have such accurate recall, the intrusion of past memories and imagery made it difficult for S to maintain attention in normal life. Images he had formed would often creep into consciousness and interfere with his ability to concentrate.

A distinction we can make concerns whether the original memory is lost *from* storage or lost *in* the memory store. If information is no longer in storage then we have a problem of *availability*, i.e. the memory is no longer there to be retrieved. If information is lost in the store, we have a problem of *accessibility*, i.e. the memory is still there but we are having trouble finding it. In practice, as long as information is not remembered it seems we cannot know for sure which of these conditions applies. As soon as information is recalled, then it suggests the problem was one of accessibility all along. However, even here, we face the problem of deciding whether the original memory has now been recovered, or whether an appropriate new memory has been constructed to fill in the gap (this is called *confabulation*). Let us turn now to consider some of the reasons why we may forget things.

Decay

Problems of availability arise if memories decay, i.e. they simply fade away. Hebb (1949) believed that incoming information would excite a pattern of neurons (brain cells) to create a neurological memory trace in the brain and that this would spontaneously fade with time. Repeated firing of this trace, however, would produce a structural change within the brain. This change occurred at the synapses (the junction between nerves), altering the ways in which nerves communicate with each other, and thereby coding memories permanently. Accordingly, repeated firing or rehearsal maintains the memory in STM until a structural change occurs in the brain, this corresponding to the creation of a new long-term memory.

Tulving (1972) tested participants recall of word lists. He found that, over three trials, participants would recall about the same number of words, but they remembered a different mix of words on each trial, with only about half the recalled words coming up on all three trials. This points to the fact that the memory trace had *not* decayed, and that different words may provide different chains of associations to combat interference and aid recall. Waugh and Norman (1965) presented sequences of 16 digits at rates varying from one to four digits per second. They used a serial probe technique in which one digit in the series was selected and participants had to report the digit that followed it. The notion of trace decay suggests that faster rates of presentation should result in better recall (less time for decay to occur). However, they found no relationship between speed of presentation and recall.

Neurological evidence supports the idea that *synaptic changes*, i.e. changes between nervous connections, do occur with repeated firing. Since Hebb believed these changes were permanent he consequently believed that decay only occurred in STM. Forgetting in LTM was therefore mainly to do with interference from other memories. However, the notion of decay has been extended to LTM, with some researchers arguing that changes to the brain may not necessarily be permanent and therefore in time a memory could fade as a result of 'decay through disuse'. But the fact that elderly people can remember events from their childhood does not support the idea of decay in LTM. Certainly, motor skills seem very resistant to decay (for example, you never forget how to ride a bike).

for and against

trace decay

+ Decay explains why we forget more as time goes by.

+ Hebb has proposed a physiological mechanism to explain decay in STM (the spontaneous fading of the neural trace).

− In practice it is very difficult to test the theory, since other explanations (repression or context-dependency) offer plausible alternatives.

− Some memories never seem to decay. This requires explaining if trace decay is a major cause of forgetting.

Repression

Problems of accessibility will arise if information is repressed. Repression is an *ego defence mechanism* (see page 135). It refers to the pushing of anxiety-provoking thoughts into the unconscious mind. This can manifest itself as a general difficulty in recalling unhappy memories and as the complete blocking out of particularly traumatic memories. Repression is sometimes referred to as a theory of *motivated forgetting*, i.e. we fail to remember some unpleasant experiences because, really, we don't want to remember. Nevertheless, these repressed memories affect us in our daily lives. Many clinicians have found great utility in the idea of repressed memories, and the focus of much psychodynamic therapy is to tap into these buried memories, dragging them into consciousness (making them accessible), where they can be examined and come to terms with.

Repression is a controversial idea, and many cognitive psychologists do not believe in its existence at all, or that if it does exist that it is extremely rare.

There is a large body of clinical case-study evidence supporting the existence of repression (see page 136). However, cognitive psychologists tend to favour highly scientific research methods and to be wary of case studies as the sole evidence for a phenomenon. Indirect support for the existence of repression comes from surveys in which people have reported that they had previously forgotten a traumatic event although they remembered it at the point of the survey. In one such study, Elliott (1995) surveyed 500 people about whether they had continuously recalled a traumatic event. The traumas reported included military combat, rape, sexual abuse and witnessing a murder. Eighty per cent of respondents said they had always remembered the trauma, but 20 per cent said that there had been a period in which they had forgotten it until another event triggered the memory. This is of course only *indirect* evidence for repression because, although it suggests that memories can be forgotten and later recovered, it does not tell about the reason *why* they were forgotten in the first place.

Until recently there was little *direct* evidence for repression as a mechanism of forgetting. However Myers and Brewin (1994) have recently developed an approach to studying forgetting under laboratory conditions that may provide rather more solid support for repression. We can look at this is detail.

research now

can we demonstrate repression in the lab?

Myers, L.B. and Brewin, C.R. (1994) Recall of early experience and the repressive coping style. *Journal of Abnormal Psychology*, 103 (2), 288–92

Aim: Repression is said to involve both the general tendency to recall traumatic or unhappy memories less well than happy memories, and the complete blocking from consciousness of particularly stressful memories. The aim of this study was to see whether individuals who appeared to have a strong tendency to defend themselves against difficult emotions had more difficulty in remembering unhappy memories than did other people.

Method: Female participants were tested for their *trait anxiety*, i.e. their individual level of anxiety and their tendency for defensiveness, using psychometric tests. Participants who scored low for anxiety but high for defensiveness were classified as *repressors*, because it was judged that the low anxiety they experienced was probably a result of their defensiveness. All participants were then asked to recall as many happy and unhappy childhood memories as quickly as they could. The time they took to recall both types of memory was recorded. Finally, to account for the possibility that repressors simply had fewer unhappy childhood memories, participants were interviewed about their childhood.

Results: The results were dramatic. Repressors took twice as long to recall unhappy memories as highly anxious but less defensive people and three times as long as low anxious–low defensive people (mean recall time 18 seconds, 9 seconds and 6 seconds respectively). No difference emerged in the time needed to recall happy childhood memories between repressors and the other groups. The results of the interviews were also significant. The repressors were more likely to have experienced indifference or hostility from their fathers than the other participants.

Conclusion: The results provide evidence for the existence of repression in its form of a general tendency to have more difficulty in recalling unhappy memories. Of course this study has no bearing on the existence of repression in the sense of completely blanking out memories. It is particularly interesting that the repressive coping style in women was associated with poor relationships with their fathers. This suggests that the tendency for repression appears in childhood and is associated with parental relationships.

The Myers and Brewin study is extremely significant in demonstrating under controlled conditions that some form of repressive coping style does exist, and that some people are more prone to it than others. We shall return to the issue of repression in *talking point* when we examine the issue of false memory syndrome.

for and against

repression

+ Many therapists over very many years have utilised the idea of repression to good effect in their therapeutic treatments with patients.

+ There is now experimental evidence for the existence of repression in the sense of general difficulty in recalling unhappy memories.

– Whilst there is a body of evidence suggesting that it is possible to forget and later recall traumatic memories (for example, Elliott, 1995), there is little direct evidence that this temporary forgetting is caused by repression. Many psychologists are thus sceptical about complete loss of memories due to repression.

– Repression is clearly not a complete explanation of forgetting as it does not easily explain why we forget more as time goes by.

Cue-dependent forgetting

The tip-of-the-tongue phenomenon (when we know that we know something but can't quite recall it), along with the common, everyday experience of having our memory jogged for all sorts of things, suggests that much forgetting is due to problems of accessibility. We understand that very often, in the right circumstances or with the right prompt, we can remember information that is otherwise difficult to recall. This possibility, that information is in storage but needs the right cue to access it, is called *cue-dependent forgetting*.

Good evidence for cue-dependent forgetting comes from Tulving and Pearlstone (1966). They read people lists of words from various categories (for example, furniture or animals). The category names were also presented but the participants were not asked to remember the category names, just the examples (table, chair, etc.). They found that, in free recall, those participants who were given paper with the category names as headings remembered more words than those who were just given a blank sheet of paper. However, when the latter were also given the category headings their recall improved. This demonstrates how cues can guide us to information in memory that we are unable to otherwise access. Tulving (1983) believed that cues are only useful if they have been encoded at the time of the original learning (though others have questioned this). He called this the *encoding specificity principle*. This helps explain things like state- and context-dependent recall.

Tulving (1974) distinguished between *context-dependent recall* and *state-dependent recall*. Context-dependent recall relates to externally generated cues in the environment. Revisiting the neighbourhood where you were raised as a child may trigger childhood memories. Abernathy (1940) found students could recall more when tested in the rooms in which they were taught than if tested in different rooms. Godden and Baddeley (1975) asked people to learn a list of words either on land or 20 feet underwater. Four minutes later participants were given a test of free recall, either on land or underwater. Godden and Baddeley found that recall was about 50 per cent better if learning and recall took place in the same environment than if they occurred in different environments. These studies show the usefulness of environmental cues in aiding recall.

State-dependent recall relates to internally generated cues such as your physical or emotional state at the time of learning. Overton (1972) found that when a person sobered up after a bout of heavy drinking they could often forget experiences that occurred when they were drunk, but that memory for these experiences could return the next time they were drunk. Bower (1981) had people keep a diary for a week, recording events that they considered to be pleasant or unpleasant. The participants were then hypnotised and it was suggested to them that they were either in a happy mood or a sad mood. When asked to recall the events of the previous week, those in a happy mood tended to recall mostly pleasant events, and those in a sad mood tended to recall mostly unpleasant ones. Similarly, Mayer *et al.* (1990) found that you are more likely to remember happy events when you are happy compared to when you are sad. In a recent study, Aggleton and Waskett (1999) tested the common belief that smells make good cues to aid recall.

research now

do smells make good memory cues?

Aggleton, J.P. and Waskett, L. (1999) The ability of odours to serve as state-dependent cues for real-world memories: Can Viking smells aid the recall of Viking experiences? *British Journal of Psychology, 90, 1–7*

Aim: To determine the extent to which re-exposure to the unique combination of smells present in a museum (the Jorvik Viking Centre in York) would aid the recall of a previous visit several years earlier.

Method: The study utilised the fact that the Jorvik Viking Centre in York provides vehicles that introduce visitors to a number of exhibits along a fixed route at a fixed pace. Visitors therefore have a number of experiences in common. Along the way, certain evocative smells are piped into the museum to aid the completeness of the 'Viking experience'. These are described as: 'burnt wood', 'apples', 'rubbish acrid', 'beef', 'fish market', 'rope/tar' and 'earthy'. Three groups of participants were used. Members of each group had all visited the museum six or seven years previously (but not subsequently).

One group of participants completed a questionnaire on the exhibits in the presence of exactly those same odours. Odours were presented in bottles which participants were asked to smell before answering the questionnaire. Participants could smell the odours in any sequence they wished for as long as they wished. Once completed, the questionnaire was removed, and, after a five-minute delay, participants then completed the same questionnaire once more in the presence of a different (control) set of odours not used in the exhibition. The second group of participants followed an identical procedure except that the odours were presented in reverse order (control odours then the original Jorvik odours). The third group completed the question-naire twice with no odours presented. All participants were tested individually.

Results: The first group (Jorvik-control) showed the best recall for the exhibit, though their accuracy on the second questionnaire was not significantly different from the first. The second group (control-Jorvik) were initially the least accurate in recall, and this group showed a signif-icant improvement on the second questionnaire, scoring more highly than the no-odour group. The no-odour group showed little improvement, and were the least accurate on the second questionnaire.

Conclusion: The results showed that exposure to those odour cues that were present at the last visit was sufficient to induce a significant improvement in the recall of the museum's contents. There is plenty of anecdotal evidence that smells can serve to trigger recall of particular events. This study is one of the first to demonstrate the effectiveness of smells as cues to memory in a real world setting involving a recall interval of several years.

for and against

cue-dependent forgetting

+ There are a wealth of studies, both in and outside of the laboratory that support the notion of cue-dependent forgetting. Eysenck (1998) has suggested that cue-dependent forgetting is probably the main reason for forgetting in LTM.

− Cues may sometimes result in confabulation, so it may difficult to know in some circumstances whether a true memory is accessed as a result of a cue, or if the memory is a reconstruction.

where to now?

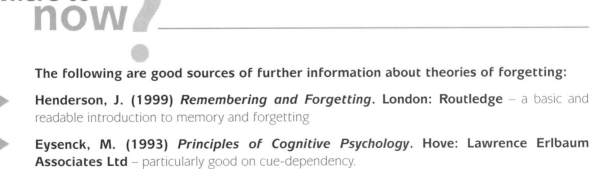

The following are good sources of further information about theories of forgetting:

▶ **Henderson, J. (1999)** *Remembering and Forgetting*. **London: Routledge** – a basic and readable introduction to memory and forgetting

▶ **Eysenck, M. (1993)** *Principles of Cognitive Psychology*. **Hove: Lawrence Erlbaum Associates Ltd** – particularly good on cue-dependency.

Eye-witness testimony

In Delaware in 1979 a Catholic priest awaited trial for several armed robberies. Seven witnesses had identified him as the man who had become known as the 'gentleman bandit' (referring to the elegant clothes and polite manners of the robber). During the trial, many other witnesses also identified the priest as the robber. The trial was brought to a sudden halt when another man confessed to the robberies (Wortman and Loftus, 1985). This case illustrates how inaccurate eye-witness testimony can be.

Even a low rate of mistaken identifications can lead to the wrongful conviction of very many people. Just how reliable is eye-witness testimony? Loftus (1983) reported that jury members tend to trust eye-witness reports more than they do fingerprint experts. In one study, Loftus (1974) found that students would be more likely to judge that an accused man was guilty even if the testimony against him came from a witness discredited as short-sighted and unable to see the face of the robber. Loftus believed jury members should be more suspicious. It is likely that there are many wrongful convictions every year as a result of faulty eye-witness testimony (Loftus, 1986).

The effects of leading questions

Loftus and Palmer (1974) demonstrated that changing the wording of questions can influence the way in which a witness responds. They showed people film of a car accident and asked participants 'about how fast were the cars going when they …?' with the final word being either 'smashed', 'collided', 'bumped', 'hit' or 'contacted'. Of course, the different wordings imply different speeds, and this affected the answers participants gave. The 'smashed' group estimated 41 m.p.h. and the 'contacted' group estimated 32 m.p.h. In a variation on Loftus and Palmer's procedure, Harris (1973) found that asking some participants 'How tall was the basketball player?' compared to 'How short was the basketball player?' produced a mean difference of 26 cm in participants' responses. These studies show how post-event information can *distort* the original memory of the event.

As part of their research, Loftus and Palmer tested other participants for 'smashed' or 'hit' (with similar results) and another group who were not asked about speed. One week later the participants were asked 'did you see any broken glass?' Thirty-two per cent of the 'smashed' group reported seeing broken glass, compared to just 14 per cent of the 'hit' group and 12 per cent of the control group. In fact there was no broken glass in the film. Even very subtle changes in wording can have an impact. Having shown people film of a car accident, Loftus and Zaani (1975) asked some of the witnesses 'Did you see *a* broken headlight?', and asked other witnesses 'Did you see *the* broken headlight?' Just 7 per cent of those asked about *a* broken headlight reported seeing one (there wasn't one in the film), compared to 17 per cent of those people asked about *the* broken headlight. These studies show how post-event information can result in information being *added* to an earlier memory. Loftus believed such information is incorporated into the original memory.

classic
research

how easy is it to mislead witnesses?

Loftus, E.F., Miller, D.G. and Burns, H.J. (1978) Semantic integration of verbal information into a visual memory. *Journal of Experimental Psychology: Human Learning and Memory*, 4 (1), 19–31

Aim: To investigate how information supplied after an event can influence a witness's memory for that event. In this study the later information was supplied in the form of misleading questions.

Method: An experiment in which 195 students from Washington University were shown a series of photographic slides in which a car (a red Datsun) travels to and stops at a junction. Half the participants saw a stop sign at this junction and half the participants saw a give-way sign. The car turned right and knocked down a pedestrian who was crossing the road. Immediately after viewing, the slides participants are given a 20-question questionnaire. For half the participants question 17 was, 'Did another car pass the red Datsun while it was stopped at the stop sign?' and for the other half of the participants the same question was asked, but with the words 'give-way sign' instead of 'stop sign'. For 95 participants, the sign mentioned in the question matched the one they had seen, while for 100 participants the sign mentioned did not match the one seen and so the question contained misleading information. All the participants then performed a 20-minute filler activity (reading and answering questions about a short story). They were then presented with 15 pairs of slides, one member of each pair being a slide they had seen earlier, and the other being new. Participants had to select the slide in each pair they had seen earlier. The critical pair was a slide showing the car at either a stop sign or a give way sign.

Results: Participants correctly selected the slide they had seen before 75 per cent of the time when the intervening question contained consistent information, and only 41 per cent of the time if it contained misleading information. If we would expect participants to guess correctly 50 per cent of the time by chance, then those given consistent information did significantly better than chance and those given misleading information did significantly worse.

Conclusion: This study provides powerful support for the idea that misleading information received after an event can alter memory for that event. It shows how one piece of information (for example, the presence of a stop sign) can be *substituted* with different information (for example, the presence of a give-way sign).

As part of this research, Loftus and Palmer decided to investigate the possibility that these results might reflect demand characteristics (i.e. the possibility that participants guessed the purpose of the research and acted in the way they thought that the experimenters wanted them to). The study was repeated with new participants and achieved broadly similar results. This time, though, after the recognition test, participants were told the aims of the study and asked whether they thought the sign mentioned in the questionnaire was the same as the one they had seen. This provided an opportunity for those who had been exposed to misleading information and selected the wrong sign to say that they thought there may have been a difference between the two, but most (88 per cent) did not. This led Loftus *et al.* (1978) to claim that the results of their research reveal a genuine change in people's memories, and are not explained by demand characteristics. Loftus believed that information received after an event can be incorporated into the memory of that event, overwriting the original memory trace. The original memory is changed, and the eye-witness believes that the updated, altered memory is what actually happened.

We should note, though, that Loftus's own research shows that misleading information that is *blatantly* incorrect is unlikely to affect a witness's memory. In one study, Loftus (1979) showed people slides of a man stealing a large, bright red purse from a woman's bag. Some participants later read a description of the event that contained a number of subtle errors about peripheral information in the slides (such as the colour of other items in the scene). Other participants read a similar description, which additionally contained the blatantly wrong information that the purse was brown. Although participants were often misled about peripheral items, Loftus found that 98 per cent of participants, when tested, correctly remembered the purse they had seen as red. The colour of the purse is clearly a central focus of the incident, and this resulted in people's memories of it being resistant to distortion.

There is debate about the effect that misleading information has on the original memory trace (does interference make the original memory hard to recover or is it irrevocably changed)? Memon and Wright (1999) have argued that, currently, the most popular explanation is that memories of details from various sources can be amalgamated with the original memory. This is referred to as *source confusion*, and occurs when information from one source cannot be distinguished from information from another source. Effectively, different memories can blend together and the memory for an event and memories for other events become confused. Once this has happened it may be impossible to sort them out back into their original form.

Confirmation bias and stereotypes

One possible source of distortion is 'confirmation bias'. People may remember an event in such a way that it conforms to their expectations rather than to what actually happened. Eysenck and Keane (1997) report that students from two universities in the USA, shown a film of a football match involving both universities, showed a strong tendency to report that their opponents had committed many more fouls than had their own team.

Stereotypes provide expectations of the world, and can influence the ways in which we interpret and remember events. In one study, participants read a narrative about a woman named Betty K. This described her life from birth to adulthood, and contained statements about her social life such as, 'Although she never had a steady boyfriend in high school, she did go out on dates'. After reading the story, participants were given further information about Betty K. that would lead to stereotyping her. Some participants were told that she later married, while others were told that she adopted a lesbian lifestyle. On a recognition test for the original story, participants told about Betty's lesbian activities were more likely to remember 'she never had a steady boyfriend' than 'she did go out on dates.' Participants told about her marriage did the reverse. It may be that participants used their stereotypes to answer questions when they could not remember the original story. Alternatively, both groups may have reconstructed their memory of the story to make it fit their stereotypes, (Bellezza and Bower, 1981; Snyder and Uranowitz, 1978).

Identity parades

We should note that laboratory tests often involve using the same stimuli (for example, photographs). However, in research on eye-witness identification based on parades or line-ups, the facial appearance of a person may be radically different between a staged incident and the subsequent line-up. Such research shows that eye-witnesses frequently make mistakes. Sanders (1984) found that, rather than using stable characteristics like height and facial features, witnesses are more likely to pick suspects who are wearing similar clothing to the clothes the culprit wore.

Fig 3.3
An identity parade

Clothing, of course, is easy to change, and in fact many criminals do change their appearance prior to an identity parade (Brigham and Malpass, 1985).

Wells (1993) argued that eye-witnesses tend to use relative judgements. They choose the member of the line-up who *most resembles* their memory of the culprit. In a real-life setting this may become even more important. People may feel it is unlikely that the police would set up an identity parade unless it was likely that the real culprit was present. They may pick the person who looks most like the criminal, even if all members of the line-up are innocent. Wells (1993) argued that, where line-ups are small and eye-witnesses are not warned that the true culprit may not be present, a false identification becomes more likely. Lindsay *et al.* (1991) found that *sequential* line-ups, in which members of the line-up are presented individually, one at a time, can reduce witnesses tendencies to use a relative judgement strategy. It has also been found that, if witnesses are less nervous, they are more accurate at picking suspect from identity parades (Ainsworth and King, 1988). Some familiarisation with the procedure, and the use of one-way mirrors should be useful here.

where to now?

The following are good sources of further information about eye-witness testimony:

▶ **Vrij, A. (1998) Psychological factors in eyewitness testimony. In Memon, A., Vrij, A. and Bull, R. (eds)** *Psychology and Law, Truthfulness, Accuracy and Credibility*. **London: McGraw-Hill** – an excellent chapter summarising some recent research findings on eye-witness testimony

▶ **Gross, R. (1998)** *Key Studies in Psychology*, **3rd edition. London: Hodder & Stoughton** – contains a detailed account of the work of Elizabeth Loftus, and reviews some more up-to-date studies.

talking point

False memory syndrome

During the 1980s and 1990s there have been a number of high-profile cases in which people have recovered or appeared to recover traumatic memories, frequently of sexual abuse. It has later turned out that these memories have been entirely false, but often not before the reputations of innocent people have been ruined and their families permanently split. Before going any further, let us look at two cases of false memories in detail.

case example 1:

Eileen Franklin Lipsker

One of the earliest cases, which helped launch the issue of recovered memories, was that of Eileen Franklin Lipsker. In 1989, Eileen was playing with her daughter, who she said reminded her of her childhood friend, a girl named Susan Nason. Susan was murdered at the age of eight. While playing with her daughter, Eileen suddenly remembered seeing her own father, George Franklin, kill Susan all those years ago. A few months after that shocking memory, Eileen also remembered that her father had committed incest with her, starting when she was three years old. Her testimony resulted in her father being convicted for first-degree murder. Her father appears to have been an alcoholic who unpredictably beat his children. But Eileen's siblings do not believe her story and have severed all contact with her. Subsequently, Eileen 'remembered' her father killing two other girls, but an investigation of this claim completely exonerated him. In 1995, George Franklin's conviction was reversed on the grounds that Eileen's testimony could have been based on information she read in newspapers rather than her own memories (a fact that was not presented to the jury).

case example 2:

Beth Rutherford

Beth Rutherford, in Missouri 1992, remembered during therapy that her father, a clergyman, had regularly raped her between the ages of seven and 14, and sometimes her mother helped him by holding her down. She remembered that this caused her to become pregnant on two occasions, and she was forced each time to abort the fetus herself with a coat hanger. These allegations forced her father to resign his post as a clergyman when they became public. Later medical examination of the daughter showed that, at 22, she was still a virgin and had never been pregnant. The daughter sued the therapist and in 1996 received $1 million in settlement.

Other studies of false memories

In both these cases there was clear evidence that the recovered memories were false. The apparent recovery of memories that have no basis in fact has become known as *false memory syndrome*. There is clear evidence from laboratory studies that it is quite possible to implant false memories. In one study Loftus and Pickrell (1995) were able to implant false memories in 24 participants aged 24–53. Using information gained from participants' relatives, they constructed for each participant a booklet containing one-paragraph stories about three events that had actually happened to the participant, and one that had not. The false story was about being lost in a shopping mall for an extended period at about the age of five, and included details about crying, being comforted by an elderly woman and, finally, reunion with the family. Participants were asked to write what they remembered about the events in the booklet after reading each one. Seven of the 24 participants 'remembered' the false event, often with vivid details.

Furthermore, even asking people to *imagine* that they witnessed an event or that they performed an action increases the likelihood that they will 'remember' that such events or actions took place (Loftus *et al.*, 1996). Some mental health professionals encourage patients to imagine childhood events as a way of recovering hidden memories. Further still, Kassin and Kiechel (1996) found that simply accusing someone of doing something may result a false memory. In one study, they falsely accused participants of damaging a computer by pressing the wrong key. Although the innocent participants initially denied the charge, when a confederate claimed to have seen them perform the deed, many participants went on to sign a confession! The researchers argued that false incriminating evidence can lead to internalised guilt, leading to the confabulation of details consistent with these guilty feelings.

Studies of genuine recovered memories

While there is clear evidence that some recovered memories are in fact false, a fierce debate is currently raging about whether or not recovered memories are *ever* genuine. There are on one hand those who believe that recovered memories are likely to be accurate (mostly though not exclusively practising therapists), and on the other hand those (mostly though not exclusively research psychologists like Loftus) who believe such memories are rarely if ever accurate. In our earlier discussion of repression we looked at one study (Elliott, 1995), which shows that a substantial minority of people who have suffered trauma report that there has been a period when they did not remember the traumatic event. There have been several such survey studies, and some have found that a far higher percentage of people report having forgotten and later recovered traumatic memories than did Elliott.

There are fundamental problems with survey studies as evidence for recovered memory. These studies depend on the respondents' understanding the questions, being able to recall accurately what they remembered several years ago and not being influenced by the social desirability of their answers or their beliefs about what the researchers wanted to hear. Thus, although all such studies have found people who said they had forgotten then recovered memories, many psychologists have refused to accept this type of evidence. Much stronger support for the existence of genuine recovered memories comes from the work of Constance Dalenberg. Dalenberg (1996) analysed in depth 17 current cases in which women were accusing their fathers of sexual abuse. Dalenberg distinguished between continuous and recovered memories and was able to compare the accuracy of recovered and continuous memories by interviewing the accused fathers and by encouraging the women to seek evidence for or against the accuracy of their memories. It emerged that in four cases, continuous memories were more accurate than recovered memories and in four cases, recovered memories were more accurate. In nine cases, no difference emerged in the accuracy of continuous and recovered memories. Two cases emerged as clearly the result of false memory syndrome. This study indicates that there are both genuine and false recovered memories, and that recovered memories are, in general, as accurate as continuous memories.

Conclusions about recovered memories

Since cases of false memory syndrome have hit the headlines, the British Psychological Society has been under pressure to adopt a position on the status of recovered memories, and a group was set up to investigate the issue. A survey of 810 psychologists found that 90 per cent believed that recovered memories are sometimes 'essentially correct'. Very few believed they are always correct, and around 66 per cent believed that false memories are possible (Andrews *et al.*, 1995). In 1999 the British Psychological Society published draft guidelines for working with recovered memories. On the status of recovered memories the following is the (draft) BPS position:

> 'there can be little doubt that at least some recovered memories of CSA are recollections of historical events. However there is a genuine cause for concern that some interventions may foster in clients false beliefs concerning CSA [childhood sexual abuse] or can lead them to develop illusory memories.'

In other words the current 'official position' of psychologists is to support the existence of both false memory syndrome and genuine recovered memories. In the absence of other, supportive evidence, it is difficult to know whether a recovered memory of, say, childhood abuse is true or false. In general in such cases, it is probably unsafe to accept that the recovered memory is true if:

- the person claims that they can, as a result of therapy, now remember abuse they suffered in the first year or two of their life

- the therapist used hypnosis, drugs, or guided imagery to help the patient remember the abuse

- the memories of the abuse become more detailed and bizarre over time.

where to now?

The following is a good source of further information about recovered memories and false memory syndrome:

▶ **Memon, A. (1998) Recovered memories: psychological issues and legal questions. In Memon, A., Vrij, A. and Bull, R. (eds)** *Psychology and Law, Truthfulness, Accuracy and Credibility***. London: McGraw-Hill** – a very balanced account of the evidence for and against recovered memory.

Conclusions

Cognitive psychology is a scientific approach to psychology that treats the human mind as a processor of information, rather like a computer. In this chapter we have looked at memory as an example of an area of study within the cognitive approach. Many psychologists have found it useful to think of separate systems of short- and long-term memory. Others have rejected this distinction and explained memory in terms of levels of information processing. One fairly recent development in memory research has been to look at memory in real-life situations rather than in the psychology laboratory. One such area of real-life memory research concerns autobiographical memory.

How we forget information is of crucial importance to understanding memory. Trace decay is an example of an availability explanation for forgetting, proposing that the physical memory trace decays with time. Repression is a psychological defence mechanism in which traumatic memories are pushed out of consciousness to prevent the unpleasant experience of recalling them. Cue-dependency is probably the common cause of forgetting. We experience this when we are unable to recall a memory without a cue, internal or external, that was present at the time when the information was committed to memory. Our understanding of forgetting is important when it comes to understanding eye-witness testimony and false memory syndrome. Both inaccurate eye-witness recall and the fabrication of false memories are important social issues to which psychologists can contribute their knowledge.

1   Briefly outline two principles underlying the cognitive approach to psychology.   (4)

2   Describe one theory or model of memory.   (10)

3   (a) Outline one theory of forgetting.   (5)

    (b) Discuss the evidence for the theory you have chosen in (a).   (5)

4   Describe two key studies from the cognitive approach.   (12)

4

The Cognitive–Developmental Approach

what's **ahead?**

If you have read Chapter 3 you will know that cognitive psychology involves the study of *cognitive* or mental processes, including perception, memory and thinking. Cognitive–developmental psychology is concerned with how these cognitive processes develop throughout the lifespan. In this chapter we are primarily concerned with the development of *thinking* as opposed to memory or perception. We shall also focus on cognitive development in childhood and adolescence, looking at the classic theories of Jean Piaget and Lev Vygotsky, and the more modern theory of Jerome Bruner. We also have a brief look at a concept of particular current interest in cognitive–developmental psychology – *theory of mind*. In our *real lives* section we see how cognitive–developmental theory has been applied to education and in *talking point* we look at the contemporary issue of the psychological implications of using computers as aids to learning.

what's it **about?**

The cognitive–developmental approach is based on the following ideas.

- Like any cognitive approach, cognitive–developmental psychology sees mental processes such as thinking as particularly important for understanding human behaviour.

- People's mental abilities change with age, not just because of increasing experience but also because of changes in the ways in which the brain is capable of handling information at different ages.

- One of the important influences on how we think, behave and feel is the type of cognitive processes of which we are capable.

Jean Piaget

The work of Jean Piaget

In this chapter we are primarily interested in the normal processes by which children develop intellectually. The best known and most influential theory of cognitive development is that of the Swiss biologist and psychologist, Jean Piaget. Piaget researched and wrote on the subject of children's cognitive development from the 1920s until the 1980s. Piaget's great contribution to psychology was his belief that the ways in which children think are not less sophisticated than those of adults simply because they have less knowledge, but that they think in an entirely different way. Piaget was interested in both how children learnt and how they thought. From this starting point Piaget went on to contribute three main areas of theory:

- the way in which children acquire knowledge
- the logical flaws in children's thinking
- stages of cognitive development through which children pass.

In this chapter we will examine each of these areas separately, although as you will see they are all closely interrelated.

The acquisition of knowledge

Piaget saw intellectual development as a process in which we actively explore the world and construct a mental representation of reality based on what we discover in our explorations. Piaget noted that even very young children are very inquisitive about their own abilities and about the details of the world. He proposed that the mind contains two types of structure: *schemas* and *operations*.

Schemas

Schemas are mental structures, each of which contains all the information the individual has relating to one aspect of the world. We have schemas for people, objects, actions and more abstract concepts. Piaget believed that we are born with a few innate schemas, which enable us to interact with others (very similar to Bowlby's idea of social releasers – see Chapter 5, page 146). During the first year of life we construct other schemas. An important early schema is the 'mum-schema' that develops as the child realises that its primary carer is a separate (and extremely important!) person.

Equilibration

When we can comprehend everything around us, we are said to be in a state of equilibrium. Look around the room for a moment and consider whether you understand as much as you need to about the contents of the room. The chances are that you do and hence you are in a state of equilibrium. However whenever we meet a new situation that cannot be explained by our existing schemas, we experience the unpleasant sensation of disequilibrium. It may be that at this moment you are in a mild state of disequilibrium as you try to grasp the details of Piagetian theory! According to Piaget we are instinctively driven to gain an understanding of the world and so escape disequilibrium. He identified two processes by which equilibration takes place:

- *assimilation*, which takes place when a new experience can be understood by altering an existing schema. For example, when an infant who has a 'bird' schema based on the family canary first encounters sparrows in the garden it will assimilate sparrows into the 'bird' schema

- *accommodation*, which takes place when a new experience is so radically different that it cannot be assimilated into existing schemas and so a new schema is formed. An example of accommodation occurs when the infant in the above example first encounters an aeroplane, and this new object is just too distinctive to incorporate into the 'bird' schema, and so an aeroplane schema is formed.

Operations

As well as knowledge of things we will encounter in the world, we also need to understand the rules by which the world operates. Piaget called these rules *operations* and, very importantly, he suggested that the reason that children think in different ways at different stages of their development is because the operations of which we are capable change with age. Piaget believed that, while schemas develop with experience, operations develop as the child's brain matures. The very young child does not have operations at all, and they are thus said to be *pre-operational*. The first operations to appear are *concrete*. This means that children can understand the rules governing something provided they can see it. Later, rules governing abstract concepts are understood. The rest of Piaget's theory is largely dependent on this idea of operations. The errors of logic that Piaget identified in children's thinking take place because of the limited operations available to them. Piaget's *stage theory of development* is based around the maturing of operations.

for and against

Piaget's view of knowledge acquisition

+ Children are certainly curious from a very young age. This fits in well with Piaget's theory.

+ The concept of the schemas as the basic unit of knowledge is widely accepted by psychologists.

– We can tolerate rather more inconsistencies and gaps in our knowledge of the world than we might expect if we suffer disequilibrium whenever we are unable to explain something.

– Piaget was largely describing the way that highly intelligent individuals such as himself operated. By definition, researchers in psychology are largely motivated by intellectual curiosity, and it is possible that Piaget over-estimated the importance of such curiosity in the rest of us.

Logical flaws in children's thinking

Piaget conducted a number of studies of children's ability to carry out tasks of logic. His earliest studies were observations of children playing. Piaget noted that different children of the same age tended to make the same mistakes, and he suggested that this was because children of the same age tended to commit the same errors in logic. From these observations was born the idea that children do not just know less but think *differently* from adults. Piaget went on to conduct experimental studies, initially on his own children but later on large numbers of children at a psychology laboratory. He also interviewed children (at least those who were old enough) to try to get an idea of how they were thinking when they committed errors in logic. We can look now at some of Piaget's major areas of research into children's thinking.

Object permanence

Piaget was interested in children's intellectual development from birth until adolescence. His best-known work on very young children concerned their understanding of *object permanence*. Object permanence refers to the understanding that objects exist permanently even when they are no longer visible. Piaget observed the behaviour of infants who were looking at an attractive object when it was removed from their sight. Until about eight months, children would immediately switch their attention away from the object once it was out of sight. From about eight months, however, they would actively look for the object. If, for example, it were pushed behind a screen within their reach they would simply push the screen aside. Piaget concluded from this that, prior to about eight months of age children do not understand that objects continue to exist once they are out of sight. Support for Piaget's idea comes from a variation in his procedure in which the hidden object is covered by a sheet, such that the object's shape is clearly visible to the child. Children still did not respond to the object, suggesting they really did not understand that the object continued to exist.

It seems that even when young children have grasped the fact that objects still exist after they cannot be seen, they continue for a time to have difficulty with locating hidden objects. In a variation on his object permanence procedure, Piaget noted that when children get used to looking behind a particular screen for the concealed object, they will sometimes continue to look behind the *same* screen even when they have seen the experimenter hide the object elsewhere. This showed that, although grasping object permanence was a significant milestone in the child's development, there are further steps to be taken in the child's understanding of the properties of objects.

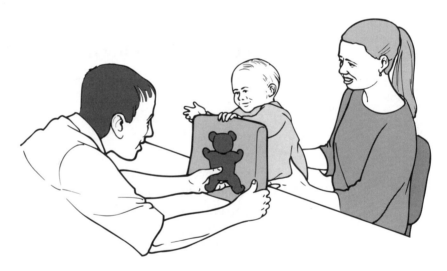

This nine-month-old has no difficulty in locating his teddy bear behind a screen!

Some later researchers have questioned the reliability of Piaget's research on object permanence and his assertion that children do not begin to understand object permanence until the age eight months. Freeman *et al.* (1980) replicated Piaget's studies showing that children will look for objects in the place they were previously found rather than where they were seen to be concealed, and found similar results. However, when they used screens featuring pictures of upside-down faces, the number of children looking in the wrong place rose from six to 13 out of the 21. This shows that the environment in which this type of study is carried out causes wild variations in the results and casts doubt on the validity of Piaget's approach. Other research has shown that children may have an understanding of object permanence at an earlier age than was suggested by Piaget. One such study was by Baillargeon and DeVos (1991).

research now

when do babies really acquire an understanding of object permanence?

Baillargeon, R. and DeVos, J. (1991) Object permanence in young infants: further evidence. *Child Development, 62, 1227–46*

Aim: Piaget believed that because infants below about eight months did not actively pursue an object once it was out of sight, this meant that they did not have an understanding of object permanence. However, there are other possible explanations for Piaget's findings. Younger children might simply not have the co-ordination or the ability to maintain their attention on an object without its being in view. This study aimed to test infants' understanding of object permanence by an alternative method.

Method: We know that infants focus their attention for longer periods on *discrepant events*, i.e. unusual or seemingly impossible events (Kagan *et al.*, 1978). The researchers aimed to set up an object permanence task in which infants witnessed an 'impossible' condition. A screen was set up with a window in the top half in front of three-month-old babies (see the diagram on page 104). Long and short carrots were passed behind the screen held vertically. This meant that the 'possible' or control condition, long carrots could be seen passing by the window and the short carrots could not be seen until they emerged at the edge of the screen. In the 'impossible' condition the long and short carrots were passed behind the screen, but neither were visible in the window, although they emerged as expected at the edge of the screen. The time the infants spent looking at the carrots in each condition was measured. The idea behind the study was that, if children looked for longer at the long carrots in the impossible condition they must have identified a discrepant event and must therefore have an understanding of object permanence.

Results: The infants looked for significantly longer at the long carrots, which had not appeared in the window during the 'impossible' condition once they had reappeared at the edge of the screen.

Conclusion: Children had presumably spotted the fact that the non-appearance of the long carrots at the window was a discrepant event, because they looked at these carrots for a longer period once they had reappeared. This suggests that they knew that the carrots were still there when they were out of sight, and hence that they had some understanding of object permanence.

Newer and more sophisticated studies like that of Baillargeon and DeVos appear to show that babies develop some concept of object permanence at a rather earlier age than was suggested by Piaget.

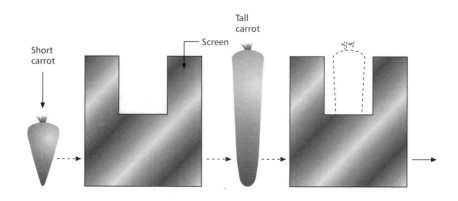

The apparatus used by Baillargeon and DeVos (1991)

Egocentrism

Egocentrism is the tendency to see the world entirely from our own perspective, and to have great difficulty in seeing the world from the viewpoint of others. Unlike difficulty with object impermanence, which is associated with specific ages, egocentrism declines gradually throughout childhood. Piaget saw egocentrism as applying to both abstract and concrete concepts. A classic study by Piaget and Inhelder (1956) illustrated egocentrism in the physical environment.

In Piaget and Inhelder's famous three mountains experiment, each model mountain had a different marker on the top – a cross, a house or a covering of snow. A doll was positioned to the side of the three mountains. Children were sat in front of the scene and shown pictures of the scene from different viewpoints. Their task was to select the picture that best matched what the doll could 'see'. Piaget and Inhelder noted that children aged less than seven years old had difficulty with this task, and tended to choose the picture of the scene from their own point of view. You can demonstrate egocentrism

Piaget and Inhelder's three mountains experiment

Children at the pre-operational stage say that the two rows contain the same number of pennies...

...but also that there are more pennies in the more spread-out, second row.

Piaget's demonstration of number conservation

for yourself by watching the news on television with a young child, and asking them what the newsreader can see. Young children will often find this difficult and believe that the newsreader can see *them*.

Related to egocentrism is the phenomenon of *animism*. Piaget (1971) reported that children aged two to four years typically attribute life-like characteristics to inanimate objects. They may for example worry about hurting or offending their toys, or indeed they may punish their toys when they are 'naughty'. By about four years children have a clear understanding of which objects around them are alive and which are not. Related to animism is *artificialism*, whereby children tend to believe that natural phenomena have been created by people. If you have ever tried to convince a child that the TV weather presenter is just reporting the weather and has not in fact created, it you will understand artificialism!

Conservation

Conservation refers to the understanding that objects remain the same in quantity even when their appearance changes. Piaget (1952) reported that young children had difficulty with tasks of conservation. He demonstrated this in a number of situations, two of which are particularly well-known.

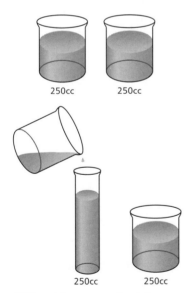

250cc   250cc

250cc   250cc

Children at the pre-operational stage believe that the volume of water is greater after it has been transferred to the taller glass.

Piaget's demonstration of liquid conservation

- *Number conservation* – Piaget found that if two rows of counters are laid out side by side, with the same number of counters spaced apart at the same distance children correctly spotted that there were the same number of counters in each row. If you want to try this at home Smarties make ideal counters (but as the child will probably eat them, check with the parents first)! If however the counters in one of the rows were pushed closer together, young children typically thought that there were now fewer counters in that row.

- *Liquid conservation* – Piaget found that if children see two glasses together with liquid coming up to the same height in each they can correctly spot the fact that they contain the same amount of liquid. However, if liquid was poured from a short, wide glass to a taller, thinner container, young children typically believe there was now more liquid in the taller container.

There have been challenges to Piaget's ideas about conservation. In a classic study, McGarrigle and Donaldson (1974) demonstrated that children's answers in conservation tasks are strongly affected by the circumstances in which the transformation of the material takes place.

classic
research

when do children really understand conservation?

McGarrigle, J. and Donaldson, M. (1974) Conservation accidents. *Cognition, 3, 341–50*

Aim: In his research on number conservation Piaget had shown that when he pushed counters closer together so that the row was shorter, children typically responded by saying that there were now fewer counters in the row. From this he had concluded that young children do not have a good understanding of number conservation. However, McGarrigle and Donaldson suggested that actually the children did understand that there were still the same number of counters, but that they had assumed that Piaget had *wanted them to say* that there were now fewer counters, otherwise why would he ask the question? They tested this idea by creating a condition in which the length of the row appeared to change accidentally rather than deliberately.

Method: There were 80 participants aged four to six years. All took part in both conditions. In the control condition, they were subjected to the standard Piagetian task, in which the experimenter presented them with the two rows of counters, asked them whether there were the same number in each row, then pushed the counters in one row closer and asked them again. In the experimental condition, once the children had been asked whether there were the same number in each row, a 'naughty teddy' ran across the table and, apparently accidentally, pushed the counters in one row closer together. The children were then asked whether there were the same number of counters in each row. The idea was that in this condition the children should not be influenced by the fact that the experimenter moved the counters then asked about them.

Results: The difference between children's apparent ability to conserve in the two conditions was dramatic. In the Piaget condition only 13 of the 80 children (16 per cent) correctly said that there were the same number of counters in the two rows. However in the experimental condition 50 of the children (62 per cent) answered correctly.

Conclusion: The results suggest that McGarrigle and Donaldson were correct to think that children acquire their understanding of number conservation at an earlier age than was believed by Piaget. They also suggest that Piaget's methods of researching conservation were flawed, because children were responding to what they thought the adult wanted to hear them say rather than what they believed.

It is worth noting that numerous researchers have attempted to replicate this study, and that not all have confirmed the results of McGarrigle and Donaldson. We are thus not really sure exactly when children begin to conserve successfully. However, we can learn much about the difficulties of conducting research with children from looking at the contrasting results obtained by Piaget and McGarrigle and Donaldson. It seems that the ways in which adults behave when interacting with children have a profound effect on the behaviour of the children, and that children can respond to adult researchers in quite subtle and unpredictable ways. It is well worth remembering that children are usually more interested in the researcher than whatever task the researcher has for them!

Formal reasoning

Piaget believed that from about 11 years of age, children became capable of abstract or formal reasoning. The term *formal* indicates that children capable of this type of reasoning can focus on the *form* of an argument and not be distracted by its content. For example if a child capable of formal reasoning is presented with the following syllogism: 'All green birds have two heads. I have a green bird called Charlie. How many heads does Charlie have?' They should be able to answer 'two' (Smith *et al.*, 1998). Before a child becomes capable of this type of reasoning they would be more likely to become distracted by the content and suggest that birds do not really have two heads.

Inhelder and Piaget (1958) gave Swiss school children some science questions with the task of devising hypotheses and carrying out experiments to test them. One such task was to investigate the pendulum problem. Children were given pendulums of different weights and string of different lengths. Their task was to determine whether the speed of the pendulum depends on its weight or the length of the string. It was found that most 11–15-year-olds were capable of setting up and carrying out this and similar tasks.

Piaget believed that we all achieve formal reasoning eventually, although there is some variation in age and some only achieve formal thinking by the age of 20. However, a number of studies have concluded that many people are not capable of formal thinking. In a longitudinal study (one in which participants are followed up over a long period), Bradmetz (1999) studied the cognitive development of 62 children until they were 15 years old. When they were 15 years old he gave them a battery of tests, including the Inhelder and Piaget science task, designed to measure formal thinking. Only one of the 62 young people proved capable of formal thinking – less than 2 per cent. Of course, if they were tested again at the age of 20 many more may demonstrate formal operational thinking, but Bradmetz's results do at least show that formal thinking tends to develop later than Piaget believed.

for and against

Piaget's research

+ From his early observational studies Piaget developed highly original and effective experimental procedures such as the three mountains experiment and the conservation tasks.

– Later research has uncovered limitations with some of Piaget's procedures. In particular he did not adequately take into account the impact of the social aspects of the experimental procedures on children's behaviour.

+ Piaget's fundamental belief that the sophistication of children's reasoning increases with age is generally supported by later research.

– There have been challenges however to Piaget's ideas about the ages at which children develop different abilities. Most contemporary psychologists believe that children achieve object permanence and conservation at an earlier age than was suggested by Piaget, but that abstract reasoning is achieved later, if at all.

Piaget's stage theory

Based on the types of logical error Piaget identified as typical of children of different ages, he proposed a stage theory of development. Piaget identified four stages of development:

1 sensorimotor stage – 0–2 years

2 pre-operational stage – 2–7 years

3 concrete operational stage – 7–11 years

4 formal operational stage – 11 years+.

Piaget believed that we all pass through all four stages in the same order, hence he referred to them as *invariant*. However, we vary considerably in the age at which we arrive at each stage, and the ages given above for each stage are intended only as broad averages. We reach each stage when our brain is mature enough to permit the use of new types of logic or *operations*. Let us look briefly at the type of thinking that takes place at each stage.

The sensorimotor stage

This lasts for approximately the first two years of life. Piaget believed that our main focus at this point is on physical sensation and on learning to co-ordinate our bodies. We learn by trial and error that certain actions have certain effects. Infants are fascinated when they realise that they can move parts of their body and eventually other objects. By the second year of life infants are quite mobile, and so are well-equipped to actively explore their environment. They are extremely curious and often experiment with actions to discover their effects. By the end of the sensorimotor stage infants are aware of themselves as separate from the rest of the world and have begun to develop language.

The pre-operational stage

By the end of the second year, the child has sufficient grasp of language for its thinking to be based around symbolic thought rather than physical sensation. However the child has not developed sufficiently to grasp logical rules or operations (hence the term *pre-operational*) and it deals with the world very much as it appears rather than as it is. Preoperational children are thus highly egocentric, have difficulty in conservation and tend to believe in animism and artificialism.

The concrete operational stage

The child's mind is now mature enough to use logical thought or operations, but children can only apply logic to objects and situations that are present and physical (hence *concrete* operational). Thus children now lose their tendency for animism and artificialism. They become less egocentric and better at conservation tasks. However, concrete operational children have great difficulty carrying out logical tasks without the physical objects in front of them. Think back for a moment to the tasks we looked at when we examined formal reasoning earlier in this chapter, such as syllogisms. Children in the concrete operational stage find syllogisms very difficult.

Formal operational stage

In the formal operational stage children become capable of formal reasoning (see earlier in this chapter). Formal operational thinkers can respond to the form of syllogisms and devise and test hypotheses. Piaget took this to mean that children had entered a new stage of adult logic, where abstract reasoning was possible. As well as systematic abstract reasoning, formal operations permits the development of a system of values and ideals, and an appreciation of philosophical issues.

Discussion

Piaget's stages have proved extremely useful for anyone who has to explain ideas to children of different ages. One area where this is clearly important is education, and we will spend some time later in this chapter looking at how Piaget's ideas, and those of other cognitive–developmental theorists, have been applied to teaching and designing programmes of study. Another important, though less well-known application of Piaget's stages is in paediatric medicine and nursing. Hurley and Whelan (1988) noted the behaviour and comments of children of different ages in severe pain, and concluded that their understanding of their pain corresponded closely to their Piagetian stage. Hurley and Whelan's findings are summarised in Table 4.1.

How children perceive the cause and effect of pain (Hurley and Whelan, 1988)	
Piagetian stage	**Perception of pain**
Pre-operational	Pain is primarily a physical experience. Children think about the magical disappearance of pain. Not able to distinguish between cause and effect of pain. Pain is often perceived as a punishment for a wrong-doing or bad thought (Gildea and Quirk, 1977), particularly if the child did something he or she was told not to immediately before the pain started. Children's egocentricity means that they hold someone else responsible for their pain and, therefore, are likely to strike out verbally or physically when they have pain. Children may tell a nurse who gave them an injection 'You are mean' (McCaffery, 1972).
Concrete operational	Relate to pain physically. Able to specify location in terms of body parts. Increased awareness of the body and internal organs means that fear of bodily harm is a strong influence in their perceptions of painful events. Fear of total annihilation (bodily destruction and death) enters their thinking (Alex and Ritchie, 1992; Schultz, 1971).
Transitional; formal	Have a perception of pain that is not quite as sophisticated as formal operational children. Their perception of pain is not as literal as would be expected in children who are in the concrete operational stage of development. Children in the transitional stage are beginning to understand the concept of 'if…then' propositions.
Formal operational	Begin to solve problems. Do not always have required coping mechanisms to facilitate consistent mature responses. Imagine the sinister implications of pain (Muller *et al.*, 1986).

Table 4.1 Children's perceptions of pain according to their Piagetian stage. Reproduced by permission from Twycross (1998)

Twycross (1998) has proposed that Piaget's stages form a good basis with which nurses can understand children's perception of pain and to inform them on how to communicate with children of different ages on the subject of pain. She goes on to suggest that current nursing procedures to assess pain in children are flawed because they do not take account of the child's developmental stage.

for and
against

Piaget's stages

+ The idea that children become capable of more advanced logic as they get older is generally accepted.

– However the Piagetian idea of *stages* is controversial. It may be that children gradually learn to tackle more complex logical tasks with greater experience and continual brain maturation.

+ Smith *et al.* (1998) reviewed studies of the concrete operational stage and concluded that there is strong support for the idea of concrete operational logic.

– More controversial is the pre-operational stage. Much post-Piagetian research, for example, McGarrigle and Donaldson (1974) has cast doubt on Piaget's findings concerning children's inability to conserve.

– Numerous studies, for example that of Bradmetz (1999), have found that most teenagers do not reach Piaget's formal operational stage.

where to
now?

The following are further sources of good information regarding Piaget's work:

▶ **Phillips, J.L. (1975)** *The Origins of Intellect: Piaget's Theory***. San Francisco: Freeman** – quite old, but still perhaps the best review of Piaget's work. In-depth coverage of the issues we have discussed, here, though of course without the newer research findings

▶ **Smith, P.K., Cowie, H. and Blades, M. (1998)** *Understanding Children's Development***. Oxford: Blackwell** – an excellent general child development text with a large chunk devoted to the work of Piaget

▶ **Lee, V. and Das Gupta, P. (1995)** *Children's Cognitive and Language Development***. Oxford: Blackwell** – the first chapter gives a good, detailed but quite easy to follow account of Piaget's major contributions.

Vygotsky's theory of cognitive development

Vygotsky was a contemporary of Piaget in Piaget's early days, though Vygotsky died young in 1934. His work was first published in the West in the 1960s, since which time it has grown hugely in influence, especially in the 1990s (Wertsch and Tulviste, 1996). Vygotsky agreed with Piaget on many key points, for example that cognitive development takes place in stages characterised by different styles of thinking. He disagreed, however, with Piaget's view of the child as exploring the world alone and instead placed a strong emphasis on social interaction during learning and the culture in which the child grows up.

The importance of culture and social interaction

Vygotsky placed far more emphasis than did Piaget on the role played by culture in the child's development. Vygotsky saw children as being born with basic mental functions such as the ability to perceive the outside world and to focus attention on particular objects. However, children lack higher mental functions such as thinking and problem-solving. These higher mental functions are seen as 'tools' of the culture in which the individual lives, and are cultural in origin. Tools are transmitted to children by older members of the culture in guided learning experiences (such as lessons in school), and include the ability to use language, art and mathematics. Experiences with other people gradually become internalised and form the child's internal representation of the world. Thus the way each child thinks and sees the world are shared with other members of its culture.

What this means is that people in different cultures will have quite different sets of tools, hence different ways of thinking. Luria and Yodovich (1971), colleagues of Vygotsky, compared styles of thinking in traditional Uzbecki people of Central Asia, some of whom had maintained their traditional culture whilst others had adopted a more modern lifestyle. Luria found that the traditional Uzbecki tended to respond to reasoning tasks by the use of concrete examples from their own experience. By contrast the educated Uzbecki used abstract reasoning. Luria's study demonstrated that when a culture changes, a different set of tools are transmitted to the next generation and the thinking of the culture changes.

The zone of proximal development

In contrast to Piaget, who emphasised how much a child can learn by exploring its environment, Vygotsky believed that children can develop far more quickly during interaction with others. Children, according to Vygotsky, could never develop formal operational thinking without the help of others. The difference between what a child can learn on its own and what it can potentially learn through interaction with others is called the *zone of proximal development* (ZPD). Whereas Piaget believed that the limiting factor in what a child could learn at any time was its stage of development, Vygotsky believed that the crucial factor was the availability of other 'experts' who could instruct the child. Unlike Piaget, Vygotsky emphasised instruction from others in how to do things in order for the child to achieve its potential. As the child progresses through a zone of proximal development or *learning cycle*, the amount of instruction from experts will reduce. At first, explicit and detailed instructions are needed but later on, prompts are sufficient to help the child progress.

The role of language

Vygotsky placed far more emphasis on the importance of language in cognitive development than did Piaget. For Piaget, language simply appeared when the child had reached a sufficiently advanced stage of development. The child's grasp of language depended on its current level of cognitive development. For Vygotsky however language developed from social interactions with others and was a very important cultural tool. At first the sole function of language is communication, and language and thought develop separately. Later, the child internalises language and learns to use it as a tool of thinking. In the pre-operational stage, as children learn to use language to solve problems, they speak aloud while solving problems (you can often hear children doing this). Once in the concrete operational stage this inner speech becomes silent.

Discussion

Vygotsky was probably correct in saying that Piaget under-estimated the importance of social interaction with more experienced people during learning. Later in this chapter, when we go on to look at the ways in which the ideas of Piaget and Vygotsky have been applied to education, we will see that children learn more quickly working together than they do alone. A more controversial aspect of Vygotsky's theory was the idea that, because tools are specific to different cultures, cultures that do not have formal schooling do not develop the ability for abstract thinking. Effectively this is saying that some cultures are better at thinking than others, an assumption that we would now consider highly *ethnocentric*, i.e. from the perspective of a single culture. Contemporary psychologists influenced by Vygotsky see different cultures as having different 'toolkits' (Wertsch, 1991), i.e. qualitatively different sets of tools rather than having more or fewer tools than one another.

for and against

Vygotsky

+ Vygotsky was probably correct in criticising Piaget for under-estimating the importance of social interaction in learning.

− However Vygotsky may have exaggerated the importance of culture. If all higher mental processes are cultural in origin, we would expect different cultures to vary far more than they do in their thinking.

+ There is considerable support for the idea that children develop more quickly with some instruction. This demonstrates the existence of the ZPD.

− Vygotsky's view of cultural differences in thinking is, by modern standards, ethnocentric because he believed that cultures who use formal schooling to transmit the tools of the culture – as happens in Europe – produce children capable of more advanced thinking than cultures which do not have formal schooling.

+ Modern Vygotskians have eliminated this flaw by seeing the tools of different cultures as qualitatively different rather than superior or inferior to one another.

where to now?

The following are good sources of information on the work of Vygotsky:

▶ **Faulkner, D., Littleton, K. and Woodhead, M. (1998)** *Learning Relationships in the Classroom*. **London: Routledge** – a collection of papers from some contemporary researchers that focus on Vygotsky's view of learning

▶ **Lee, V. and Das Gupta, P. (1995)** *Children's Cognitive and Language Development*. **Oxford: Blackwell** – the first chapter gives a good, detailed by quite easy to follow account of Vygotsky's major contributions.

Bruner's theory of cognitive development

Bruner has written more recently than Piaget or Vygotsky and he has applied and adapted aspects of both theories. Bruner rejected the idea of developmental stages as used by both Piaget and Vygotsky. Instead he preferred to look at cognitive development in terms of the way information is represented in the mind at different ages.

Modes of representation

Bruner (1966) placed much emphasis on *modes of representation*. A mode of representation is the *form* in which information is kept in the mind. When we think, we mentally manipulate information. As a child's mind develops it becomes capable of manipulating information in different forms, and this affects the type of reasoning of which they are capable. Bruner identified three modes of representation, each of which appears at a specific age.

Enactive representation

This is the first type of representation to appear in children's minds and corresponds to the type of representation that Piaget believed to be present in children at the early sensorimotor stage. Thinking in the first year is based entirely on physical actions. What knowledge we have during our first year is entirely dependent on what we can do with our bodies. We thus experience thinking as motor actions. This type of thinking does not disappear once other modes of representation develop, but is present in adults as what we sometimes call 'muscle memory'. Thus when we think of performing a physical task, such as tying a shoelace, we may think in terms of the necessary hand movements.

Iconic representation

This is the representation of information in the mind in the form of pictures or *mental images*. According to Bruner this appears at about one year of age. Piaget described this type of representation in the second half of his sensorimotor stage. As children the development of iconic representation allows us to reproduce images, thus drawing becomes possible. However holding images in the mind does not help us solve problems. Bruner and Kenney (1966) demonstrated that children relying on iconic representation could not perform a *transposition task*. We look at this in *classic research* on page 116.

Symbolic representation

Whereas Piaget saw the transition in children's thinking that takes place at around seven years as a result of the development of concrete operations, Bruner saw it as dependent on the development of *symbolic thinking*. Symbolic thinking means that language (and other symbolic forms such as numbers and music) can now be used for thinking. This use of symbols allows the child to categorise things and start to think logically. Bruner believed that symbolic thought became possible when the child had achieved a certain level of mastery of language. Language was thus very important to Bruner, as it was to Vygotsky.

classic
research

what can children do once they develop symbolic thought?

Bruner, J.S. and Kenney, H. (1966) The Development of the Concepts of Order and Proportion in Children. New York, Wiley

Aim: Bruner and Kenney set out to demonstrate the differences in the abilities of children who were dependent on iconic thought and those who had achieved the more advanced symbolic thought. The experiment also demonstrated the age at which children achieved symbolic thinking.

Method: Three groups of children, one group aged five, the second aged six and the third aged seven years, were presented with a grid of nine squares and nine glasses (see opposite). The nine glasses increased in height in each row and width in each column of the matrix. Children all took part in two conditions. In the first condition they performed a *reproduction task*. The glasses were scrambled and children had to put them back in the positions they were in originally. In the second condition, the glasses were removed from the grid and children were instructed to put them back on the grid *back-to-front*, i.e. with the three tallest glasses in the squares previously occupied by the three shortest glasses and vice versa. This is called a *transposition task*. The idea behind the study was that the reproduction task involved iconic thinking whereas the transposition task required symbolic thinking.

Results: Children tended to succeed on the reproduction task at an earlier age than the transposition task. Of the five-year-olds, 60 per cent succeeded in the reproduction task and none succeeded in the transposition task. Of the six-year-olds, 72 per cent succeeded in the reproduction task and 27 per cent in the transposition task. By the age of seven years it seemed that children's thinking had taken a leap forward and 80 per cent succeeded in *both* the tasks. They no longer found the transposition task any harder than the reproduction task.

Conclusion: By seven years, the children could perform both the tasks, but although most five-year-olds could perform the reproduction task, none of them could perform the transformation task successfully. Bruner and Kenney took this to mean that symbolic thought, which was necessary for the type of mental manipulation required to swap the position of the glasses around, appeared at around six to seven years. The younger children could not perform the transformation task because they were dependent on iconic thought.

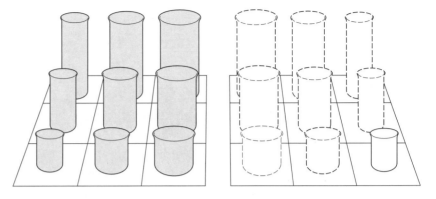

Bruner and Kenney's apparatus

Scaffolding

Bruner built on Vygotsky's idea of the ZPD, introducing the concept of *scaffolding*. Scaffolding has been defined as 'the wide range of activities through which the adult, or more experienced peer, assists the learner to achieve goals that would otherwise be beyond them' (Smith *et al.*, 1998). Scaffolding thus describes the ways in which adults help the child through the zone of proximal development. We will return to the concept of scaffolding in more detail later in this chapter when we look at the ways in which theories of cognitive development can be applied to education.

Discussion

Bruner's main influence is in education, and when we revisit his work later in the chapter you should get more of a flavour of how useful his ideas have been. On a theoretical level, Bruner's idea that mode of representation changes with age seems credible and is supported by research. It does seem, however, that logic gets more advanced with age for quite a time after children have mastered language. If Bruner's ideas were the whole story we would expect children to be capable of more advanced logic as soon as they can use language effectively. In fact, abstract reasoning tasks only become possible much later in children's development. One way in which Bruner has undoubtedly contributed to our understanding of cognitive development is in his idea of scaffolding. This plugs a gap in the work of Vygotsky, who emphasised a role for adults but did not explain well how adults go about guiding children through the ZPD.

for and against

Bruner

+ Bruner's ideas have been extremely useful in education.

+ Bruner is probably correct that as children mature they become capable of different types of mental representation, and that this affects their ability to reason.

− It seems likely however that other factors apart from mode of representation influence the type of reasoning of which a child is capable. We know that some cognitive abilities like abstract reasoning appear a long time after the appearance of symbolic functioning.

where to now?

The following are good sources of further information on the work of Bruner:

▶ **Bruner, J. (1971) The course of cognitive growth. In Richardson, K. and Sheldon, S. (eds)** *Cognitive Development to Adolescence*. **Hove: Lawrence Erlbaum Associates Ltd** – a set of readings including one by Bruner himself, in which he summarises some of his major points

▶ **Smith, P.K., Cowie, H. and Blades, M .(1998)** *Understanding Children's Development*. **Oxford: Blackwell** – a generally excellent book on child development with a good section on Bruner.

what's new?

the development of children's theory of mind

One thing the theories of Piaget, Vygotsky and Bruner have in common is that they are *domain-general*. This means that they see all the changes in mental abilities that take place during a child's cognitive development as happening because of the same underlying developmental process. Thus for Piaget, the child's increasing ability to conserve, their declining egocentrism and their loss of artificialism are all results of a general increase in cognitive ability that comes with the maturation of the brain. Similarly, to Bruner, all the mental abilities in which the child achieves mastery after the age of seven can be explained by the transition to symbolic thinking.

In recent years, however, another approach has been gaining in popularity. This is the *domain-specific* approach, which sees different mental abilities as developing independently of one another. One cognitive ability that has attracted particular attention because it does appear to develop independently of general cognitive functioning is the child's *theory of mind*. Children are said to have a theory of mind once they have an understanding of what other people believe, think and know. In other words they develop their own concept (or theory) of the minds of other people.

A classic demonstration of the sudden development of theory of mind comes from Wimmer and Perner (1983). They presented children with a story in which a boy called Maxi had left his chocolate in a green container in the kitchen. Maxi's mother had taken some of the chocolate for cooking and put the rest in a blue container. The child's task was to say which container Maxi would look in when he returned. Of course the correct answer is the green container, because Maxi wouldn't know his mother had moved it. However this task requires an understanding of the concept of other people's minds, and Wimmer and Perner found that very few three-year-olds gave the correct answer, although the majority of four-year-olds did so. Avis and Harris (1991) replicated the study with children of the Baka people, who live in a remote part of the Cameroon, suggesting that the sudden appearance of theory of mind at four years is universal.

Leslie (1994) has suggested that the sudden appearance of theory of mind in four-year-olds occurs because a particular *module* of the brain suddenly becomes active at that age. Much of the research on theory of mind takes place with *autistic* children. Autism is a genetic condition that appears in early childhood and is characterised by difficulty in communication, repetitive movements and lack of interest and skill in social interaction and emotional attachment. Baron-Cohen (1995) has suggested that autism is associated with impaired theory of mind. Certainly autistic children generally fail the Wimmer and Perner test. The study of autistic children who never develop a theory of mind, although they may go on to develop some mental abilities to very high levels, is important because it provides powerful evidence of *domain-specific* cognitive development. In Piaget's terms, Wimmer and Perner's results could be explained by a decline in egocentrism. However, we would not expect autistic children, who do not develop a theory of mind, to go on to develop other mental abilities to a high level unless theory of mind develops independently of other mental abilities.

where to now?

The following are good sources of further information about theory of mind:

▶ **Bryant, P. (1998) Cognitive development. In Eysenck, M. (1998) (ed.) *Psychology: An Integrated Approach*. Harlow: Longman** – contains an excellent chapter on cognitive development, including a detailed but very clear account of theory of mind research

▶ **Frith, U. and Happe, F. (1994) Autism: beyond theory of mind. In Messer, D. and Dockrell, J. (1999) *Developmental Psychology: A Reader*. London: Arnold** – an interesting paper concerning research on theory of mind and autism.

real
lives

Applying theories of cognitive development to education

Think back to the ways in which you have been taught at school, college and perhaps university. You will by now have experienced a variety of teaching styles, and it might have occurred to you to wonder how teachers decide to teach. You may at times have also wondered who decides what is taught and chooses what you have to study. In fact, both teaching methods and the curriculum (the content of what you learn) have been powerfully influenced by cognitive–developmental theories. In this section we can consider both teaching style and curriculum development. Briefly though, let us look first at the Plowden Report, which began the move towards cognitive–developmental models of teaching and learning.

The Plowden Report

You may have heard about or seen film of the ways in which people used to be taught in primary schools. Pupils typically sat in rows and learnt material by rote, i.e. they repeated it in unison until they knew it by heart. Children not able to keep up with the pace at which the majority learnt were often punished. In the 1960s however the Plowden Committee was set up in order to examine ways of improving primary education. and they investigated the work of Piaget and incorporated his ideas into their report. The final report, published in 1967, recommended a shift away from traditional teaching towards *child-centred teaching*, i.e. teaching based on the abilities and wishes of children. We can pick out three main messages from the Plowden Report:

- Children need to be given individual attention and cannot all be treated in the same way.

- Children should not be taught things until they are developed enough intellectually to cope with them.

- Children mature intellectually, physically and emotionally at different rates. Teachers should be aware of the stage of development each child has reached, and should treat them accordingly.

Implications of Piagetian theory for education

Piaget's research was generally not aimed at education. However, following the Plowden Report, teachers began to put Piaget's ideas into practice in the classroom. The following are some of the main implications of Piagetian theory for classroom practice and curriculum development (adapted from Smith *et al.*, 1998; Child, 1997 and Faulkner, 1995).

Classroom practice

- As children think in quite different and less logical ways than do adults, teachers should adapt to the ways in which children think rather than expect children to adapt to them. One way in which this can be achieved is for the teacher to create situations where the child can learn for itself rather than simply telling children facts. It is also important to create situations that are appropriate for children of the particular age. We would not, for example, give children still in the concrete operational stage tasks that require skills of abstract reasoning. Such tasks would become appropriate only after the children had achieved formal operations.

- Children learn best by discovery. The role of the teacher is thus to facilitate learning situations in which children can find things out for themselves. This does not mean, of course, simply leaving children to their own devices. In effective child-centred learning the teacher presents children with tasks specifically designed to lead them to discover things for themselves. A wide variety of such tasks needs to be given, in order for the child to construct their knowledge of all necessary aspects of the world. In nursery and primary school, materials like water, sand, bricks and crayons all help children build physical and hence mental constructions. Later, projects and science practicals help children explore the nature of their world.

- The aim of education is to develop children's thinking rather than just to increase their level of knowledge. This means that, when children try to work things out, what is important is their reasoning rather than the answer. It is therefore important that teachers encourage children for producing answers that are wrong but well thought-out.

Curriculum development

- Clearly if children are capable of understanding different concepts at different stages of development then the curriculum should be tailored so that children encounter new ideas when they can cope with them. This was one of the aims of the *National Curriculum*, which governs what children are taught in both primary and secondary school in this country. The curriculum also needs to be flexible enough to allow for the fact that all children do not reach the same stage of development at the same age.

- In the primary curriculum, it is important to allow for the transition from pre-operational thinking to concrete operational thinking. Concepts should be included that allow children to test and develop their logical abilities. In practice this means that the curriculum must permit some discovery learning.

- In the secondary curriculum, the concepts that children encounter should reflect children's predominantly concrete thinking. Introducing tasks involving abstract reasoning should be done with caution.

121

for and against

applying Piagetian principles to education

+ The principle that children are not passive receivers of knowledge but need somehow to construct their own knowledge is generally accepted in educational circles.

– There is however considerable disagreement over whether child-centred learning does this best. Modern 'chalk and talk' teaching is much more interactive than the pre-Piaget 'traditional' styles and may be at least as effective as child-centred learning.

– Whereas Piaget believed that children could learn in isolation and this is encouraged in some schools, modern research shows clearly that children learn faster when working in groups and with the intervention of adults. We will look at some such research later in this section.

+ Piaget has given us a good base for developing the curriculum, although modern curricula take account of the current belief that Piaget tended to under-estimate the abilities of younger children and over-estimate the abilities of older children.

Implications of Vygotsky's and Bruner's theories for education

Unlike Piaget, both Vygotsky and Bruner were interested in applying their ideas to education. We can consider them together here as their ideas are closely related. The following are some of the major implications of Vygotsky's and Bruner's work for teaching.

Classroom practice

● Vygotsky and Bruner have proposed a more important role for adults in children's learning than did Piaget. Like Piaget however they proposed that children should be actively involved in their learning rather than behaving as passive receivers of knowledge. What this means in practice is that teachers should actively assist children who are engaged in learning tasks. In theoretical terms this means that children are working within their zone of proximal development and teachers provide the scaffolding to enable children to move through the ZPD.

- From a Bruner–Vygotsky perspective, peers as well as teachers can be important influences on children's cognitive development. Co-operative group work as opposed to individual discovery learning appears to speed up children's development. An extension of the idea of co-operative group work is peer-tutoring, where one child instructs another who is slightly less advanced. Foot *et al.* (1990) have explained the success of peer tutoring using Vygotsky's theory. One child can be effective in guiding another through the ZPD because, having only recently made that advance themselves, they are in a good position to see the difficulties faced by the other child and provide appropriate scaffolding. On page 124 we look at a study by Nichols (1996) which examined the success of co-operative group work.

- Computer-assisted learning can be used to provide scaffolding, both from the use of the computer itself and the social interaction stimulated by computers. When children use educational software the computer provides detailed help or prompts as required according to the child's position in the ZPD. Certain children in the class are inevitably more skilled in the use of computers and so take on the role of peer tutors. With pupils working on computers, the teacher is free to target individuals who require help and target appropriate scaffolding to each child. We can return to look in more detail at the effectiveness of computer-assisted learning later in this chapter.

Curriculum development

- Vygotsky has emphasised that rather than waiting for children to reach a level of cognitive development where they can cope with concepts and tasks on their own, we can be more ambitious in what we expect of children if teachers provide scaffolding. This means that a Vygotskian curriculum would introduce children to new concepts at an earlier age than would a Piagetian curriculum.

- Bruner (1963) emphasised that how something is taught is more important than when it is taught. This means that provided children are presented with concepts in a way that they can understand them we need not worry too much about when to place concepts on the curriculum. Bruner and Kenney (1966) have proposed the idea of the spiral curriculum, in which ideas are revisited throughout a child's schooling. Each time an idea is revisited, children encounter it in a more sophisticated form, deepening their understanding.

research
now

does co-operative group work improve motivation?

Nichols, J.D. (1996) Cooperative learning: a motivational tool to enhance student persistence, self-regulation, and efforts to please teachers and parents. *Educational Research and Evaluation*, 2 (3), 246–60

Aim: Previous research has shown that children generally learn faster and achieve more when they work in co-operative groups rather than alone by discovery learning. More controversial is whether children learn better in child-centred classrooms or in traditional 'chalk and talk' lessons. What we do know is that the motivation of learners is enormously important. This study aimed to test whether adolescents of secondary school age were more motivated to learn in traditional lessons or lessons based on co-operative group work.

Method: Eighty-one students from an American high school participated in the study. They were randomly assigned to one of three groups. Each group made up one of the three geometry classes. The study was run across 18 weeks (one semester, or American term). One group of 27 students had nine weeks of co-operative group learning followed by nine weeks of traditional teaching. A second group had nine weeks of traditional teaching followed by nine weeks of co-operative group learning. This meant that if motivation changed when the teaching method the researchers would know that results were not affected by the order in which the two styles of teaching were used. The co-operative group activity involved students being divided into small groups and given problems to solve together. The control group had 18 weeks of traditional teaching. The motivation of each group was measured at the start, after nine weeks and after 18 weeks. Motivation was judged by measuring the students' persistence, self-regulation and effort to please teachers and parents.

Results: The two groups who had experienced co-operative group learning scored significantly higher at the end of the semester on all measures of motivation. Within the two groups that had experienced 9 weeks of co-operative group work, it could be seen that the greatest increases in motivation took place during the nine-week period when they were working in groups rather than the nine weeks when they were having traditional lessons.

Conclusion: The results clearly showed that co-operative group work led to improved motivation in the high school students. In theoretical terms, the study supports the effectiveness of student-centred learning and in particular the approach of Vygotsky and Bruner who emphasised how much children can learn from one another.

for and against

applying the Vygotsky–Bruner approach to education

+ Research has shown clearly that children learn more effectively in groups, and that adults and peers can effectively provide scaffolding.

+ The idea of scaffolding has provided teachers with a way of intervening actively in children's learning without resorting to traditional teaching.

+ The effectiveness of co-operative group work and computer-aided learning have generally been supported by research findings.

– There are practical problems with the use of co-operative group work. There are more opportunities for children to be off-task in group work, and there are 'free-riders' who do not contribute to the work of the group.

where to now?

We recommend the following as good sources of information about cognitive development and education:

 Child, D. (1997) *Psychology and the Teacher*. **London: Cassell** – a book intended to give teachers a grounding in general psychology. It is particularly useful for relating psychological theory, including the cognitive-developmental approach to education

 Hartley, J. (1998) *Learning and Studying*. **London: Routledge** – this is not focused particularly on a cognitive–developmental approach to education, but is useful in drawing together different psychological approaches and showing how each have influenced educational practice

Borich, G.D. and Tombari, M.L. (1997) *Educational Psychology: A Contemporary Approach*. **New York: Longman** – a detailed and up-to-date text covering many aspects of psychology and education. Particularly good information on applying Piaget, Bruner and Vygotsky to teaching.

talking

point

Do computers help people learn?

If you are or have recently been a student, the chances are that you have encountered computers at some point in your education. *Computer-assisted learning* is a tremendous growth area at the turn of the century, and a large body of research is currently being generated about its effectiveness. Think for a moment about the variety of ways in which you have used computers in the course of your studies. You have probably word-processed assignments. You may have used statistical programs to analyse the results of research. You may also have taken part in or administered studies that present tasks to participants by computer. Packages are available that guide students through sequences of tasks that allow one to master a skill or a topic. Revision tests are also available via computer, and there are now even computer packages available that will mark your essays! You may have had the opportunity to program computers in the course of your study. The usefulness of computers in teaching and learning is interesting in its own right. In this section, however, we are interested specifically in understanding the processes of computer-aided learning using ideas from cognitive–developmental psychology.

Theoretical background

Piaget and Vygotsky both died before the use of computers in education became an issue, therefore we cannot say what they would have thought. However, contemporary psychologists have applied both Piaget's ideas and those of the Vygotsky–Bruner model to understanding the processes of computer-assisted learning. From a Piagetian perspective, computers offer a highly versatile tool for individual discovery learning. If you have ever used CD-ROMs or the Internet to research a topic on your own, you have experienced computer-aided discovery. It has also been suggested that programming helps develop thinking skills – we will return to this idea shortly when we look in detail at programming. From a Vygotsky–Bruner perspective, computers provide opportunities for co-operative learning. Both teacher intervention and on-screen instructions also provide scaffolding. We can look here at studies of both scaffolding and co-operative learning based on computers.

On-screen scaffolding

Whenever we use educational software, there are a series of on-screen prompts which help us progress through the task at hand. Crook (1994) has suggested that these prompts constitute a form of scaffolding, which serve to move learners through a zone of proximal development. There are normally choices that the learner can make as to how much detail they require from prompts. This means that, just as a teacher will reduce the amount of help they give as the learner moves through the ZPD, the computer-aided learner can select a declining level of detail in their on-screen prompts.

Grammar checkers, a feature of most modern word-processing systems, are a familiar example of on-screen scaffolding (Hartley, 1998). If, for example, you use Microsoft Word 97 you will be familiar with a green underlining function, which identifies possibly suspect grammar in your writing. According to your level of expertise, you can respond to this by ignoring it, selecting the text and considering the options suggested by the computer or simply going with the computer's advice. From a Brunerian perspective, which option you take will depend on where you are in your word-processing or prose-writing ZPD. If you are new to word-processing or writing extended prose, you will probably just take the computer's advice. As you progress, however, you will probably require less and less scaffolding and use the prompts less often.

Co-operative learning with computers

Another way in which computer-aided learning can be beneficial is in fostering social interaction. According to the Vygotsky–Bruner model, co-operative learning in pairs or groups will achieve greater gains than solo study. Mevarech et al. (1991) tested this idea by seeing whether students working together sharing a computer do better than students working alone. Twelve-year-olds worked on computer-based arithmetic tasks for five months. Half the students had their own computer and the other half shared a computer and worked in pairs. The latter group did significantly better when tested later on their arithmetic ability. This finding runs counter to common sense which would suggest that the students who had their own computer would do better than those who had to share. Mevarech et al.'s study is also significant in that it lends support to the Vygotsky–Bruner model of education as opposed to the Piaget model.

Programming and the development of thinking skills

Papert (1980) suggested that children can acquire new thinking skills when they learn to programme computers. Papert was one of a team that developed the child-friendly programming language Logo. An example of a child-friendly feature of Logo is a turtle graphic that can be directed to draw lines by typed commands. For example, the command FORWARD 50, LEFT 90 would direct the turtle graphic to draw a 50 mm straight line then turn 90° to the left. Papert proposed that the use of the turtle to draw

Students who share computers may do better than those who work alone

lines enhances children's mathematical abilities. Papert was influenced by Piaget rather than by Vygotsky and Bruner, and he believed that using Logo helped children's thinking by developing their ability to use formal operational thinking as opposed to concrete operational thought. In line with Piaget's thinking, Papert suggested that the teacher's role in computer-aided learning should be confined to creating a suitable environment for children to work in.

Since Papert's claims, most researchers have failed to find that children trained in the use of Logo show any significant advantage in their thinking abilities over other children. However, a recent study by Kramarski and Mevarech (1997) has shown that Logo programming can be used to enhance one particular aspect of learning – *metacognition*. Metacognition refers to our knowledge of how our mind operates and an awareness of the strategies we use to solve problems. In the Kramarski and Mevarech study, 68 12–14-year-old pupils were randomly assigned to one of four groups. All the students studied a computer-based course in statistics using Logo for one 45-minute lesson per week over 30 weeks. Two of the classes had training in metacognition and two did not. Metacognitive training consisted of lessons in which the teacher explored with the students all their possible methods of solving problems. At the end of the year the groups instructed in metacognition performed better in their use of Logo *and* were found to have enhanced their own metacognitive abilities.

for and against

computer-aided learning

+ Computers can provide opportunities for both discovery learning and co-operative learning. They also provide opportunities for both developing individual thinking skills and scaffolding the development of skills. This means that computer-assisted learning is compatible with both the Piagetian view of education and the Vygotsky–Bruner model.

– It has been suggested that the excessive use of computers in the classroom may lead to social isolation and the breakdown of the essential teacher–learner relationship.

– However, if the majority of learners are receiving on-screen scaffolding this frees the teacher to spend more time with each learner. Provided computer-assisted learning does not lead to the phasing out of teachers, it appears that it will probably not lead to social problems.

where to now?

The following are good sources of further information about computer-aided learning:

▶ **Bancroft, D. and Carr, R. (eds) (1995)** *Influencing Children's Development*. **Milton-Keynes: Open University** – contains an excellent chapter by Karen Littleton on various aspects of computer-assisted learning

▶ **Messer, D. and Millar, S. (eds) (1999)** *Exploring Developmental Psychology*. **London: Arnold** – contains a great chapter by Charles Crook, one of the leading researchers in the area of computer-aided learning.

Conclusions

The cognitive–developmental approach to psychology has centred around the development of thinking in children. The most famous theory, that of Piaget, emphasised children's tendency to explore and learn from their environment and the gradual acquisition of logical thought through brain maturation. Vygotsky and Bruner have placed much greater emphasis on the importance of other people in learning. All these theories are domain-general in nature, i.e. they see all aspects of cognitive development as taking place together, controlled by the same underlying processes. An alternative modern approach is to look at domain-specific development, i.e. the separate development of different cognitive abilities. The most extensively researched specific cognitive ability is *theory of mind*. It seems that the child's awareness of the minds of others appears very suddenly at around four years and cannot be explained by general cognitive development.

The major application of the cognitive–developmental approach has been in education. The approaches of Piaget, Vygotsky and Bruner all point towards an active role for children as discoverers of knowledge rather than passive receivers. However, Vygotsky and Bruner have proposed a more active role for teachers than have followers of Piaget. The use of computers in education provides opportunities for enhanced learning. Piagetians emphasise the opportunities provided by computers for discovery learning and the development of thinking, whereas followers of Vygotsky and Bruner place more emphasis on the opportunities for scaffolding and co-operative learning provided by computers.

1 (a) Describe in detail *two* studies from the cognitive-developmental approach. *(12)*

(b) Outline one limitation in experimental studies involving young children. *(2)*

2 Outline two differences between the approach of Piaget and one alternative theory. *(5)*

3 Describe *two* ways in which *one* cognitive–developmental theory *other than that of Piaget* has been applied in education. *(4)*

4 Discuss how the cognitive–developmental approach has helped us understand *one* contemporary issue of your choice in psychology.

5

The Psychodynamic Approach

what's
ahead?

This chapter concerns the psychodynamic approach to psychology. This is one of the oldest approaches, dating back to the 1890s. Nowadays psychodynamic approaches still flourish, but most commonly outside mainstream psychology, being more popular in the fields of psychiatry, psychotherapy and counselling. In this chapter you will come across the term 'psychoanalytic' as well as 'psychodynamic'. Distinguishing between the two terms can be confusing, but here we have used the word *psychoanalytic* to refer to the body of theory underlying psychodynamic psychology (a broad term covering the whole approach) and to the therapies derived from it. We will look at three influential psychoanalytic theories, those of Sigmund Freud, Erik Erikson and the Object Relations School. We also have a brief look at the recent work of Alessandra Piontelli. In our *real lives* section we see how we can apply a psychodynamic understanding to mental health issues and in *talking point* we look at an issue currently being debated in psychology – how effective are psychological therapies based on the psychodynamic approach.

what's it
about?

The psychodynamic approach is based on the following ideas.

- Our behaviour and feelings as adults (both normal and in the case of psychological problems) are largely rooted in our early childhood experiences.

132

- Relationships (especially those with our parents) are of great importance in determining how we feel and behave.

- Our behaviour and feelings are strongly affected by our unconscious mind, i.e. mental processes of which we are not consciously aware. These unconscious influences come from past experiences and instincts, with which we are born.

- Unlike the other branches of psychology which place a strong emphasis on systematic, scientific research, psychodynamic psychologists take a broader approach and also look for information in dreams, symptoms, irrational behaviour and what patients say in therapy.

Sigmund Freud

The work of Sigmund Freud

Sigmund Freud, who wrote from the 1890s to the 1930s, remains the best known and perhaps the most argued-about psychologist of all time. He developed a collection of theories, which have together formed the basis of the psychodynamic approach to psychology. Freud was a therapist and his theories are based on what his patients told him during therapy, together with reflections on his own life. Freud wrote on a wide variety of topics and developed his ideas throughout the period of his writing. It is not possible to look at all or even most of Freud's ideas in this chapter, but we can examine four of his more important theories:

- the structure of personality

- psychological defence mechanisms

- stages of children's development

- dreams.

The structure of personality

Perhaps Freud's single most important idea was that the human personality has more than one aspect. We reveal this when we say things like 'part of me wants to do it, but part of me is afraid to…' Freud described his approach as 'depth psychology'. Whilst we are fully aware of what is going on in our *conscious* mind, our feelings, motives and decisions are actually powerfully influenced by our past experiences and instincts which operate in the *unconscious* mind. We use the term 'unconscious mind' to describe the influence of instinct and past experience, because we are not *conscious* of how they are influencing us.

Freud (1933) tried to show how instinct and past experience affects a person by dissecting the personality into three parts: *I*, *it* and *above-I*. Each of these parts represents a different aspect of the person and plays a different role in deciding on a course of action. *It* represents the instinctive aspect of the personality, present from birth. *It* wants to be satisfied, and *it* does not willingly tolerate delay or denial of its wishes. *I* is the aspect of the person that is aware of both the demands of *it* and the outside world, and which makes decisions. *I* develops through experience of dealing with the world, and has the capacity to think logically. *Above-I* is the aspect of the personality formed from the experience with authority figures such as the parent, which poses restrictions on what actions are allowed. Your *Above-I* can reward you with pride and punish you with guilt, according to whether you go along with its restrictions. These three aspects of the personality are sometimes called the *id* (it), the *ego* (I) and the *superego* (above-I).

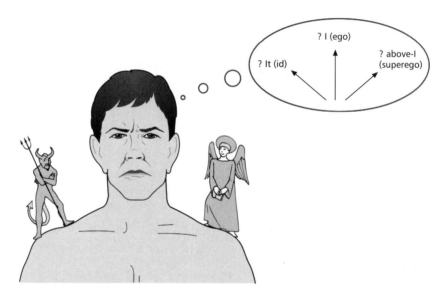

Freud's three aspects of the person

Freud saw his model of personality as having two major strengths. Firstly, it provided an explanation for the experience of being pulled in different directions by different aspects of the self when making decisions, especially decisions with moral implications. Secondly, the idea of the *above-I* aspect of personality is useful in showing how relationships with others affect our personality. Someone with a harsh and punitive upbringing is thus likely to feel guilty a lot of the time – because the *above-I* aspect of their personality is powerful and punitive. Numerous psychologists from more scientific backgrounds have commented on the lack of any objective way in which to isolate, measure and study the *id*, *ego* and *superego*. However, this attitude probably fails to understand what Freud intended when he 'dissected' the personality – he was not literally dividing the mind into three parts, but describing the *experience* of being pulled in different directions by conflicting influences.

for and against

personality theory

+ Freud has successfully described the experience of being pulled in different directions when making decisions.

+ Freud was almost certainly correct in saying that we are affected by instinct and by past experience, and that we are not usually aware of these influences.

− Ideas like *id* and *ego* – and even instinct – are rather abstract and very difficult to study scientifically. Most psychologists are more comfortable with ideas that can easily be researched.

Psychological defences

An important aspect of Freudian theory, which has become quite well accepted in mainstream psychology, is the idea of psychological defences. These are unconscious mechanisms by which we protect ourselves from painful, frightening or guilty feelings. You may, for example, have heard of *denial*, which occurs when a smoker refuses to admit to themselves that they are endangering their life by smoking, or *regression*, in which we use childlike strategies in order to comfort ourselves when under stress – see the photograph below. Other defences include *repression*, *displacement* and *reaction formation*. We can look at these defences in a little more detail.

This woman is showing several tell-tale signs of regression. Note the curled up foetal position, the chocolate and the tears

Repression

Repression occurs when a memory, such as that of a traumatic event or a guilt-provoking sexual fantasy, is forcibly blocked from being remembered. We thus have no conscious recollection of the event or fantasy, although the memory may exert a powerful influence on us, sometimes leading to serious symptoms. Bateman and Holmes (1995) gave an example of repression in a man who came for therapy for depression. When talking about the death of his mother many years earlier, he suddenly remembered – for the first time as an adult – that his mother had committed suicide. Once he had retrieved this memory his symptoms lessened.

Displacement

Displacement takes place when we redirect emotions, most commonly anger, away from those who have caused them on to a third party. Displacement is easy to see in everyday life – most of us tend to take out our bad moods on unfortunate colleagues, friends and family, even when they were not the cause of the bad mood. Displacement can have more serious consequences, however. One psychodynamic perspective on racial violence is that those who have had harsh, violent parenting and who thus carry a lot of anger that they dare not express to their parents look for a convenient target for their anger.

Reaction formation

Reaction formation occurs when we go beyond denial and adopt an attitude that is directly opposed to our real feelings. The classic example is homophobia, in which people who worry that they might have homosexual feelings deal with the resulting anxiety by adopting a harsh anti-homosexual attitude, which helps convince them of their heterosexuality. A fascinating recent study by Adams *et al.* (1996) confirms the link between reaction formation and homophobia (see opposite).

The general principle of psychological defences is probably the most widely accepted of Freud's ideas, and they have proved useful in understanding a range of psychological phenomena. However, Freud believed that the most important of the defences was repression. Of all the defence mechanisms, repression is the most controversial in contemporary psychology, and the issue of repression has become something of a battlefield between psychodynamic practitioners and memory researchers. Memory researchers have pointed out that there is no direct evidence that repression exists. However, memory researchers favour *experimental* research, i.e. putting someone in a particular controlled situation and systematically noting what occurs in those circumstances. For ethical reasons, memory researchers have not been able to recreate the traumatic conditions in which repression is alleged to occur. Psychodynamic psychologists would therefore argue that we simply would not expect to see the type of direct evidence for repression that memory researchers would find convincing. See Chapter 3 for a detailed review of the evidence for repression.

research
now

is homophobia caused by reaction formation?

Adams, H.E., Wright, L.W. and Lohr, B.A. (1996) Is homophobia associated with homosexual arousal? *Journal of Abnormal Psychology*, 105 (3), 440–5

Aim: Freud's theory would predict that men who have strong feelings of hostility towards gay men are those who either have strong homosexual feelings themselves or have particular difficulty in dealing with normal homosexual feelings. A more common sense explanation would be that homophobes are just particularly aggressive people. This study aimed to test whether homophobic men were more aggressive than others and whether they were more likely to become aroused by gay erotica, which would indicate strong homosexual feelings.

Method: A group of heterosexual men were assessed for their attitudes to homosexuality using a questionnaire called the Index of Homophobia. Thirty-five particularly homophobic and 29 non-homophobic men were identified and went on to take part in an experimental procedure. Both groups were shown explicit videos featuring scenes of heterosexual, lesbian and gay sex. The sexual arousal of each man in response to each category of sex was measured using a penile plethysmograph. This is a pressure sensitive ring that is placed on the penis. How aroused the men became in response to each category of sex was measured by the pressure exerted on the plethysmograph. Each man was asked to estimate how aroused they were whilst watching each type of sex scene. All the participants also completed a questionnaire designed to measure aggression. The homophobic and non-homophobic groups were compared on their general aggression, their arousal as measured by the plethysmograph in response to each type of sex scene and their reported arousal at each scene.

Results: There was no difference in the levels of general aggression expressed by the homophobic and non-homophobic men. Neither was there a difference in the arousal level as measured by the plethysmograph when watching the heterosexual and lesbian scenes. However there was a large difference in the response to the gay scenes. Eighty per cent of the homophobic group as opposed to only 33 per cent of the non-homophobic group had erections during the gay scenes. The homophobic group significantly under-estimated their levels of arousal in response to the gay scenes.

Conclusion: Results strongly support the idea that homophobia is associated with reaction formation. There was no evidence for a link between homophobia and general levels of aggression. Of course there are probably a number of other factors influencing homophobia other than reaction formation. Remember, for example, that homophobia is so much more socially acceptable than most prejudices.

for and against

psychological defences

+ Everyday experience tells us that we use psychological defences to make ourselves feel better. We have probably all kicked the cat when in a bad mood (displacement) or comforted ourselves with tears or chocolate (regression).

+ Some of the defence mechanisms have strong supporting evidence, like the Adams *et al.* study of reaction formation.

— Freud almost certainly over-estimated the importance of repression as a defence. Repression has turned out to be difficult to study, and some psychologists don't believe in it at all.

Stages of children's development

Freud (1905) proposed that psychological development in childhood takes place in a series of fixed stages. These are called *psychosexual stages* because each stage represents the fixation of libido (roughly translated as sexual drives or instincts) on a different area of the body. If this sounds slightly odd, it is important to realise that Freud's use of the word 'sexual' was quite broad in meaning, and he did not mean that the child experiences these instincts as 'sexual' in the adult sense. Libido is manifested in childhood as *organ-pleasure*, centred on a different organ in each of the first three stages of development.

The oral stage (0–1 year)

In the *oral stage*, while the child is breast-feeding and being weaned, the focus of organ-pleasure is the mouth. As well as taking nourishment through the mouth, children in the oral stage are taking comfort and their knowledge of the world via the mouth. Freud proposed that if the person experiences a trauma in the first year they can become fixated in the oral stage and continue to display oral characteristics into adulthood. Oral habits can include thumb-sucking, smoking, tastes such as oral sex and attitudes such as *gullibility*, which represents the unquestioning taking in of information as children do in their first year.

The anal stage (2–3 years)

In the *anal stage*, the focus of organ-pleasure now shifts to the anus. The child is now fully aware that they are a person in their own right and that their wishes can bring them into conflict with the demands of the outside world. Freud believed that this type of conflict tends to come to a head in potty-training, in which adults impose restrictions – for the first time in the child's experience – on when and where the child can defecate. The nature of this first encounter with authority can determine the child's future relationship with all forms of authority. Early or harsh potty-training can lead to the child becoming an *anal-retentive personality* who hates mess, is obsessively tidy, punctual and respectful of authority. Alternatively the child may turn out an *anal-expulsive personality*, who is messy, disorganised and rebellious.

The phallic stage (3–6 years)

In the *phallic stage*, the focus of organ-pleasure has shifted to the genitals, as the child becomes fully aware of its gender. This coincides with a growing awareness of the child's exclusion from some aspects of its parents' lives, such as sleeping in the same room. The resulting three-way relationship is known as the *Oedipus complex*, named after Oedipus, who in a Greek legend killed his father and married his mother (not realising who they were). In the Oedipus complex, a rivalry relationship develops between the child and the same-sex parent for the affection of the opposite-sex parent. Freud believed that on an *unconscious level*, the child is expressing instinctive wishes to have sex with his mother and kill his father. This is not to suggest that children possess a conscious awareness of sexual intercourse or death in the adult sense. One of Freud's case studies, Little Hans (Freud, 1909) illustrates Freud's ideas about the Oedipus complex (see page 140).

Freud believed that the phallic stage was the most important of the developmental stages. When boys realise that they have a penis and girls do not, their unconscious response is *castration anxiety*, the belief that girls have already been castrated and the fear that they might share the same fate! Their response is to repress their desire for the mother and identify with the father (in much the same way as we might identify with a bully and become like them in order to overcome our fear of them). Freud was somewhat perplexed by how girls dealt with the Oedipus complex on an unconscious level. He speculated (Freud, 1924) that when girls discover they lack a penis they feel that they have somehow come off worse, and are left with a sense of *penis envy*, the wish to have a penis. Penis envy is later sublimated into the wish to have a baby, and eventually relieved by actually having a baby.

Feminist writers have objected vigorously to Freud's speculation that women are motivated by feelings of inferiority because of their lack of a penis. If Freud is to be taken literally then this is quite justified. However, the later French psychoanalyst Lacan (1966) has suggested that the idea of penis envy is not intended to be taken literally, but rather to mean envy of the penis as a *symbol of male dominance* in society. From Lacan's perspective, penis envy is not envy of the penis itself, but of men's position in the male-dominated society.

classic
research

a case of the Oedipus complex?

Freud, S. (1909) Analysis of a phobia in a five-year old boy. *Collected Papers,* Vol. III, 149–295

Aim: Little Hans, a five-year-old boy, was taken to Freud suffering from a phobia of horses. As in all clinical case studies, Freud's most important aim was to treat the phobia. However, Freud's therapeutic input in this case was extremely minimal, and a secondary aim of the study was to explore what factors might have led to the phobia in the first place, and what factors led to its remission. By 1909 Freud's ideas about the Oedipus complex were well-established and Freud interpreted this case in line with his theory.

Case history: Freud's information about the course of Hans' condition was derived partially from observation of Hans himself, but mostly from Hans' father, who was familiar with Freud's work, and who gave him weekly reports. Hans' father reported that from the age of three, Hans had developed considerable interest in his own penis or 'widdler' and that at age five his mother had threatened to cut it off if he didn't stop playing with it. At about the same time Hans developed a morbid fear that a white horse would bite him. Hans' father reported that his fear seemed to be related to the horse's large penis. At the time Hans' phobia developed his father began to object to Hans' habit of getting into bed with his parents in the morning. Over a period of weeks Hans' phobia got worse and he feared going out of the house in case he encountered a horse. He also suffered attacks of more generalised anxiety.

Over the next few weeks Hans' phobia gradually began to improve. His fear became limited to horses with black harnesses over their noses. Hans' father interpreted this as related to his own black moustache. The end of Hans' phobia of horses was accompanied by two significant fantasies, which he told to his father. In the first, Hans had several imaginary children. When asked who their mother was, Hans replied 'Why, mummy, and you're their Grandaddy' (p.238). In the second fantasy, which occurred the next day, Hans imagined that a plumber had come and fitted him with a bigger widdler. These fantasies marked the end of Hans' phobia.

Interpretation: Freud saw Hans' phobia as an expression of the Oedipus complex. Horses, particularly horses with black harnesses, symbolised his father. Horses were particularly appropriate father-symbols because of their large penises. The fear began as an Oedipal conflict was developing around Hans being allowed in the parents' bed. Freud saw the Oedipus complex happily resolved as Hans fantasised himself with a big penis like his father's and married to his mother with his father present in the role of grandfather.

Discussion: The case of Little Hans does appear to provide support for Freud's theory of the Oedipus complex. However, there are difficulties with this type of evidence. Hans' father, who provided Freud with most of his evidence, was already familiar with the Oedipus complex and interpreted the case in the light of this. It is also possible therefore that he supplied Hans with clues that led to his fantasies of marriage to his mother and his new large widdler. There are also other explanations for Hans' fear of horses. It has been reported for example that he saw a horse die in pain and was frightened by it. This might have been sufficient to trigger a fear of horses. Of course even if Hans did have a fully-fledged Oedipus complex, this shows that the Oedipus complex *exists* but not how *common* it is. Freud believed it to be universal.

A balanced appraisal of Freud's psychosexual development comes from Brown and Pedder (1991). They suggested that Freud's labels of oral, anal and phallic were too narrow to describe what occurs in these stages. They suggested that we should think of the oral stage as a stage of complete *dependency* on the caregiver(s), the anal stage as a period of *separation* from the care-giver and the phallic stage as a time of passionate emotions in which a *rivalry* may form between the child and the same-sex parent for the affection of the opposite-sex parent. The concepts of dependency, separation and rivalry are extremely useful in understanding the developing relationship between a child and its parents.

for and against

Freud's stages of child development

+ Freud was probably correct to say that our early years and our early relationships with our families are extremely important in affecting our development. He is also probably correct that the themes of dependency, separation and rivalry can be important aspects of the child's development.

− It seems very likely that Freud over-estimated the importance of body-parts and the 'sexual' nature of children's development.

− Freud's emphasis on the phallic stage and the Oedipus complex appears to be misplaced. Although rivalry relationships certainly do develop sometimes, they are not universal and probably rarely as significant as Freud believed.

Dream theory

Freud famously called dreams 'the royal road to a knowledge of the activities of the unconscious mind' (Freud, 1900, p.769). He believed that dreams both perform important functions for the unconscious mind *and* give us valuable clues to how the unconscious mind operates. Freud (1900) went on to propose that a major function of dreams was the fulfilment of wishes. Freud elaborated this idea and distinguished between the manifest content of a dream – what the dreamer remembers, and the latent content – the underlying wish. The manifest content is often based upon the events of the day. The process whereby the underlying wish is translated into the manifest content is called *dream-work*. The purpose of dream-work is to transform the forbidden wish into a non-threatening form, so reducing anxiety and allowing us to continue to sleep.

Dream-work

Dream-work involves three processes: displacement, condensation and secondary elaboration.

- *Displacement* takes place when we change the person or object we are *really* bothered about into someone or something else. An example of displacement comes from one of Freud's patients, who was extremely resentful of his sister-in-law. He used to refer to her as a dog, and once dreamed of strangling a small white dog. Freud interpreted this as representing his wish to kill his sister-in-law. As you can see, had the patient actually dreamed of killing his sister-in-law, the patient would probably have felt guilty. It appears that the patient's unconscious mind, in transforming her into a dog, protected him from this guilt.

- *Condensation* takes place when we combine different factors into one aspect of the manifest content. Thus a woman who has angry feelings towards her husband and father might dream of punishing a single man, who represents both the father and husband. This man would embody aspects of both the father and husband.

- *Secondary elaboration* is the final part of dream-work, and occurs when the unconscious mind strings together wish-fulfilling images into a logical succession of events, further obscuring the latent content. According to Freud this is why the manifest content of dreams can be in the form of plausible chains of events.

Symbols in dreams

In Freud's later work on dreams, he toyed with the possibility of universal symbols in dreams. Some of these were sexual in nature, including poles, guns and swords representing penises, and horse-riding and dancing representing intercourse. However, Freud was cautious about these symbols and believed that in general symbols were unique to the individual rather than universal, and that one could not interpret what the manifest content of a dream symbolised without knowing about the person's circumstances. 'Dream dictionaries,' which are still popular now, were a source of irritation to Freud. In an amusing example of the limitations of universal symbols, one of Freud's patients dreamed about holding a wriggling fish, and said to him 'that's a Freudian symbol – it must be a penis!' Freud however explored further and it soon turned out that the woman's mother – who was a passionate astrologer and a Pisces – was on the patient's mind because she disapproved of her daughter being in analysis. It seems much more likely that, as Freud suggested, the fish represented the patient's mother rather than a penis!

Contrary to what you might read in dream dictionaries, Freud did not believe that fish were penis-symbols!

Since Freud's time there has been a shift in psychodynamic circles away from concentrating on the *function* of dreams as wish-fulfilment towards looking more closely at their *meaning* to the dreamer. Jung (1923) suggested that characters in dreams can represent different aspects of the person. This is now a more popular approach to the interpretation of dreams than wish-fulfilment. More serious criticisms of Freud's dream theory come from psychologists of other theoretical backgrounds.

Contemporary psychologists have studied dreams from other perspectives and suggested that dreaming may have more to do with random brain-cell activity than psychological functioning. We look more closely at theories of dreaming in Chapter 1.

for and against

dream theory

+ Freud was probably correct that the content of some of our dreams reflects things that are on our mind. Remember that Freud never believed that *all* dreams could be interpreted.

− There are almost certainly other reasons for dreaming as well as wish-fulfilment.

+ The idea that things in dreams can represent other things is quite credible. Freud's example of the fish dream is a good example.

− There is, however, no way of knowing whether a particular interpretation of a dream is correct, therefore symbols in dreams defy scientific study.

Discussion of Freud's work

Nobody doubts the historical importance of Freud's work, but evaluations of its value to psychology a hundred years on vary widely, from complete acceptance to complete rejection! Freud's ideas have won more favour amongst therapists than in academic psychology. Although there are a number of 'schools' of therapy (and some of these reject Freud's ideas utterly), many therapists have found an understanding of unconscious desires, family relationships and dreams invaluable to understanding what is going on in the minds of their patients.

The major criticism levelled against Freud concerns the unscientific nature of his work. Freud, being a practising doctor and medical researcher, was trained in the methods of science. However, despite agonising over his slackness as a scientist (Jones, 1951), Freud rejected scientific methods as simply too clumsy to tackle the issues he was interested in. How for example would you perform a laboratory experiment of the sort favoured by many psychologists to see whether a particular dream really represented wish-fulfilment? The result of Freud's rejection of scientific psychology is that many of his ideas are untestable. This is a source of great annoyance to psychologists, although as we have seen, some ideas such as reaction formation have been successfully researched. A further difficulty with many of Freud's ideas is that they are derived from looking at a very small sample of people (his patients). Furthermore, as a group Freud's patients were quite unrepresentative of the population at large, being highly neurotic middle-class Austrians. This means that, even if we accept Freud's observations as regards his patients, there are problems in applying his ideas to people in general.

where to now?

The following are further sources of good information regarding Freud's work:

▶ **Jacobs, M. (1992)** *Sigmund Freud*. **London: Sage** – a detailed but readable account of the life and work of Freud. Includes lots of good material on criticisms made of Freud and arguments that can be made in his defence

▶ **Stevens, R. (1983)** *Freud and Psychoanalysis*. **Milton Keynes: Open University Press** – a good overview of Freudian theory with convincing arguments for the value of Freud's work

▶ **Gay, P. (1989)** *The Freud Reader*. **New York: Norton** – introduces the reader to some manageable chunks of Freud's writing. Be prepared for the hundred-year-old style of writing, but there is usually nothing like going back to original sources to really understand what the writer was trying to put across.

MEDIA WATCH

Melons feel the squeeze at Tesco

Libby Brooks

The supermarket psychologists who brought us the theories of trolley daze and aisle alignment, who calculate the relative spend increase induced by the smell of freshly baked bread, have surpassed themselves: they have entered the realm of the psycho-sexual.

As a consequence, Tesco, Britain's biggest supermarket chain, has asked its suppliers to grow smaller melons after focus groups of shoppers revealed that shoppers subconsciously selected fruit according to the trend in breast size.

After investigating a marked drop in melon sales, a retail psychologist's report for Tesco suggested that the modern preference for smaller breasts, as modelled by the likes of the superwaif Kate Moss, is informing customers' decisions to reject larger melons.

The company has instructed growers in Spain to produce galia melons of no more than 0.55 kg, rather than the 1 kg melons that were proving slow to sell.

A Tesco spokesman yesterday said the findings surprised him, but insisted that the sales results spoke for themselves.

"Since we introduced the smaller melons two months ago we have sold more than a million."

The possibility of a subconscious relationship between breast and melon size was first raised by a member of an all-female focus group, set up when Tesco buyers sought to find out why customers consistently picked the smallest fruit from store displays.

The theory was then tested by the retail psychologist, who found that seven out of 10 women questioned agreed that breast size was "the most likely subconscious factor when selecting size of melon". Half of the women went further, attesting that breast size was a conscious thought when choosing melons.

Most of the women believed that the modern obsession with small-breasted models made it more "comforting" to choose smaller melons. Gender proved irrelevant to the subconscious influence: an all-male focus group produced similar results.

The report also noted that customers liked to feel around the "blossom end" – the nipple-like scar where the flower fell off during growth – claiming that the relative softness of the melon proved a good indicator of ripeness.

(from *The Guardian*, March 1999)

Object relations theory

The greatest influence on modern psychodynamic thinking in Britain is not the work of Freud, but rather that of a group of British psychoanalysts collectively called the *Object Relations School*. The word 'object' in psychoanalysis means person, so *object relations theory* (or ORT) literally means a theory of relations with others. The key figures in the Object Relations School are Ronald Fairbairn, Donald Winnicott, Harry Guntrip and John Bowlby. Object relations theory evolved gradually from Freud's ideas (this development is still going on), but there are some key points that distinguish the approach from Freud's ideas.

- We are born with a powerful instinct to form relationships with other people. This is known as *object-seeking*.

- We have a mental representation of the world of other people with whom we have had significant relationships. This is known as the *inner* or *internal world*. How we react to new people and the nature of the relationships we form is powerfully influenced by our inner world.

- The relationship with our primary care-giver is of particular importance in our psychological development.

The object-seeking tendency

Whereas Freud saw people as being born as 'bundles of it' that are motivated to satisfy biological needs like hunger, Fairbairn (1952) proposed instead that we are born with an intact sense of identity (Freud's

'I'), and an instinct to seek out relationships with other people. Babies are thus object-seeking rather than pleasure-seeking. The ways in which the child behaves in order to satisfy its object-seeking tendency depend on its age. From birth, infants have a tendency to fix their gaze on human faces in preference to other objects, and behaviours like crying, cooing and grasping all help to facilitate meaningful interactions with the primary care-giver. Bowlby (1969) called these behaviours *social releasers* and suggested that adults respond with instinctive parenting behaviour when they encounter social releasers.

The inner world

Whereas Freud saw the unconscious mind as containing a combination of instinct and past experience, ORT sees the most important part of the unconscious as the inner world. We all carry around with us a mental representation of the world. To the OR theorists the most important aspect of this representation of the world involves our relationships with others. The *inner world* is populated by mental representations of ourselves and all the people with whom we have – or have had – significant relationships. These representations of significant people are called *internal objects*. The inner world is extremely important in affecting our responses to new people and our ability to have relationships. Our internal objects serve as templates for future relationships. Thus if we have experienced abusive relationships and so have abusive internal objects, the likelihood is that we will fall into further abusive relationships. If however our experiences of relationships have been generally positive, we have a much better chance of forming further successful relationships. The more our emotional needs are successfully met in early relationships, the less will be the influence of the inner world.

The first relationship

In ORT, the first relationship is crucial for the healthy development of the child. The over-riding factor in the development of the child's identity is the quality of mothering, i.e. how well the primary care-giver picks up and responds to the baby's needs. Winnicott (1965) called the mother who can adjust to the baby's needs the *good enough mother*. Winnicott suggested that if the mother fails to respond to the infant's needs and instead makes the infant fit in with her demands, healthy ego development does not occur and instead the child develops a *false self*. This is a kind of smokescreen behind which the child and later the adult hides because it has failed to develop a true sense of identity. The false self is dominated by a tendency for compliance as it has developed through serving the emotional needs of someone else and denying its own needs.

The adult with a strong false self and weak ego continues to comply with the wishes of others and fails to assert their own wishes.

In contrast to Freud, the OR theorists played down the importance of the child's relationship with its father and emphasised the maternal relationship above all else. Object relations theory evolved in the 1950s and 1960s when families in Britain were much more likely than nowadays to have a traditional family structure with a full-time working father and a full-time mother at home. Contemporary OR theorists such as Nancy Chodorow (1996) believe that where parents both play active roles in parenting the child, both the parental relationships will impact on its development.

Research findings

There is considerable support from psychological research for many of the major aspects of object relations theory. Goren *et al.* (1975) showed that infants as young as nine minutes old will focus their attention on an object resembling a human face in preference to any other object. This suggests that the baby has an instinctive attraction to other people, as suggested by OR theory.

This mother has had no problems in forming a good relationship with her baby. Object relations theorists would suggest that her past experiences of successful relationships has contributed to this

There is evidence for the importance of our mental representations of past relationships in affecting our ability to develop new relationships. This was demonstrated in a study by Fonagy *et al.* (1993). They assessed pregnant women's mental representations of their parental relationships using a standard interview called the adult attachment interview (AAI). They then measured how securely attached their babies were to them at 12 and 18 months. It emerged that those mothers who reported poor mental representations of their relationships with their own parents tended to be those whose babies displayed insecure attachment towards them.

Recent studies have also supported the idea that the failure to form a successful relationship with an adult can have serious effects on the psychological development of the child. Main (1996) followed up the progress of children who displayed very pathological behaviour towards their primary care-giver as toddlers (many had been abused or neglected), and found that these children were more likely than others to develop a mental disorder by the age of 17. However, recent research has also shown that children are often tougher than OR theorists have suggested. In a recent study of Romanian orphans adopted in Britain prior to their second birthdays, Rutter *et al.* (1998) found that, although they had had no primary care-giver for up to two years, by the age of four they were experiencing no difficulties.

for and against

object relations theory

+ Many aspects of ORT have support from psychological research.

– Some key concepts such as the internal world have proved very difficult to study scientifically.

+ ORT has enhanced our understanding of people's patterns of relationships and the link between mental health and early experience.

– ORT is reductionist in that it places huge emphasis on mental representation of early relationships and ignores the numerous other factors that affect child development and mental health.

where to now?

The following are good sources of further information about object relations theory:

Bateman, A. and Holmes, J. (1995) *Introduction to Psychoanalysis*. **London: Routledge** – a detailed but relatively clear account of a variety of psychoanalytic theories, including their links to mental health and therapy

Gomez, L. (1997) *An Introduction to Object Relations*. **London: Free Association Books** – a detailed account of the work of each of the major OR theorists

Lemma-Wright, A. (1995) *Invitation to Psychodynamic Psychology*. **London: Whurr** – written for the layperson as well as the student this book discusses well the issue of human relationships and in particular the importance of the first relationship.

Erikson's theory of lifespan development

Let us now look at another classic theory, that of Erik Erikson. While the object relations theorists were examining the importance of very early life, Erikson developed psychoanalysis in the opposite direction and looked at development throughout the entire lifespan. Freud believed that the individual personality was largely established by the age of six, and the object relations theorists saw the first year as of primary importance. Erikson, by contrast, saw the personality as developing throughout life on predetermined lines.

Erikson (1959) identified a number of *psychosocial stages* to the human life, each of which is characterised by a particular conflict that must be overcome if the individual's ego is to develop. Table 5.1 shows Erikson's eight psychosocial stages.

Age	Psychosocial stage	Developmental task
0–1	basic trust v. mistrust	to gain a basic sense of trust in the world
1–3	autonomy v. shame and doubt	to establish an independent identity
4–6	initiative v. guilt	to feel free to explore the world
7–12	industry v. inferiority	to be busy in order to learn to achieve
12–18	identity v. identity-diffusion	to develop an adult social and sexual identity
19–25	intimacy v. self-absorbtion	to establish healthy adult relationships
26–40s	generativity v. stagnation	to surrender youth and focus on the next generation
40s+	integrity v. despair	to accept one's own life and impending death

Table 5.1 Erikson's psychosocial stages of development

Basic trust v. mistrust

The child's focus in its first year is its relationship with its primary carer. It is this first relationship which gives a child a sense of security or *basic trust* in the world and in other people. If the primary carer manages to create a secure, reliable and comfortable environment the child will trust them and transfer this trust to its dealings with the rest of the world. Inconsistent, neglectful or abusive care on the other hand will leave the child with a sense of mistrust that will affect its later development. This is very much how Freud thought of the oral stage, although Erikson placed less emphasis on organ pleasure and the mouth.

Autonomy v. shame and doubt

The child is now aware of its identity as a separate person. This brings with it the challenge to assert its own wishes and to 'do its own thing', i.e. to have *autonomy* whilst maintaining a close relationship with its parents. Freud saw this period as the anal stage, dominated by the conflict of potty-training. Erikson agreed that potty-training was important, but saw the stage in slightly broader terms. The child is developing its own identity at this point and this risks being crushed by heavy-handed or overly critical parenting. Accidents, for example in toilet training, can be a source of shame to the child and it is essential that this shame does not overwhelm the child's developing sense of self. Firm but gentle parenting is needed to get the child past this period.

Initiative v. guilt

At this point the child is developing physically and intellectually very rapidly, and the child is generally keen to explore the world and its own abilities. Having established in the previous stage that it is a person the child now needs to find out what *sort* of person it is. The child is thus very inquisitive and starts to show curiosity about sex. The child also indulges in considerable fantasy play at this stage as a way of exploring its place in the world. This fantasy typically includes imagining taking the place of the same-sex parent in the relationship with the opposite-sex parent – Freud's Oedipus complex. However, whilst Erikson believed in the Oedipus complex, he did not afford it the same importance as did Freud. If parents respond to the child's curiosity and fantasy with embarrassment or treat the child as a nuisance, it can develop a sense of guilt. If, however, it is encouraged in these activities it will develop a sense of initiative which will continue into adulthood.

Industry v. inferiority

At this stage the child is focusing on what it can learn about the world. Erikson believed that all cultures have the equivalent of school where the child can learn the practical and technological skills emphasised by the particular culture. The word 'technological' in this context means anything from weapons through manual tools to computers, depending on the culture. Relationships with others outside the family start to assume particular importance at this stage as the child compares its developing skills with those of its peers and begins to form significant relationships with its teachers. If the child succeeds in forming new relationships outside the family and in its mastery of technology, it develops a sense of industry, i.e. the capacity to be busy. If it fails to achieve these goals, however, the child can be left with a sense of inferiority.

Identity v. identity-diffusion

This is adolescence, a time of rapid change for the individual, on a physical, psychological and social level. Erikson believed that the developmental task of adolescence is to maintain a stable identity in the face of these changes. At the physical level the young person experiences rapid and dramatic changes in their body – this requires a period of adjustment. On a social level adolescence is a *moratorium*, i.e. a period where we delay responsibilities such as work and marriage in order to give the adolescent time to adjust. However, this moratorium can cause as much difficulty as it prevents; young people are expected to act in an adult manner and to make adult career decisions, yet they are excluded from the benefits of adulthood. Matters are not helped by the fact that different adult agencies do not agree on when we become adults. For example, you have to pay full fare on the buses at 16, and you may be required to work full-time, yet you are not allowed to participate in adult privileges such as voting or drinking for a further two years. The adolescent who overcomes all these difficulties develops a stable adult identity. However, there is a risk of *identity-diffusion* in which during the struggle for identity they identify with labels such as 'delinquent' or extreme youth cultures such as violent gangs.

Intimacy v. self-absorbtion

The developmental task at this age is to develop successful platonic, romantic and erotic relationships. Erikson believed that this could only be achieved if the individual had successfully achieved an identity during adolescence. While Erikson emphasised the importance of sexual relationships, he applied the same principles to the establishment of adult friendships and adult relationships to other family members. The developmental conflict of early adulthood is to achieve intimacy in relationships while retaining one's autonomy. Unsuccessful outcomes of this conflict include isolation and loneliness (or superficial, meaningless relationships) at one extreme and, at the other end of the spectrum, submerging one's individuality in a relationship and becoming 'under the thumb'. Erikson considered the capacity for *distantation* very important. Distantation refers to the ability to distance oneself from and to oppose others and what they represent, when necessary even going to war.

Generativity v. stagnation

Generativity refers to the capacity to maintain interest in the next generation. This is manifested in an interest in work, family and the world as a whole, but particularly in one's children and in that which will affect future generations of humanity. A failure in generativity or *stagnation* may lead to loss of the will to work or in impoverished interpersonal relationships. Erikson (1959) observed that many parents he saw in his child-guidance work had been unable to maintain an appropriate interest in their children because of their own parenting. Erikson believed that those who did not have children but who channelled their energies into creative or altruistic work were still displaying generativity and could successfully negotiate this stage of development.

Ego integrity v. despair and disgust

As one enters the second half of one's life and most of what one is going to achieve has been achieved, and as one's physical and cognitive abilities begin to decline, the psychosocial conflict that must be overcome is between *ego integrity*, as one looks back at one's achievements with contentment, and *despair and disgust* as the unsatisfied individual looks back with regret. Despair results from the awareness that life is too short to start again. The despairing individual may also feel disgust at their own lack of achievement. This feeling of disgust is commonly projected on to others, thus the individual may appear to be angry, critical and contemptuous of others. Erikson believed that the main determinant of whether a state of integrity or despair and disgust results in the individual is whether generativity has been achieved in the previous stage. If one has thrown oneself wholeheartedly into the development of the next generation one is more likely to sit back and watch contentedly as they take their turn in achievement.

Discussion of Erikson's stages

Erikson's ideas have found wide popularity and his is perhaps the most widely accepted psychoanalytic theory within mainstream psychology. One reason for the greater acceptance of Erikson's ideas is that he has avoided issues like infant sexuality, which tend to make us uncomfortable. Another is that his ideas are a little more easily testable and have a body of supporting research. In one longitudinal study (i.e. one conducted on the same participants over a long period of time), Whitbourne *et al.* (1992) demonstrated that people's sense of identity and intimate relationships do indeed become stronger in middle adulthood after a shaky adolescence and early adulthood (see opposite).

A further advantage of Erikson's ideas over those of other psychoanalytic theories is that they were conceived with a range of cultures in mind. His theory is less *culture-bound* than those of Freud or the object relations theorists. On the downside, however, Erikson does appear to have somewhat neglected differences in the development of men and women. Marcia (1993) has suggested that Erikson's views on identity and intimacy are useful for understanding men, but that different rules seem to apply for women. This is supported by a study by Kahn *et al.* (1985) in which it was found that scores of identity in early adulthood predicted different relationship patterns for men and women. Men who scored low in identity were less likely to marry, but it was no more or less likely that the marriages would survive. For women, however, low scores for identity were not associated with reduced likelihood of getting married, but they *were* associated with a higher probability of the marriage breaking down.

research
now

do identity and intimacy really change with age?

Whitbourne, S.K., Zuschlag, M.K., Elliot, L.B. and Waterman, A.S. (1992)
Psychosocial development in adulthood: a 22-year sequential study. *Journal of Personality and Social Psychology*, 63, 260–71

Aim: The aim of this study was to look at changes in people's sense of identity and the intimacy of their relationships with age. Participants were followed over a 22-year period in order to assess changes in their identity and intimacy. However, just following one group of people would have left open the possibility that changes in society were responsible for any changes seen in their identity. Therefore, three cohorts were looked at: one group aged 20 in 1966, a second group aged 20 in 1977 and a further group aged 20 in 1988. If any changes in identity were consistent across the three groups this would suggest these changes are a product of universal lifespan development rather than changes in society during the period of the study.

Method: Twenty-year-old college students were recruited in 1966 and assessed using psychometric tests measuring their sense of identity and the intimacy of their close relationships. In 1977 this first cohort was re-assessed using the same psychometric tests and a further cohort of 20-year-old students was also assessed. In 1988 a third cohort of 20-year-old students was assessed and the first two cohorts were assessed again. Scores for identity and intimacy were thus available for the first cohort at ages 20, 31 and 42, for the second cohort at ages 20 and 31, and for the third cohort at age 20. The scores were compared within each cohort and between the three cohorts.

Results: For both intimacy and identity, scores for all three cohorts were relatively low at age 20. For cohorts 1 and 2 there was a substantial increase in scores on the identity scale between 20 and 31, and for cohort 1 there was a further increase between 31 and 42. For scores of intimacy the same pattern was seen except that in cohort 1 intimacy remained stable rather than increasing between 31 and 42 years. Interestingly the scores for each age varied very little between the three cohorts (they were virtually identical for identity).

Conclusion: The results strongly supported Erikson's ideas about identity and intimacy. As his theory would predict people's sense of identity and intimacy were relatively weak at the transition of adolescence and early adulthood and they picked up by the thirties. Most significantly, the massive social changes that took place between 1966 and 1988 had little impact on scores of either identity or intimacy, particularly identity. This suggests that these aspects of development are more dependent on age than external factors – as Erikson's theory would predict.

for and against

Erikson's theory

+ Erikson extended the psychodynamic approach to the study of adulthood, and has given us an understanding of personality development in adults.

+ Erikson based his ideas on the study of different cultures and his theory is less culture-bound than other psychoanalytic theories.

— There is some evidence however that Erikson's theory applied much better to men than women, and that further work is required to understand adult development in women.

+ There is sound research supporting some of Erikson's ideas. The Whitbourne *et al.* study is a good example.

— Erikson's stages, like those of other stage theories are rather rigid, and underplay the importance of individual differences in lifespan development.

where to now?

The following are good sources of further information on Erikson's theory of development:

▶ **Erikson, E.H. (1959)** *Identity and the Life-cycle*. **New York: Norton** – Erikson's writing is quite easy to follow, and as always it is ultimately best to read the original material in order to see what the author really meant to say

▶ **Schaie, K.W. and Willis, S.L. (1996)** *Adult Development and Ageing*. **New York: Harper Collins** – an excellent account of research into adulthood, largely based on Erikson's theory.

what's new?

Alessandra Piontelli and life in the womb

At the heart of the psychodynamic approach to psychology is the assumption that early experiences, especially those with other people, are central in shaping the person we become. Until recently we have assumed that experience – certainly experience of relationships – begins at birth or later. However, the Italian psychoanalyst Alessandra Piontelli has used the modern technique of ultrasound to observe interactions between twins in the womb, and it appears that distinct patterns of interaction between the twins can be observed, and that these patterns continue following birth.

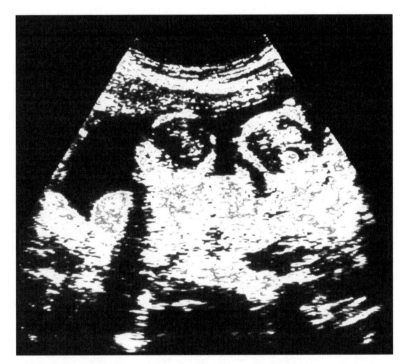

An ultrasound picture of twins in the womb

Piontelli (1992) followed a number of pairs of twins through pregnancy and for three years after birth. Ultrasound observations began 18 weeks into the pregnancy and continued at monthly intervals until birth. The twins were distinguished from each other by their size, sex and position. It was seen that distinct patterns of interaction emerged between the twins through the pregnancy. Some would nestle together whilst others 'fought' for position. In observations of the twins after birth, Piontelli found that many of the patterns of behaviour and 'relationships' in the womb appeared to have continued after birth. Foetuses who had established dominance and occupied more space in the womb continued to be the dominant twin. Apparently aggressive and affectionate relationships in the womb continued in the same vein in the first three years of life.

Although Piontelli's research is radical in its use of technology, it is in other ways typical of the psychodynamic approach, and carries with it the same strengths and weaknesses as other research in psychoanalysis. Piontelli has conducted long, detailed and painstaking observations, which have yielded very detailed results. However, she has focused on a relatively small number of children and made rather subjective judgements about the behaviour of the foetuses, classing them as affectionate and aggressive on the basis of behaviour that *could* in fact be simply a series of reflexes.

Applying the psychodynamic approach to mental health

The psychodynamic approach to psychology is most influential in the field of mental health, although it tends to be more popular amongst psychiatrists and psychotherapists than amongst psychologists. Psycho-analysis has contributed to our understanding of mental health issues by showing how experience and relationships in our early life can affect our later mental health, and in some cases how symptoms of mental disorder can represent unconscious conflicts.

Family relationships and mental health

Central to psychoanalysis is the assumption that the child's developing personality is determined largely by its relationships with its parents. Later mental disorder can represent a failure in normal personality development or the lasting effects of unhappy childhood memories, often a direct consequence of the nature of the parental relationship. Lemma-Wright (1995) has provided us with an example of a woman called Alex who experienced a panic attack, and explained this in terms of unconscious conflicts dating back to Alex's childhood.

case example:

Alex (Lemma-Wright, 1995)

Alex was the older of two sisters. One weekend Alex organised a sea boat-trip to celebrate her sister's birthday. The trip went well, but Alex suffered a panic attack on the boat. Alex had always loved her sister dearly, but she had also resented her a little, believing that her family had always doted on her while ignoring Alex. On one occasion as a child, Alex had become so angry with her sister for being the centre of attention that she dragged her into the sea, frightening her badly. As an adult, Alex frequently felt obliged to organise her sister's life and to help her out of financial difficulties. She had no idea why she suffered the panic attack until a few days later when she had a dream in which she had a fight with a friend (who reminded her of her sister) and wished her dead. It then became apparent to Alex that the boat-trip, in which Alex had once again taken her sister into the sea, had stirred up guilty memories of the time she had dragged her into the sea.

Looking at the case of Alex we can see that long-buried childhood memories appear to have returned to produce anxiety in the form of a panic attack. This case illustrates well the usefulness of a psychodynamic understanding of mental health, but also its limitations. On one hand, it is likely that Alex's panic attack was the result of a rush of guilt triggered by the boat trip with her sister. You can imagine that, if this was the case, understanding it could be invaluable in helping Alex overcome her symptoms. On the other hand, what evidence do we have that Alex's panic attack, her dream and her childhood experiences are really linked in this way? Psychologists, who in the main think of themselves as scientists, tend to have reservations about accepting this style of linking apparently unrelated events together.

Despite this difficulty with adopting a psychodynamic approach, there is a wealth of evidence linking dysfunctional relationships in early childhood to later mental health problems. We have already looked at Main's (1996) study in which toddlers who had failed to develop normal attachments following neglect or abuse were more likely to go on to develop mental health problems than were other children.

Early trauma and mental health problems

There is a large body of research linking susceptibility to mental disorder in adulthood to traumatic experiences in childhood. Depression may too be particularly linked to early experience. Freud (1917) proposed that, while some cases of depression were biological in origin, others were linked to early experiences of loss, in which the sense of loss is so powerful that it affects the developing personality and manifests in later childhood or adulthood as depression. A classic study from Brown and Harris (1978) supports this idea.

classic
research

are early experiences associated with later depression?

Brown, G.W. and Harris, T.O. (1978) *The Social Origins of Depression: A Study of Psychiatric Disorder in Women.* London: Tavistock

Aim: Brown and Harris aimed to investigate the link between depression and both current and past stress in the lives of sufferers. They focused on working-class women, as women tend to experience more stress than men, and working-class people tend to experience more stress than the middle classes.

Method: A complex structured interview called the Life Events and Difficulties Scale (LEDS) was developed. Interviewers were trained in the use of the LEDS. Five hundred and thirty-nine women in Camberwell, London were interviewed using the LEDS. Interviewers obtained details of what stressful events had occurred in the previous year, along with the background circumstances in which they occurred. The LEDS also aimed to uncover stressful childhood events. Interviewers had to prepare a written account of each event of source of stress, which could be rated by a panel of researchers for how stressful it would be for a typical person. To avoid bias, these raters had no knowledge of whether the person they were looking at had suffered depression. It was later ascertained which interviewees suffered from depression. Researchers then looked for associations between who suffered depression and who had recently had a stressful life and who had had stressful events in their childhood.

Results: It emerged that both recent high levels of stress and having suffered a stressful childhood event left people particularly vulnerable to depression. Eighty per cent of the women who suffered depression had had a major stressful life-event in the previous year, as opposed to 40 per cent of those who did not suffer depression. Three of the four factors that had the strongest associations with depression involved recent levels of stress. These were the lack of an intimate relationship, lack of paid employment and the presence of three or more children in the home. However, childhood events were also important, especially the death of the woman's mother before she reached the age of 11.

Conclusions: It was concluded that there was a link between life events and the onset of depression. It was also concluded that loss in childhood, especially of the mother, also made women more vulnerable to depression. This latter finding supports both Freud's idea that depression in adults is linked to loss in childhood and the ORT principle that the relationship with the primary care-giver is of paramount importance for the developing child.

The Brown and Harris study is important because, unlike the case studies that make up the bulk of psychodynamic research, it was performed on a large group of participants and there was a degree of scientific rigour. For example, the researchers assessing the degree of stress the participants had endured had not met the women and did not know whether they were suffering depression. This meant that the likelihood of bias in their assessment was reduced considerably. However, like all structured interview studies, Brown and Harris' work still has the limitation that it relies on participants' ability to report accurately and truthfully their experiences, including those many years in the past. Many psychologists prefer to rely on *prospective* studies (like that of Main, 1996), in which people who have been identified as meeting certain criteria are followed up for a period of years in order to see what happens to them.

Following the classic Brown and Harris study, Bifulco *et al.* (1991) reported that depression was more common in women who had lost their mothers by death or by family re-ordering (i.e. changes to the family such as separation, divorce and remarriage). Interestingly, death of the mother was more likely than loss by family re-ordering to precede depression. In a large-scale study on patients suffering from depression, Kessler and Magee (1993) found that several childhood factors, including parental heavy drinking, domestic violence, the death of a parent and the lack of a close relationship with an adult all increased the probability of suffering depression in adulthood. These studies clearly show that childhood stress, traumatic experiences and lack of good relationships – we can collectively call these *psychodynamic factors* – increase the probability of later mental disorder.

Discussion

From what we have seen so far, it is clear that there is an important role for psychodynamic psychology in the field of mental health. Many patients seek help for mental health problems already believing that childhood experiences are at the root of their problems, and many people in such a position benefit from exploring their early lives. Research firmly supports the idea that stress, trauma and poor relationships in childhood are risk factors for later mental health problems.

That said, there are also drawbacks and risks to adopting a purely psycho-dynamic approach to mental health. There is an increasing body of research showing that genes can also be important in predisposing people to mental disorder (see Chapter 1 for a description of genes and their influence). There are also some conditions that appear to be the result of faulty learning of behaviours (see Chapter 2 for an account of learning). Psychodynamic factors are thus not the only factors that we need to be aware of in working with people with mental health difficulties, and there is a risk of wasting time looking for links with early experience where there are none.

for and against

the psychodynamic approach to mental health

+ In many cases patients can benefit from an understanding of the links between their early experiences and their later symptoms.

+ There is clear evidence that both dysfunctional family relationships and early trauma are major risk factors for developing mental health problems. There is particularly strong evidence for the link between depression and experiences of loss.

– Adopting a purely psychodynamic approach to mental health can mean ignoring other important risk factors such as genetic predisposition to mental disorder.

– The emphasis placed on parenting in psychodynamic approaches can lead to blaming parents for any later mental health problems their child develops. This is a particular problem when we consider how many other factors also affect mental health.

where to now?

We recommend the following as good sources of information on the psychodynamic approach to mental health:

 Bateman, A. and Holmes, J. (1995) *Introduction to Psychoanalysis*. **London: Routledge** – although written by two psychoanalysts, this excellent book provides a very balanced account of the usefulness of a psychodynamic approach to mental health

Fancher, R.T. (1995) *Cultures of Healing*. **New York: Freeman** – a very critical look at how all the major psychological approaches are applied to mental health. This account is biased against the usefulness of all the major psychological approaches including psychoanalysis, but if you are prepared for this it makes an interesting read and provides a good counterpoint for the positive attitude adopted in this chapter

Lemma, A. (1996) *Introduction to Psychopathology*. **London: Sage** – a well-written and comprehensible account of some major classes of mental health problem, including very good accounts of the psychodynamic explanations for each condition.

talking
point

Psychoanalytic therapies – do they work?

We have already seen that psychodynamic ideas are of great value in understanding issues of mental health. Psychoanalytic therapists can make use of these ideas in conducting psychotherapy with people suffering mental health problems. Psychotherapy is sometimes called the 'talking cure'. It involves working with patients by talking in an attempt to alleviate psychological distress. There are several approaches to psychotherapy, the psychoanalytic therapies being the oldest and best-known.

The distinguishing feature of a psychoanalytic approach to therapy is exploration of the links between current psychological distress and/or maladaptive patterns of behaviour and early experiences. Patients explore their past and may re-enact significant past relationships with the therapist. This is called *transference* because patients' feelings left over from significant past relationships are *transferred* on to the therapist, and the patient relates to them *as if they were* that significant person. The aim of psychoanalytic therapies is for patients to gain insight into the ways they relate to others, and to work through the 'baggage' they have been carrying from their childhoods. Psychoanalytic therapy can be conducted individually or in groups, and can often be quite long-term, lasting up to several years, although recently short-term psychodynamic therapies have been developed and are growing in popularity.

Psychoanalytic therapies have been provided in the British National Health Service since the 1940s, as well as privately. However, for almost as long as the NHS has provided psychoanalytic therapies there has been some doubt as to whether they are in fact are effective treatments. Hans Eysenck (1952) published a review of early studies into the effectiveness of psychoanalytic therapies and claimed that there was no evidence that people treated psychodynamically improved any more than people who received no treatment. He produced figures showing that 66 per cent of people improve following psychoanalytic therapy but 66 per cent get better anyway, given no treatment! Actually, Eysenck's study was flawed in several ways. He included in his review some studies with serious design-errors which should have been disregarded. He also took any evidence of improvement in patients who were not undergoing therapy as a 'cure' whilst patients undergoing therapy had to move very substantially before they were counted as improved. Bergin and Lambert (1971) re-analysed Eysenck's own data using the same criteria for improvement in patients with and without psychotherapy, and found that about 80 per cent of those given therapy showed significant improvement as opposed to about 30 per cent of patients receiving no treatment.

Although Eysenck's findings have been discredited, there has never been a large body of evidence for the effectiveness of psychoanalytic therapies. One reason for this is that psychologists, who are trained researchers, have shown relatively little interest in the psychodynamic approach, whilst psychoanalytic therapists have often not been trained or interested in conducting scientific research. However, in a major review of psychotherapy in the NHS, Glenys Parry (1996) pointed out that a more substantial body of research needed to be established if the NHS was to continue to provide psychodynamic therapies. In response to this, a number of studies were conducted in the late 1990s and the results of these have been extremely favourable towards psychoanalytic therapies. One such study by Bateman and Fonagy (1999) showed that psychoanalytic psychotherapy is effective in treating borderline personality disorder.

research now

do psychoanalytic therapies really work?

Bateman, A. and Fonagy, P. (1999) Effectiveness of partial hospitalisation in the treatment of borderline personality disorder: a randomised control trial. *American Journal of Psychiatry,* 156, 1563–9

Aim: Borderline personality disorder is a psychiatric condition characterised by difficulty with relationships, suicidal and self-harming behaviour and drug-abuse. The borderline personality is notoriously hard to treat. The aim of this study was to see whether patients given psychoanalytic therapy would show greater improvements than those receiving standard hospital care.

Method: Thirty-eight patients were diagnosed as having borderline personality disorder using standard psychiatric criteria. They were randomly allocated to one of two conditions. One group was admitted as full-time psychiatric in-patients and remained in hospital for the course of the study. The other group spent part of the time as in-patients but the rest of the time living at home and attending individual and group psychoanalytic psychotherapy. This treatment lasted 18 months. Improvement in each group was assessed by looking at the incidence of drug-use, depression, self-harming, anxiety and suicide attempts. How often the patients needed to be readmitted after treatment was also compared.

Results: The group undergoing psychoanalytic therapy did significantly better on all the measures of outcome than did those in standard psychiatric in-patient care. The therapy group generally showed substantial improvement whereas in general those in the standard treatment condition did not.

Conclusion: Long-term psychoanalytic psychotherapy is effective in treating borderline personality disorder. Significantly it was more effective than standard in-patient care and resulted in fewer re-admissions to hospital. This is important because one of the questions asked about long-term psychotherapy is whether it justifies its high cost. Clearly in this case it did because it reduced the need for more expensive in-patient treatment.

Other studies have investigated the effectiveness of psychodynamic therapies for depression and anxiety disorders. Holm-Hadulla *et al.* (1997) allocated 117 patients suffering from depression and anxiety disorders to a condition of brief psychodynamic therapy, whilst a control group of 116 patients received no therapy. Six months after the course of therapy the control group showed little or no improvement, whilst the therapy group displayed very substantial improvements.

In conclusion, recent studies have been highly supportive of the effectiveness of both short and long-term psychoanalytic therapies for use with a variety of conditions. One recent trend in the use of psychodynamic approaches to therapy in the NHS has been in the growth of short-term treatments. It seems that, although some patients do require long-term psychoanalytic therapy, many people can benefit from short-term therapy. One of the major tasks of researchers in the next few years is to establish precisely *when* long-term treatment is required.

for and against

psychoanalytic therapies

+ There is now a body evidence for the effectiveness of psychoanalytic therapies.

− This body of evidence is still considerably smaller than that for the effectiveness of other types of treatment.

− There are alternative approaches to psychological therapy that may in some cases be equally effective and are quicker and cheaper than psychoanalytic approaches.

+ New short-term forms of psychodynamic treatment have now been developed. These are as effective as other short-term psychological therapies.

+ Studies looking at the cost-effectiveness of psychoanalytic therapies (for example, Bateman and Fonagy, 1999) show that they significantly reduce the use of psychiatric services, therefore justifying the expense.

where to now?

We recommend the following as good sources of further information on psychoanalytic therapies:

▶ **Gross, R. (1998)** *Key Studies in Psychology*. **London: Hodder & Stoughton** – contains a good chapter on psychotherapy research, looking in some detail at the Eysenck study and moving on to some more recent research

▶ **Malan, D. (1995)** *Individual Psychotherapy and the Science of Psychodynamics*. **London: Butterworth-Heinemann** – a detailed but readable account of psychoanalytic therapies. Includes numerous case examples which make the ideas behind psychoanalytic therapies clear

▶ **Molnos, A. (1995)** *A Question of Time*. **London: Karnac** – a good account of brief psychodynamic therapies.

Conclusions

Psychoanalysis remains a controversial approach to psychology. Its dominant research method – the case study – is considered unscientific by many psychologists, and many aspects of psychoanalytic theory remain difficult to test by more scientific methods. However, psychoanalytic ideas have proved extremely valuable for people seeking to understand what is going on in the mind of the individual, hence they remain popular with therapists. As we have seen, some aspects of psychoanalytic theory (such as reaction-formation) do have firm scientific support.

Our understanding of mental health has been enriched by the study of how psychodynamic factors such as early trauma and early relationships impact on later mental health. However, it is also clear that we cannot fully understand mental health with reference to psychodynamic ideas alone. There is no longer any suggestion that psychoanalytic therapies do not work, but *when* they should be used and whether they are *cost-effective* in comparison with other types of psychological therapy are ongoing research questions.

what do you know?

---

1 (a) Describe in detail one study from the psychodynamic approach to psychology.   *(10)*

     (b) Outline one strength and one limitation of case studies.   *(4)*

2 Outline Freud's explanation of dreams.   *(5)*

3 Briefly discuss one way in which a post-Freudian psychoanalytic theory, for example ORT, differs from Freud's theories.   *(4)*

4 Discuss how a psychodynamic approach can be applied to understanding mental health problems.   *(10)*

6

The Social Approach

what's ahead?

This chapter concerns social psychology and the social approach to psychology. *Social psychology* is the study of the ways in which people impact on one another. A *social approach* to psychology is any approach which emphasises the influence of human society or social situations on human behaviour as opposed to the influence of genes, learning, information processing or early relationships. In this chapter we can look at two classic areas of social psychology, prejudice and obedience to authority, and see how both social and alternative approaches can help us to understand these behaviours. In our *real lives* section we look at ways in which we can tackle the problem of prejudice and in *talking point* we look at a new and fascinating area of research – the social psychology of the Internet.

what's it about?

The social approach is based on the following ideas.

- Understanding human social behaviour is central to understanding human nature.

- Our thoughts, feelings and behaviour are strongly influenced by the nature of the social situation in which we find ourselves.

- Social–psychological research is highly varied in nature, and includes the use of laboratory and field experiments, surveys and discourse analysis.

Prejudice

The word 'prejudice' can be broken down to *pre* (meaning before) and *judice* (meaning judgement). You can see therefore that to be prejudiced means to *prejudge* someone, in other words to form a judgement about them before finding out anything about them as an individual. A prejudice is an attitude towards a group that causes us to prejudge anyone just based on their membership of that group. Like all attitudes, prejudices consist of three elements:

- the *cognitive element* – this involves the beliefs held about the group. These beliefs will be in the form of *stereotypes*, common but oversimple views of what particular groups of people are like

- the *affective element* – this involves the feelings experienced in response to the group. If we are prejudiced against a group we may experience anger, fear, hate or disgust when we encounter a member of that group

- the *behavioural element* – this consists of our actions towards the object of our prejudice. Behaving differently towards people based on their membership of a group is called *discrimination*. Our actions against members of a group against which we hold a prejudice can range from avoidance and verbal criticism to mass extermination.

We can illustrate these three elements with the example of prejudice against university students. Stereotyped views of students might include that they are lazy and spoilt, that they make inconsiderate neighbours and that they are heavy drinkers. People who subscribe to those stereotypes are likely to feel angry (and perhaps jealous!) in response to students. The resulting behaviour will probably include verbally criticising students and avoiding places where students congregate. In a minority of people with strong anti-student views, behaviour extends to physical violence.

What stereotyped views might you hold about these students?

There is still much overt racism in Britain today

The targets of prejudice

Prejudice is universal. However much value we might place personally on being tolerant of people's differences, we are bound to have stereotyped views about some groups of people and to prefer the company of some groups over others. If your politics are left-wing then you probably have some degree of prejudice against people with more right-wing views (and vice versa). If you are a full-time student of psychology then you probably have a preference for other psychology students over sociology students and perhaps for social science students in general over mathematicians. Although prejudice is universal, and perhaps to some extent inevitable, it is important not to lose sight of the terrible harm it causes. Prejudice in 1940s Germany led to the systematic extermination of six million Jewish people as well as gypsies, communists and trade unionists. Currently AIDS patients in America receive less attention from health professionals than do other patients (Hunter and Ross, 1991). Twenty per cent of black men in Britain hold managerial positions as opposed to 36 per cent of white men (Skellington, 1995), and sponsorship deals for female athletes go almost exclusively to conventionally attractive heterosexual women (Krane, 1998). Prejudice is of great concern to psychologists because it is an undesirable aspect of our behaviour and one that psychology can contribute to tackling.

The most extensively studied prejudice is racism. Racism exists in a range of cultures and situations, including between Tamils and Sinhalese in Sri Lanka, Catholics and Protestants in Northern Ireland and Albanians and Serbs in the former Yugoslavia. A recent Gallup Poll in Britain (reported in Skellington, 1995) aimed to discover the extent to which racist attitudes are held by a sample of 959 white British people. Questions aimed at discovering whether participants held racist personal views (for example, whether they would object to living next door to a non-white person), their views on the law in relation to race (for example, whether anti-racist laws should be strengthened or abolished), and their perception of race relations in Britain. Results showed a very wide spectrum of both views about issues of race and personal attitudes towards non-white people. Seventy-five per cent of participants rated race relations in 1990s Britain as 'fair' or 'poor'. Only 25 per cent believed that race relations were good. A sizeable minority of participants expressed openly racist views. Twenty-five per cent of people questioned said they would object to a non-white person living next door and 10 per cent of people wanted anti-racism laws to be abolished. On a more encouraging note, 40 per cent of participants wanted anti-racism laws strengthened.

Explanations for prejudice

Psychological approaches to explaining prejudice fall into two broad areas. *Social approaches* centre on the social factors that contribute to prejudice in general, whilst *individual approaches* centre on what factors make one person more prejudiced than another. To understand prejudice fully we need to take into account both of social and individual factors. First let us look at social factors. Perhaps the most-researched social theory of prejudice is social identity theory, proposed by Tajfel and Turner (1979).

Social identity theory

Tajfel and Turner (1979) proposed that many of our social behaviours, in particular prejudice, can be explained by our tendency to identify ourselves as part of a group, and to classify other people as either within or outside that group. This means that we tend to make sharp judgements of people as either one of 'us or them'. The exact nature of the groups we see ourselves as belonging to varies widely according to our individual experience and the culture we live in. However, according to social identity theory, our tendency to think of ourselves as belonging to one or more groups is a fundamental part of human nature. As social animals we have evolved the tendency to identify with a group to aid co-operation and so help us form societies. Tajfel and Turner's theory was based on a series of laboratory experiments called the *minimal group studies*. We look at the idea of minimal group research in *classic research* opposite.

Based on the minimal group experiments, Tajfel and Turner (1979) proposed that there are three cognitive processes involved in evaluating others as either one of 'us or them'. These are:

- *Social categorisation.* In the first stage of the social identity process we *categorise* other people as members of particular social groups. Categories we all tend to subscribe to involve gender, race and social class. Others are more relevant to some people than others, for example football-supporting and cat-loving. Although the categories we consider most important vary according to the individual, we do not make up categories individually. Instead we take categories that we have learned to be important. We can, of course, categorise ourselves as part of several groups, for example one could be a Southampton supporter, a cat-lover and a parent.

- *Social identification.* In the second stage, we adopt the identity of the group we have categorised ourselves as belonging to. If, for example, you have categorised yourself as a Southampton supporter, the chances are you will adopt the identity of a supporter and begin to act in the ways you believe Southampton supporters act, for example, wearing red and white scarves and watching Southampton matches.

There will be an emotional significance to your identification with a group, and your self-esteem will become bound up with group membership.

● *Social comparison.* This is the final stage of the social identity process. Once we have categorised ourselves as part of a group and identified emotionally with that group, we then tend to compare that group with other groups. If our self-esteem is to be maintained our group needs to compare well against other groups. This is critical to under-

classic
research

is just being part of a group sufficient to lead to prejudice?

Tajfel, H. (1970) Experiments in intergroup discrimination. *Scientific American*, 223, 96–102

Aim: Tajfel was interested in whether being categorised as belonging to one of two groups was sufficient to induce prejudice against the other group. Previous studies had clearly established that two groups in competition would show prejudice towards one another, but Tajfel's study deliberately set out to create situations in which two groups were clearly identifiable but were not in competition.

Method: Two experiments were set up, using 14–15-year-old British schoolboys as participants. The first is reported here. In the first experiment 64 participants were told that the researchers were investigating vision. They were shown clusters of dots on a screen and asked to estimate the number of dots. The boys were then told that they were being divided into two groups (underestimators and overestimators in one condition, and accurate and inaccurate in another condition), on the basis of their number-estimates. In fact they were randomly divided into two groups. The boys were then given the task of allocating points to each other, choosing which one of a pair of boys should receive points for their estimates of the numbers of dots. They were told that points could later be converted into money. The participants did not know which individuals they were allotting the money to but they *did* know which group each boy was in. In one condition, the choice was between two boys in the in-group, in the second condition the choice was between two boys in the out-group and in the third condition it was between one boy from the in-group and one from the out-group.

Results: Tajfel was primarily interested in the choices made between allocating money to a boy in either the in-group or one in the out-group. It was found that boys overwhelmingly chose to allocate points to boys who had been identified as in the same group as themselves. This was irrespective of the accuracy of the boys' estimates.

Conclusion: In spite of the fact that there was no competition between groups, the participants consistently displayed a prejudice towards those who were identified as being in the same group as themselves, and against those identified as in a different group.

standing prejudice, because once two groups identify themselves as rivals they become forced to compete in order for the members of each group to maintain their self-esteem. Competition and hostility between groups is thus not only a matter of competing for resources like jobs, but also the result of competing identities.

Discussion of social identity theory

Social identity theory explains a whole host of social phenomena, ranging from racism and class conflict to the sense of togetherness we get from following a football club or band. Significantly, social identity theory provides at least a partial explanation for the tendency for people to discriminate in favour of people from their own country and against those from other countries. We can look at one study of this phenomenon in detail.

research now

do Europeans perceive their own nationality as more competent and moral than other European nationalities?

Poppe, E. and Linssen, H. (1999) In-group favouritism and the reflection of realistic dimensions of difference between national states in Central and Eastern European nationality stereotypes. *British Journal of Social Psychology,* 38, 85–102

Aim: The researchers were interested in what stereotypes European adolescents held regarding the morality and competence of their own and other European nationalities. Social identity theory would predict that the young people questioned would favour their own country. However, differences in the economic status and recent history of different European countries would suggest that people in some states should rate other countries as more competent and/or moral than their own.

Method: One thousand one hundred and forty-three 15–18-year-old students from Russia, Bulgaria, Hungary, Poland, Belaruss and Czechoslovakia answered a questionnaire which examined beliefs about the characteristics of people from European countries including all those from which participants were taken plus Italy, Germany and England. The questionnaires required participants to rate each nationality according their competence and their morality. *Counterbalancing* was employed, i.e. the questionnaires given to different participants listed the various nationalities in different order. This ensured that the participants were not influenced by the order in which the nationalities were presented. The responses were analysed to see whether people tended to favour their own nationality over others or whether general national stereotypes (such as German efficiency) proved a more important factor in judgements.

Results: Results showed that social identity appeared to be one factor affecting people's judgements about other nationalities. The Eastern Europeans tended to favour their own nationality over those of other Eastern Europeans, but not over Western Europeans. Overall, national stereotypes were upheld, and participants consistently rated Germans as the most competent (though least moral) and the English as the most moral people.

Conclusion: Social identity theory correctly predicted that the Eastern European countries would show in-group favouritism in relation to other East European countries. However, people did not blindly favour their own nationality, and economic and historical factors proved important in creating national stereotypes.

We can see from the Poppe and Linssen study that although social identity is one factor influencing prejudice, economic and historical factors are also important in the affecting the ways in which we evaluate people from other countries. A closer look at the minimal group studies also tells us that individual participants differed considerably in the extent to which they favoured the in-group over the out-group. Platow *et al.* (1990) assessed individual differences in responses to the minimal group situation and concluded that participants assessed as highly competitive showed greater in-group favouritism than those assessed as highly co-operative. The latter tended to favour fair distribution of resources rather than the interests of the in-group. Although social identity theory has proved useful in understanding relations between groups, the studies of Poppe and Linssen and Platow *et al.* show clearly that social identity alone is not sufficient to explain prejudice in its entirety.

for and against

social identity theory

+ There is clear evidence from the minimal group studies that being part of a group is sufficient to lead to prejudice against people not within that group.

+ Social identity explains a wide range of phenomena and can be applied to a range of social and cultural situations.

− Not all cultures show equal bias towards in-groups (Wetherall, 1997).

− Social identity theory does not explain individual differences in prejudice. A closer look at the results of the minimal group studies shows wide variations in the degree to which people discriminate against the out-group.

The prejudiced personality

We have already established that social explanations of prejudice have the limitation that they do not readily explain individual differences in prejudice. To understand this aspect of prejudice we need to turn to another approach, the idea of the *prejudiced personality*. Adorno *et al.* (1950) proposed that individual differences in prejudice could be explained by the idea of *authoritarianism*. Authoritarianism is characterised by political conservatism, hostility, rigid morality, strong racial in-group favouritism (ethnocentrism) and intolerance of challenges to authority or deviations from conventional behaviour (totalitarianism). Adorno was interested in the characteristics of the Nazis who in 1940s Germany had taken prejudice to its extreme, systematically murdering six million Jewish people as well as numerous gypsies, communists and trade unionists.

Adorno and his colleagues devised tests to measure ethnocentrism, anti-Semitism (anti-Jewish prejudice), political conservatism and totalitarianism. As expected, the same people tended to score highly on all these characteristics, indicating that there indeed people with an authoritarian personality. The four scales were collectively called the F-Scale (F stands for Fascist, the political ideology of the Nazis). The items in Adorno's original F-Scale were very much tied up with the social and political situation in the 1940s and 1950s, and the scale in its original form is probably not of much use today. However, Ray (1972) has produced an updated version that relies less on current affairs. Some items from Ray's scale are shown below.

	Strongly agree	Agree	Don't know	Disagree	Strongly disagree
If everybody would talk less and work more, everybody would be better off.	_____	_____	_____	_____	_____
Disobedience to the government is sometimes justified.	_____	_____	_____	_____	_____
Young people sometimes get rebellious ideas but as they grow up they should get over them and settle down.	_____	_____	_____	_____	_____
Obedience and respect for authority are the most important virtues a child can learn.	_____	_____	_____	_____	_____

Items from Ray's updated F-Scale (Ray, 1972)

Having established a test of authoritarianism, Adorno and his colleagues went on to interview individuals who had been identified as authoritarian, in order to get an idea of what factors might have led to their developing this type of personality. It emerged strongly from these interviews that authoritarians tended to have had a distinctive style of upbringing. They were generally from cold, unloving homes with a hostile atmosphere. Parents of authoritarians tended to be aloof and controlling, and they typically insisted on high levels of achievement and self-discipline in their children. The primary strategy for ensuring that children complied with their wishes was the withdrawal of affection.

Cold, harsh parenting may be linked to the development of highly prejudiced individuals

Adorno *et al.* proposed that this power-oriented, authoritarian pattern established in childhood spills over into other aspects of the individual's life, leaving them cold and conventional and carrying unexpressed anger that needs to be taken out on a convenient group. The child that has learned to respect only uncompromising strength will have a tendency in adulthood to orient themselves towards institutions like extreme right-wing political groups, which extol the virtues of strength and are themselves uncompromising. Because Adorno's theory is centred on the effects of family relationships on later behaviour, we can describe it as a *psychodynamic* theory (see Chapter 5 for details of the psychodynamic approach to psychology).

Discussion of the authoritarian personality

We need to remember two things when evaluating Adorno's theory. Firstly, he did not propose that authoritarian upbringing led *directly* to prejudice, just that it could lead to a personality type that was *liable* to acquire prejudices. Because of this we would expect research to show only a moderate correspondence between those who had authoritarian upbringings and those who displayed high levels of prejudice. A large body of research has supported such a relationship (McKnight and Sutton, 1994). Secondly, the idea of the authoritarian personality is not intended as a complete explanation of the phenomenon of prejudice, just as an explanation of which individuals are most likely to acquire prejudices. Clearly there are social-psychological factors such as social identity which affect prejudice, along with historical, political and economic realities, as we saw in the Poppe and Linssen study. Theories of the prejudiced personality, based just on the psychological development of the individual, cannot easily explain large-scale conflict between groups such as we have recently seen between Serbs and Albanians in the former Yugoslavia.

Although Adorno's research and theory has been highly influential, there have been many attempts to refine it. Rokeach (1960) suggested that, because the F-Scale includes a scale of political conservatism it only measures authoritarianism in extreme right-wingers. Rokeach proposed that those with extreme left-wing or progressive politics can be equally authoritarian and that therefore Adorno's idea of *authoritarianism* should be replaced with that of *dogmatism*. Dogmatism refers to rigidity of one's views coupled with intolerance of the views of others. More recently, Ray (1989) has suggested that the core personality characteristic associated with authoritarianism is *directiveness*, defined as the tendency to impose one's will on others.

The Nazi personality

Perhaps the fundamental question on which the usefulness of the concept of the prejudiced personality hangs is whether we can demonstrate that people known to be highly prejudiced have common and distinctive personality characteristics. A unique opportunity to investigate this comes from the records of extensive psychological testing which was carried out on Nazi war criminals. Resnick (1984) reported that a sample of Nazi prisoners did indeed score highly on Adorno's F-Scale. Zillmer *et al.* (1995) reviewed the results of tests of the Nazi elite and found that although the prisoners were remarkably undistinctive given their actions, they did broadly tend to have certain characteristics in common. Zillmer *et al.* went on to look at the personalities of rank-and-file Nazis and collaborators, using the *Rorschach ink-blot test*. This is a tool for assessing certain characteristics of the individual personality. A series of ten patterns made up of folded coloured ink-blots are presented to the individual, and their personal interpretation of what each blot shows is recorded.

Paper fold

An example of an ink-blot similar to those used in the Rorschach test

research
now

were **Nazi soldiers and collaborators a particular type of person?**

Zillmer, E.A., Harrower, M., Ritzler, B.A. and Archer, R.P. (1995) *The Quest for the Nazi Personality: A Psychological Investigation of Nazi War Criminals.* Hillsdale, New Jersey: Lawrence Erlbaum Associates

Aim: A large volume of psychological data, including Rorschach tests, was collected on Nazi war criminals immediately after the Second World War. However, early studies using this data tended to involve small numbers of participants, and, in the case of Rorschach ink-blot tests, primitive scoring methods and inadequately trained assessors. In this study, a large volume of Rorschach results from Nazi rank-and-file soldiers and Danish collaborators were gathered and assessed by a small number of researchers with specialist training.

Method: Rorschach results from 207 Nazi soldiers and collaborators were obtained. Twenty were eliminated because they were incomplete or incorrectly completed. Of the 187 remaining, 22 were from military personnel on trial for war crimes in Denmark. The rest were from Danish citizens on trial for collaboration. These included 16 accused of multiple murder, 39 of up to two murders and 34 accused of torture or brutality not leading to death. The remaining participants were accused of non-violent collaboration. One researcher and several research assistants scored the Rorschach results using a modern scoring system. Twenty per cent of the Rorschachs were assessed by two people in order to establish *inter-rater reliability*, i.e. the extent to which they agreed on what the Rorschachs showed. An 85 per cent agreement between the assessors was recorded. The Rorschach tests were scored to test a number of participants' characteristics, including tolerance of stress, interpersonal relationships, self-perception and problem-solving style. These were compared to scores from the normal population.

Results: The war criminals differed significantly from the normal population in several ways. They emerged as less able to make decisions under stress and more prone to following the advice of others (46 per cent of the sample as opposed to 3 per cent of the normal population). In relationships, the Nazi sample emerged as significantly more likely to be very passive (33 per cent of the sample as compared to less than 1 per cent of the normal population). Seventy-five per cent of the Nazis as opposed to 13 per cent of the normal population showed a deficit in self-esteem. Forty-six per cent of the sample emerged as ambitent in their problem-solving style as opposed to 23 per cent of the normal population. No significant differences emerged between the military personnel and the collaborators.

Conclusion: Although a single distinctive personality type did not emerge in the Nazi group, there were certain characteristics including poor decision-making ability, low self-esteem and passivity that characterised the group and may have predisposed them to falling under Nazi influence.

Although the Zillmer *et al.* study does provide evidence for an association between personality characteristics and participation in extreme race discrimination, there are serious methodological problems. The 'normal' population with which Rorschach results were compared with was taken from Americans in the 1990s. Ideally they should have been taken from non-Nazi Danes from the 1940s, and it is difficult to say whether the results obtained from the Nazis would have differed significantly from a proper comparison group. Furthermore the tests were performed while the Nazis were awaiting trial, so it is perhaps not surprising that they showed low self-esteem and difficulty in making decisions! We cannot say for certain that these were characteristics of the group before they became Nazis.

There is a further problem in using studies of this type as evidence for the idea of the prejudiced personality. Whilst it may be apparent that there are certain characteristics that predispose people to go along with discrimination instituted by others, it is quite possible that what we are looking at is primarily a weak-willed and highly *conforming* personality rather than a *prejudiced* personality.

for and against

the prejudiced personality

+ There do appear to be certain characteristics, including rigidity and conservatism, that are associated with particularly prejudiced people.

+ There is a large body of research supporting Adorno's idea that cold, authoritarian upbringing predisposes people to rigid, conservative thinking.

− The prejudiced personality cannot easily explain conflict between groups of people, and is therefore not a complete explanation of prejudice.

+ Studies of Nazi war criminals, such as that by Zillmer *et al*, support the idea that certain personality characteristics are associated with affiliation to prejudiced groups such as the Nazis.

− Studies like that of Zillmer *et al.* are unavoidably flawed in their methodology, and there is some question as to whether they are actually identifying a *prejudiced* personality or some other personality type.

where to now?

The following are good sources of further information about the psychology of prejudice:

▶ **McKnight, J. and Sutton, J. (1994)** *Social Psychology*. **Sydney: Prentice Hall** – particularly useful up-to-date information on the study of the prejudiced personality. Also has information on social identity theory

▶ **Wetherall, M. (ed.) (1996)** *Identities, Groups and Social Issues*. **Milton Keynes: Open University** – great information on both social identity theory and the prejudiced personality. Very detailed and up-to-date, but nonetheless clear and readable

▶ **Hayes, N. (1998)** *Foundations of Psychology*, **2nd edition. Walton-on-Thames: Nelson** – a good general psychology text, particularly strong on social psychology, including theories of prejudice.

what's new?

understanding the language of prejudice

The *discursive psychology* approach takes a very different angle on prejudice from that of social identity theory or prejudiced personality theory. Discursive psychologists study the ways in which our perceptions of the social world are shaped by *discourse*. 'Discourse' simply means the nature of the language we use when we speak, write or sing about a topic. The central idea behind the discursive approach to prejudice is that the language we use to discuss issues like race, gender, age and sexual orientation promotes stereotyped views of the groups involved. To begin with, let us take our use of the word 'race'. We use the term 'race' rather like we do the word 'species' to mean a distinct group but, unlike 'species', which has a precise scientific definition, the term 'race' is scientifically meaningless. There is far more variation between the members of any 'race' than there is between any two 'races', and to classify people as different on the basis of their 'race' is actually just as arbitrary as dividing the world into people with blue and brown eyes, or shorter and taller people. By using the term 'race', we are *socially constructing* a way of classifying people.

The major research technique in discursive psychology is called *discourse analysis*. Discourse analysts 'unpack' as much hidden meaning as possible from the language we use in relation to an issue. A discourse analysis from Burns (1998) shows how the lyrics of popular music help construct stereotypes of how men and women conduct themselves in relationships. Burns unpacked the lyrics to Aqua's 'Barbie Girl', which reached No. 1 in the UK charts in 1997. Verses 2, 3 and 4 are reproduced below.

I'm a blonde bimbo girl
In a fantasy world
Dress me up
Make it tight
I'm your doll.

(Ken) You're my doll
rock'n'roll
feel the glamour and pain
Kiss me there
Touch me there
Hanky panky

(Barbie) You can touch
You can play
If you say
I'm always yours

(Reproduced by permission of MCA Records Ltd)

You may remember the song as irritating but light-hearted, happy and extremely harmless. However, Burns has revealed how some worrying beliefs about male–female relationships are expressed in these lyrics. Firstly, here is a discourse in which love, sex and ownership are tied together. Barbie is constructed as a self-confessed blonde bimbo who describes herself as 'your dolly', thus reducing herself to something less than a person and as the property of Ken. She offers herself as a sexual plaything ('you can touch, you can play'), on the condition that Ken gives a lasting commitment to her ('if you say I'm always yours'). Ken on the other hand is constructed as relatively unemotional. He makes no declarations of love, but instead demands sexual services ('kiss me there, touch me there'). Here is a representation of relationships in which women want love and men want sex and worse, in which men swap love for sex and women give sex in exchange for love.

You can see that a very unhealthily stereotypical and sad account of human relationships is being played out here. You might say 'so what, it's just a song?' However, to a social constructionist people construct their perceptions of relationships from the discourse of relationships they encounter. This means that songs like 'Barbie Girl' may perpetuate unhealthy stereotypes of what men and women want from relationships.

Using this as an example you can see some of the difficulties with the technique of discourse analysis. It is highly subjective, i.e. different psychologists might analyse the same lyrics and come up with different interpretations. Furthermore, we don't know just from analysing the lyrics what the song-writer intended people to get from the song, or how it was perceived by fans. Was it in fact intended to be taken literally, or was the writer having a go at stereotypical views on relationships? Social constructionism is currently a very influential approach to social psychology, but it is also highly controversial because of its subjective nature.

where to now?

The following are good sources of further information about discursive psychology and social constructionism:

▶ **Gross, R., Humphreys, P. and Petkova, B. (1997)** *Challenges in Psychology*. **London: Hodder & Stoughton** – an excellent starting point as it addresses simply and clearly the very complex issues raised by social constructionism. Particularly good on prejudice

▶ **Burr, V. (1995)** *An Introduction to Social Constructionism*. **London: Routledge** – a detailed account of the social constructionist approach to psychology and of discourse analysis.

Obedience

Following the Holocaust, in which large numbers of Nazis and their collaborators obeyed unquestioningly when ordered to perform monstrous acts, psychologists set out to investigate the phenomenon of human obedience. Like Adorno, Stanley Milgram was one of an international network of researchers committed to investigating the psychology underlying the Holocaust with the intention of preventing anything like it happening again. Early attempts to explain the Holocaust focused on the idea that there was something distinctive about German culture that had allowed the Holocaust to take place. Stanley Milgram initially set out to test the idea that the German people were unusual in their response to orders from authority figures, but he quickly found that people in general are surprisingly obedient to people in authority. In one of the most famous series of experiments in psychology, Milgram (1963; 1974) demonstrated that most participants would give a helpless victim fatal electric shocks when ordered to. The original study is described here in detail.

The Milgram studies

Milgram set out to investigate how obedient people would be in a situation where following orders would mean breaking participants' moral code and harming another person. In his original study, Milgram advertised for male volunteers to take part in a memory experiment for a fee of $5. When they arrived at the university, the participants were told they would be either a teacher or a learner. They were then introduced to 'Mr Wallace', a mild-mannered and pleasant middle-aged man who was in fact an actor working for Milgram. By fiddling an apparently random procedure, Milgram ensured that the participant was always the teacher and 'Mr Wallace' was always the learner. Mr Wallace was then strapped into a chair and given a memory task involving remembering pairs of words. Every time Wallace made a mistake Milgram ordered the participant to give him an electric shock. Of course there were no real shocks, but there was no way for the participant to realise this. Following each mistake the level of the 'shock' appeared to increase. The shock levels on the machine were labelled from 0–450 volts and also had signs saying 'Danger – severe shock' and, at 450 volts XXX. Milgram ordered participants to continue giving increased shocks whilst the learner shouted and screamed in pain then appeared to collapse. When participants protested Milgram told them 'the experiment requires that you continue'.

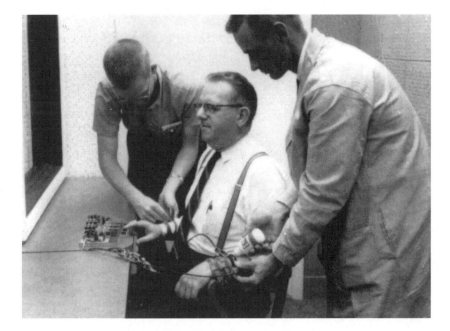

Milgram's apparatus (© 1965 by Stanley Milgram. From the film *Obedience*, distributed by Penn State Media Sales)

To Milgram's great surprise, all the participants gave Mr Wallace some electric shocks and 65 per cent went the distance, giving the full 450 volts to an apparently dead Mr Wallace! Most participants protested and some wept and begged in their distress, obviously believing that they had killed Mr Wallace. However most people did not feel that they could stop when ordered to continue by Milgram. This dramatic study demonstrates the power of authority over our behaviour. What is particularly remarkable about the results is that participants were clearly very upset by what they had to do, but *saw no alternative except to obey*.

In a series of variations on the original experiment, Milgram found that the circumstances affected the percentage of people who would follow orders to the point of killing. When the setting was moved from a prestigious university to a run-down office-block the number of people willing to give 450 volt shocks declined to 47.5 per cent. When Milgram gave orders by telephone from another room the percentage dropped to 20.5 per cent. When the teacher was required to force Mr Wallace's hand down on to an electrode, the percentage willing to go to 450 volts was 30 per cent. We can see then that the situation is important in determining how obedient we are to authority.

Later studies of obedience

Other studies, including those carried out in real-life settings have confirmed that people have a remarkable tendency to obey those in authority. One real-life setting where a degree of obedience is necessary for smooth running is in medicine. In a classic field-experiment, Hofling *et al.* (1966) demonstrated that nurses would obey doctors even when doing so would be likely to endanger patients (see page 183).

An understanding of the power relationships between doctors and nurses, and the development of systems where nurses obey doctors only when it is appropriate can be extremely important for patients' health. In a survey of 7,000 nurses, Raven and Haley (1982) found that 40 per cent of respondents said they would obey an order to move a patient out of isolation while still infectious and 23 per cent said they would obey an order to leave a catheter in after it had caused an infection. This shows that the traditional hierarchy of medicine, in which nurses are encouraged to obey doctors without question, is not necessarily the most efficient approach.

An understanding of obedience is also important in law enforcement. Bushman (1988) performed a field experiment in which a female researcher, dressed either in a police-type uniform, as a business executive or as a beggar instructed people in the street to give some change to another researcher for a parking meter. Seventy-two per cent of people obeyed her when she was dressed in uniform. Fewer people obeyed in the other conditions. Interestingly, whether she was dressed as a business executive or a beggar made very little difference. The rates of obedience were 48 per cent and 52 per cent respectively. This showed that people were not simply responding to the social status of the person giving the order. When interviewed afterwards, participants tended to report that they had obeyed the woman in uniform simply because *she appeared to have authority*.

classic
research

do nurses always obey doctors' orders?

Hofling, K.C., Brotzman, E., Dalrymple, S., Graves, N. and Pierce, C.M. (1966) An experimental study in the nurse–physician relationship. *Journal of Nervous and Mental Disorders*, 143, 171–80

Aim: Researchers were interested in whether nurses would obey a doctor when doing so would breach hospital regulations and endanger the lives of patients. On a practical level, this would have implications for nurse training and hospital policy, and on a theoretical level it is interesting to see whether the high levels of obedience reported in Milgram's laboratory studies would be replicated in a real-life setting.

Method: Boxes of capsules labelled 'Astrofen' were placed with other medicines in 22 hospital wards of American hospitals. In the capsules was glucose, which would be harmless to the vast majority of patients, but the label said that the maximum safe daily dose was only 10 mg. A researcher calling himself 'Dr Smith from the psychiatric department' telephoned nurses on duty on each ward and instructed them to give a patient, Mr Jones, 20 mg of Astrofen. Although written authorisation was normally required before nurses were allowed give drugs, Dr Smith said that he was running late and would get there and sign the necessary authorisation shortly. Meanwhile 22 other nurses not involved in the field experiment were interviewed and asked whether, if a doctor telephoned when they were on duty and instructed them to administer more than the maximum safe dose they would do so.

Results: There was a dramatic difference between what the nurses interviewed said they would do and the behaviour of the nurses actually put in the situation. Twenty-one of the 22 nurses interviewed said that they would not obey the doctor's instructions, yet 21 of the 22 nurses told by telephone to give a large dose of Astrofen did so! When questioned later, 11 of these nurses said that they had not noticed the discrepancy between the maximum dose and the dose they were told to give. The other ten did noticed but judged that it must be safe if the doctor ordered them to give it.

Conclusion: Although the nurses believed that they would not obey a doctor unquestioningly if they were ordered to do something that breached regulations and endangered patients, it appeared that in fact they did just that.

Explanations for obedience

We can look here at two very different explanations for the phenomenon of obedience. Milgram (1974) has proposed a broad theory for our general tendency to obey people who we identify as being in positions of authority. An alternative angle on explaining obedience comes from studies of *charismatic leaders*, people who seem to have exceptional abilities to command obedience in others.

Milgram's agency theory

Milgram (1974) proposed that our general tendency to obey those who we perceive to be in authority is an evolutionary mechanism for maintaining a stable society. For us to exist in complex societies we need social rules, and sticking to these rules requires that at least some of the time we give up a degree of our free will. Milgram proposed that in order to accomplish this we have evolved two social states. In the *autonomous state* we are free to act as we wish, including how our conscience dictates. However, in our *agentic state* we surrender our free will and conscience in order to serve the interests of the wider group. When we are in an agentic state we see ourselves as primarily the agents of those in authority and only secondarily as individuals.

We are socialised into developing the capacity for the agentic state during childhood. In school, we learn to put aside our individual wishes in favour of maintaining order, and so putting the good of the class as a whole first. Milgram believed that, like children in the classroom, we are all constantly subordinating our own needs and wishes to those of society. We can see this tendency in our job-related behaviour. In theory, most people would say that they work for their own benefit and would not go out of their way for their employers. In reality however, once people are in a job and they identify themselves as part of an organisation, they have a tendency to put the needs of their employers above their own.

An important aspect of the agentic state is the strategies we use to deal with *moral strain*. Moral strain results when we have to do something we believe to be immoral in order to function as an agent of authority, and so benefit society. Milgram suggested that we use Freudian defence mechanisms (see page 135) to avoid the distress of having to perform acts we would normally find abhorrent. *Denial* was found to be particularly common in participants in the Milgram studies, and in the Holocaust as perpetrators refused to confront what they were doing.

If we accept that human behaviour can be a product of evolution, then it is quite a credible idea that we have evolved the tendency to obey those in authority in order to help create stable human societies. Agency theory does explain a wide range of social behaviours, ranging from how we act at work to the way in which peaceful people can go to war, and of course how 'normal' people become involved in atrocities such as the Holocaust.

for and against

agency theory

+ The idea that obedience serves the function of allowing complex human societies to develop is highly credible.

+ Support for agency theory comes from interview studies such as that of Bushman (1988), because they confirm the principle that we will obey unquestioningly those who we see as acting on behalf of society as a whole.

– There is little direct evidence that human social behaviour is a product of evolution.

– The idea of an identifiable agentic state has proved very difficult to pin down. Simply saying that someone is in an agentic state because they obey and that they obey because they are in a agentic state is circular logic.

– Agency theory does not explain individual differences in obedience. Milgram has neglected the minority of people who did *not* obey him.

Hitler's charismatic leadership of Nazi Germany may have been a factor in the people's obedience in exterminating six million Jewish people

Charismatic leadership

House *et al.* (1991) have defined charisma as 'the ability of a leader to exercise diffuse and intensive influence over the beliefs, values, behaviour and performance of others' (p.366). It appears that some leaders can induce especially high levels of obedience. This extraordinary obedience can have positive or negative consequences according to the situation. On the downside, charisma enhances people's tendency towards destructive obedience, and it seems likely that Hitler's charisma may have contributed to obedience in Nazi Germany that permitted the Second World War and the Holocaust. Historically, many of the national leaders that we associate with particularly violent or immoral actions – including Hitler, Stalin and Thatcher – were charismatic leaders. However, we should remember that charismatic leadership can also bring about positive change, as evinced by the achievements of Ghandi and Martin Luther King.

Charisma does not exclusively belong to political leaders. Business benefits from utilising charismatic leaders to boost productivity. In a recent study, Geyer and Speyrer (1997) measured the charisma of managers in 116 Austrian banks, using reports from a total of 1,456 employees, and found a strong relationship between charisma and the productivity of the bank. It appears that introducing a charismatic manager is an extremely effective way of increasing productivity in an under-achieving workforce.

We can understand charisma in terms of both the characteristics of the leader and the relationship they have with their followers. House *et al.* (1991) identified charismatic leaders as having excellent communication skills, a high level of concern for the needs of their followers and a mastery of impression management (the skill of making others see us as we wish them to). These attributes all help in obtaining obedience. However, personal characteristics seem to be only part of the story, and most contemporary social psychologists place more weight on the *processes* by which charismatic leaders obtain obedience from others. Such leaders tend to establish a clear vision of what they are trying to achieve and how they intend to achieve it. This enhances the motivation of followers to obey their instructions. Charismatic leaders also tend to frame their orders in terms of achieving their goal, so that there are clear reasons to obey them. Charismatic leaders also tend to use emotive language that fires up followers to the extent that they tend to obey instructions without pausing to reflect on them.

It is important to understand the relationship between charisma and obedience, because many of those who demand our obedience – such as politicians – use charisma to obtain our obedience. However, charisma is clearly not a complete explanation of obedience. The classic studies of obedience have shown that in general we obey regardless of the charisma of the person giving the orders, provided the person giving the orders is identifiable as being in a position of authority. In Hofling's study for example, nurses obeyed simple telephone instructions and had no basis on which to judge and respond to the doctor's charisma.

for and against

charismatic leadership as an explanation of obedience

+ It does appear that certain individual characteristics are associated with the ability to obtain a greater than usual level of obedience from others.

+ We have some understanding of the social processes by which charismatic leaders obtain obedience from their followers.

− Charisma is not a complete explanation for obedience because people do obey those in authority regardless of their charisma.

where to now?

The following are good sources of further information about research and theory regarding obedience:

 Baron, R.A. and Byrne, D. (1994) *Social Psychology: Understanding Human Interaction*. **Boston: Allyn & Bacon** – an undergraduate-level text with comprehensive coverage of studies of obedience and charismatic leadership

 Gross, R. (1998) *Key Studies in Psychology*, **3rd edition. London: Hodder & Stoughton** – excellent detailed coverage of the Milgram studies and later research on obedience.

real lives

Tackling the problem of prejudice

We have already said that prejudice is universal and probably to some extent inevitable. This does not mean, however, that we should adopt an attitude of helplessness towards it. Psychologists have been involved in many attempts to reduce prejudice. We can look here at two approaches to prejudice-reduction, increasing contact and co-operation, and collective action.

Intergroup contact and co-operation

If we accept that the negative stereotypes held by different groups towards one another are inaccurate, common sense would suggest that increasing the contact these groups have with each other should allow people to see for themselves the inaccuracy of their stereotypes and so to get on better. Research has shown that in real-life the situation is a little more complicated. Deutsch and Collins (1951) surveyed white Americans who lived in housing projects that were either racially segregated or mixed and found that people in the mixed projects had significantly more positive attitudes towards black people. In this instance, intergroup contact succeeded in breaking down boundaries.

At around the same time, in 1954, the law was changed in America to make racially segregated schooling illegal. It was expected that this would have a similar effect to the mixed housing projects, but unfortunately this was not the case and prejudice between groups of children actually increased. This piece of history tells us that simply increasing intergroup contact is not always sufficient to reduce prejudice. Aronson *et al.* (1994) has identified six conditions that need to be met before contact will reduce prejudice:

- The groups must depend on each other.

- The groups must have common goals.

- The groups must have equal status.

- The groups must be able to interact informally and on a one-to-one basis.

- Members of the groups must have multiple contacts with different members of the other group(s).

- A social norm of tolerance of differences between groups must be established.

In real life it can be extremely difficult to establish all these conditions. If historically, one group has had higher socio-economic status than another, then interactions are more likely to be of the boss–employee type rather than equal status. Historical factors may mean that one group has been used to profiting at the expense of the other, and accepting equal status may require a reduction in some variable such as wealth.

The common in-group identity model

A more sophisticated approach to prejudice reduction than the simple increased contact hypothesis comes from Gaertner *et al.* (1989), who proposed a way of reducing racism based on social identity theory. The rationale of Gaertner's approach is that we should be able to reduce racism by stopping people classifying each other as part of an in-group or out-group. According to Gaertner, weakening the 'us-and-them' boundaries should initiate a process where more positive attitudes lead to an increase in contact between groups. From there prejudice should naturally reduce.

So how do we get people to redraw their boundaries so that members of different groups will be perceived as one group? According to Gaertner one way is to establish *co-operative interaction* between different groups. In practice this means getting groups to work together towards achieving the same goal. In one experiment, Gaertner *et al.* (1990) demonstrated that co-operative interaction leads people to redraw in-group/out-group boundaries. The researchers established two groups of three people. In the experimental condition the two groups were brought into contact so that they could work together. In the control condition, the two groups were brought into contact but did not work together. When the groups were later surveyed about their perceptions of who was in the group, the groups who had worked together identified themselves as one group of six, whereas the groups who had not worked together identified themselves as two groups of three.

A problem with laboratory experiments like this one is that they lack *ecological validity*, i.e. they are not representative of real-life situations. There is a difference between groups thrown together for an experiment and naturally-occurring cultural groups who have identified themselves as distinct groups for their whole lives, and who may have experienced conflict with other groups. However a later study by Gaertner and colleagues shows that, even in real-life settings, people's experience of co-operative interaction can be related to their perception of themselves as one large group rather than several small groups. Gaertner *et al.* (1993) gave 1,300 pupils at a multicultural American high school a survey that measured co-operative interaction and attitudes to their own and other cultural groups. It was found that the pupils that had engaged in most co-operative interaction were most likely to identify the pupils at the school as a single body rather than several smaller cultural groups.

Where practical, Gaertner *et al.*'s model seems to be an effective way of reducing prejudice. There is, however, a serious limitation to the approach. Once two groups have actually fallen out, and are actively engaged in hostilities, it would be difficult to persuade them to come together in common aims. This approach is perhaps most effective as a preventative way of tackling racism, for example in school settings.

for and against

intergroup contact

+ Under some circumstances, increased contact is sufficient to reduce prejudice.

− A number of conditions need to be met before intergroup contact works, and historical factors sometimes prevent these being met.

+ Gaertner *et al.* have devised an effective strategy based on intergroup co-operation to increase contact under optimum circumstances.

− Gaertner *et al.*'s approach relies on the members of different groups being prepared to co-operate. This may not be practical when groups have already fallen out.

Collective action

Whereas strategies to increase intergroup contact are aimed at reducing prejudice in individuals and targeted communities, collective action has a more ambitious purpose – to reform the attitudes of society as a whole and prevent discrimination on a national or world level. Collective action takes place whenever an individual acts as a representative of a group and their action is directed towards improving conditions for that group (Wright *et al.*, 1990). Collective action takes the form of political movements, and may use strategies ranging from generating literature through public protest (for example, marches and demonstrations) to violence. Whenever people perceive that they are disadvantaged because of their membership of a group rather than because of individual circumstances (this is called *relative deprivation*), collective action becomes likely.

In the light of social identity theory, it is interesting to see that, in one sense, collective action operates in the opposite way to intergroup contact. Rather than blurring boundaries between groups, collective action *strengthens* the group identity of members of the disadvantaged group, and asserts the rights of that group for equal status. A good example of collective action comes from the feminist movement. Research into the beliefs and feelings of feminist activists has supported the idea that both relative deprivation and social identity are important psychological factors underlying collective action. Kelly and Breinlinger (1996) interviewed a sample of feminist activists in order to try to understand what factors influenced their political activism. They found that most of the activists interviewed reported that their initial reason for taking action was their perception of women as a group suffering discrimination (relative deprivation). Once they were politically active, however, and had formed links with other activists, it seemed that social identity was the most important single factor maintaining their activism. Not standing up to be counted would be incompatible with feminists' social identity as both feminists and as women.

Kelly and Breinlinger (1996) have suggested that in contemporary British culture, collective action is frowned upon by the majority. Thus, whilst in principle most people would support equal rights for women, perceptions of feminists *as individuals* seem to be largely unrelated to the aims of the feminist movement and are surprisingly negative. Our tendency to see activists as an out-group irrespective of their aims is exploited by politicians. Reicher and Hopkins (1996) have used discourse analysis to show how in the 1984 miners' strike Prime Minister Margaret Thatcher and the opposition leader Neil Kinnock both tried to construct a public perception of a large in-group including themselves and a smaller out-group. For Thatcher, the in-group was the law-abiding public and the out-group a small group of extremists – the miners. For Kinnock, the in-group was society as a whole and out-group an oppressive Thatcher. Given society's distrust of political activists, Thatcher always had the advantage. When university students in the late 1980s and 1990s took to the streets to protest against shrinking (and eventually abolished) grants, they were similarly constructed as a small out-group of extremists.

Collective action on the part of the miners in the 1980s failed

So what does history tell us about the success of collective action as a strategy to reduce discrimination? The miners' strike failed and student grants have been abolished, so clearly collective action is not always effective. However, anti-discrimination laws protecting the rights of women and minority ethnic groups have been passed following collective action (although of course these laws have not been entirely effective at eliminating discrimination), and there has been a gradual shift in public opinion away from traditional racist and sexist views. In general then it seems that, although the effects of collective action are long-term rather than immediate and, although there are no guarantees of success, it is a valid strategy for effecting social change.

for and against

collective action

+ Because collective action tends to emerge in response to relative deprivation, it provides a way of identifying and addressing social inequality.

− In Britain we tend to have negative stereotypical views of political activists, reducing the effectiveness of collective action. This conservatism can be exploited by politicians to marginalise those taking part in collective action.

+ Collective action has led to anti-discriminatory laws, and a gradual shift in public attitudes.

− Anti-discrimination laws have failed to eliminate discrimination.

where to now?

The following are good sources of further information on the reduction of prejudice:

▶ **Aronson, E., Wilson, T.D. and Akert, R.M. (1994)** *Social Psychology: The Heart and the Mind*. **New York: Harper Collins** – a very well-written American social psychology text, featuring particularly good information on intergroup contact

▶ **Eysenck, M. (ed.) (1998)** *Psychology: An Integrated Approach*. **Harlow: Longman** – has a particularly detailed and up-to-date social psychology section, and features some excellent material on collective action.

talking point

Prejudice, social identity and the Internet

At the turn of the Millennium the Internet is growing rapidly, both in the extent of its use and its importance in people's lives. Internet use has implications for society as a whole and the social psychology of the individual. Social interaction on the Internet is now highly sophisticated and many people have 'virtual lives' that rival their 'real lives' in importance. Friendships and even romantic relationships in cyberspace are now common, and highly cohesive groups form among people who may never meet in 'real life'. Research has begun into these social-psychological aspects of Internet use and fascinating results are emerging, including in some of the areas we have looked at in this chapter.

Forming impressions in Internet interaction

Despite the lack of visual cues, it does seem that we are highly motivated to form impressions of people we encounter in cyberspace, just as we are in 'real life'. In one study, Walther (1993) compared the impressions people formed of one another when engaged in joint tasks, communicating face-to-face or by Internet alone. Groups of three people were asked to co-produce policy recommendations for a range of social issues. In one condition the triads were allowed to communicate face-to-face and in the other they could communicate only by the Internet. After making recommendations on each issue, group members were asked to complete a questionnaire about their co-workers. The questionnaire included a 'don't know' option for each question. It was found that after a single session the face-to-face teams formed strong opinions of their co-workers. After one Internet session the teams tended to opt for 'don't know' responses. However, after the third session they had formed just as strong impressions of co-workers as had the face-to-face group. Walther's study is important to understanding prejudice on the Internet because it shows us that our usual tendency to form impressions quickly and make judgements about people is not inhibited by Internet interaction.

Social identity in Internet groups

A further line of research has explored social identity in groups of Net users. Given that the usual visual cues for group membership are not easily available in Internet interaction, in-groups tend to use different criteria for distinguishing themselves from out-groups and excluding outsiders. One such strategy is *expertism*. Insiders such as members of newsgroups taunt would-be group members by demonstrating their expertise in whatever topic has brought the newsgroup together. They may lay traps to humiliate outsiders. This is called *trolling*, and an example comes from Wallace (1999). In a Star Trek discussion group a troll was set by pointing out that light does not travel in space, hence the shadows shown on the hull of the *Enterprise* were a technical error. Of course this is nonsense – light does travel in space, but unsuspecting outsiders who point this out are immediately identified and humiliated by their lack of understanding of the troll.

One group of Internet users with a particularly strong social identity are the *hackers*. Hackers are dedicated to extracting confidential information from databases in order to promote freedom of information. Their aims are idealistic and they assert vigorously the distinction between themselves and *crackers* who penetrate computer systems for personal gain. An anonymous hacker wrote:

> 'We spread what we find because segregated knowledge is our common enemy…It is our moral obligation to keep our noble, if somewhat naïve aspirations from becoming subverted by those who truly don't understand.' (Anon, 1994, p.4)

Hackers adopt aggressive tactics to prevent incursions into their in-group. Gilboa (1996) reported that her attempts to infiltrate a group of hackers resulted in hacking-reprisals. Her e-mail was intercepted and deleted and her phone was disconnected.

An interesting question about social identity and the Net concerns the extent to which Internet users are themselves an in-group. Katz (1997) tested this idea in a major survey of Internet users. Katz identified a hardcore of regular and expert 'Digital citizens' who were surprisingly homogeneous in their characteristics. Digital citizens emerged in the Katz survey as well-informed, outspoken and proud of the culture of the

Internet. This does support the idea of at least some Internet-users as an in-group. However, Latane and Bourgeois (1996) demonstrated that it is quite easy to sow dissension among Internet users. They established groups of 24 people who communicated by e-mail. Their task was to identify whether the majority of the group would arrive at a consensus for or against surface mining. In all cases, the majority went one way but a minority held firm and refused to conform.

The Internet as a medium for tackling prejudice

One of the most positive aspects of interacting with other people on the Net is that we need only give away whatever information we choose to about ourselves. This means that some of the usual highly visible characteristics we use to form judgements about people need not be factors in Internet interaction. Although e-mail addresses may give away gender and the signature file may reveal occupation, information about age and race are not automatically available as they are in face-to-face interaction. Although in social interactions on the Net, people do sometimes ask the age of people with whom they are communicating, enquiries about race are rare (Wallace, 1999).

Studies have also shown that differences between the status of individuals do not produce the same barriers to communication in Internet discussions as they do in face-to-face discussions. In one of the earliest studies of Internet communication, Kiesler *et al.* (1984) compared three-way conversations under two conditions, face-to-face and by e-mail. They found that face-to-face conversations tended to be dominated by the individual with the highest status, but that this phenomenon was much reduced when communication took place by e-mail. You may recall that when we looked at intergroup contact we said that equal status contact was a necessary condition for reducing prejudice. This means that the Internet may be an effective medium for tackling prejudice. As Wallace (1999) puts it, if you are a rich lawyer who dabbles in Internet interaction as a hobby, and you find that one of your 'cyber-companions' is an unemployed youth, you might reappraise your stereotypes of unemployed people.

The Internet is also an effective facilitator for collective action. Eng (1995) has reported that in response to California's new anti-immigration laws of the mid-1990s, the Internet was the means by which information was quickly disseminated and protests organised. No other medium would have allowed such an efficiently organised response by protestors. Other protests, including the Tianamen Square pro-democracy demonstration of 1989 have been co-ordinated by use of the Internet.

Stigmatised groups may find material on the Net that they find offensive and oppressive, but there is also a wealth of support available. The appeal of Internet-based support is that it is relatively anonymous so people can disclose facts with less embarrassment. A study by Mickelson (1997) into parents of children with special needs found that those who sought help on-line differed from those who sought face-to-face help. The on-line group showed higher levels of stress and a greater tendency to feel stigmatised by having a child with special needs. A particularly significant finding was that men were much more likely to use an on-line support service than face-to-face support. McKenna and Bargh (1998) studied activity in newsgroups and found a difference between those dealing with visible stigmas including obesity, baldness and stuttering, and those dealing with invisible stigmas such as homosexuality. Individuals in the latter group made much more use of the newsgroups, which appeared to play a much more important role in their lives. McKenna and Bargh suggested that this is because the participants with the invisible stigmas had not 'come out' to friends and family and hence had less 'real-life' support.

where to now?

The following is a good source of further information about the social psychology of the Internet:

▶ **Wallace, P. (1999)** *The Psychology of the Internet*. **Cambridge: Cambridge University Press** – a very readable general introduction to the ways in which basic psychology has been applied to understanding Internet use.

Conclusions

Social psychology is a wide field of study, focusing on how and why humans interact with and impact on one another. In this chapter we have looked at two aspects of social interaction, prejudice and obedience to authority. Social identity theory provides us with a good basis from which to study and understand prejudice, although it does not explain individual differences in prejudice. This is addressed by a complementary approach, prejudiced personality theory. Another feature of human social behaviour is our tendency for obedience to authority. Milgram has explained this in his agency theory as an evolutionary strategy, which helps us form stable societies. Some individuals – charismatic leaders –

appear to have a particular ability to obtain obedience from their followers.

Although prejudice is very much part of human nature, it is undesirable and psychologists have been involved in a variety of strategies designed to reduce it. We have focused here on just two approaches, intergroup contact and collective action. Both of these can be understood in the light of social identity theory. Whereas intergroup contact aims to blur the boundaries between groups, collective action strengthens the social identity of groups and encourages them to assert their rights. Both intergroup contact and collective action *can* be effective means of tackling prejudice.

A rapidly growing and fascinating field of study in social psychology involves the study of Internet use. Internet psychology has many aspects, and in this chapter we have focused on prejudice and social identity, as these topics are particularly relevant to the rest of the chapter. In some ways, social behaviour on the Internet is similar to that in other social settings, in particular our tendency to make quick judgements about people and to establish in-groups and out-groups. However there are many ways in which the Net is well-adapted to tackling prejudice, for example in effecting equal-status contact and challenging stereotyped views of groups of people.

what do you know?

1 Briefly outline two key studies from the social approach to psychology. *(10)*

2 Outline one explanation for human obedience. *(6)*

3 Describe and evaluate social identity theory as an explanation of prejudice. *(10)*

4 Discuss one contemporary issue in social psychology. *(12)*

7

Conducting Your Own Research

what's
ahead?

If you are studying AS-level Psychology, a key part of your course is to design and conduct your own data-gathering exercise. In other words, you get to conduct your own psychological study just like those you have read about in the last six chapters. Doing your own research should provide you with invaluable insights into the research process that has underpinned so much of what you have read in this book. Empirical research is fundamental to most approaches to psychology. It is what sets the study of psychology apart from common sense opinion. Psychologists do not simply tell you their own opinions. They base these opinions on research that has been carried out. They also seek to test their opinions by conducting their own research.

In this chapter we will consider the main methods that are used in psychological research, as well as related ethical issues. We will look at how you might design your study, handle the data and write the report. But first we will reflect on what we mean by 'research'.

Introduction

What is research?

The simple answer is 'any systematic attempt to discover facts'. The term 'research' is not the same as 'scientific' or 'experiment'. You can conduct research by looking something up in an encyclopaedia or by trying out different soap powders to see which produces the best results. The more systematic the input, the richer the outcome in terms of what we find out. To research is to find out.

There are two main kinds of scientific research. One involves collecting data through direct experience or observation. This is *empirical research*. The other kind involves constructing reasoned arguments and is called *rationalism*. Both are perfectly valid but the former is regarded as more objective. By 'objective' we mean that it is less likely to be influenced by personal opinions – people often 'see' what they expect to see so psychologists try to conduct research that is not influenced by personal opinions or 'biases'.

The process of conducting scientific research

The term 'science' refers to the systematic collection of data and organising these into theories. The scientific process can be summarised as follows:

1   We make observations.

2   These potential 'facts' are organised into theories.

3   Theories generate expectations (hypotheses).

4   Data is collected to test expectations.

5   Theories are adjusted in response.

In this way theories are consistently refined to better fit new findings.

Forming an hypothesis

An hypothesis is a prediction generated by a theory. It is a statement of what you believe to be true and a basis for conducting research. Consider the following example of research from Piaget (see Chapter 3). Piaget developed a theory that children over a certain age will be able to perform certain cognitive tasks, whereas younger children will not. To test the truth of this theory, Piaget would state his hypothesis in such a way that a research study could be designed, for example:

Children under the age of seven cannot conserve volume.

This is a statement of belief generated by the theory. Note that it is quite *specific*. If the hypothesis was 'Younger children can't do some cognitive tasks that older children can do', we would not be in a position to design a study. Psychologists use the term 'operationalise' to describe the fact that a hypothesis is highly specific. 'Operationalise' means spelling out the various 'operations'. In the example above, the concept of a 'younger child' was operationalised as 'a child under the age of seven' and 'a cognitive task' as specified as 'the conservation of volume'.

Psychologists write highly specific hypotheses, whereas fortune tellers do exactly the opposite. They produce rather vague statements which are impossible to test directly and therefore the hypotheses always appear partly correct

Proof and disproof

The aim of testing an hypothesis is to find out if it is right or wrong. This sounds simple but there is a logical glitch. Consider this example:

We play a game with coins. You give me £1 every time the coin lands head side up and I give you £1 every time it lands tail side up. The first 5 throws are all heads and you begin to suspect that there are no tails on this coin (i.e. you have formed an hypothesis), after another 10 throws which are still heads you have good reason to believe that your hypothesis has been proved correct. However, if the next throw comes up tails, then your hypothesis is disproved. You could never 100 per cent prove the hypothesis but disproof is clear! This explains why psychologists never use the word 'proof'.

In fact in the above example there were two hypotheses:

● There are tails on this coin.

● There are no tails on this coin.

The two hypotheses are mutually exclusive, and only one can be correct. This illustrates the concept of *falsifiability*. Scientific theories cannot be proved to be true, they can only be subjected to attempts to prove them false. You may find this concept troublesome! You might wonder why no one just looked at both sides of the coin. In psychological research we simply do not have recourse to direct verification – you can't tell that a child can or cannot conserve just by looking at them.

The null and alternative hypotheses

The concept of falsifiability means that we state our hypothesis and then state it in what is called its *null* form. The hypothesis is 'there are tails', the null form is that 'there are no tails'. In research our aim is to reject the null form thereby supporting the 'actual' hypothesis or vice versa. The 'actual' hypothesis is called the *alternative* or *experimental* hypothesis because it is the alternative to the null hypothesis. It is also referred to as the experimental hypothesis when it is used as the starting point for an experiment.

- H_1 stands for the alternate or experimental hypothesis.

- H_0 stands for the null hypothesis, the statement of what you 'don't expect' to happen if your prediction is correct.

In the example given earlier of a study related to cognitive development, H_1 was 'Children under the age of seven cannot conserve volume'. H_0 would not be 'children over the age of seven can conserve volume'. This is the opposite of H_1 not its negation. H_0 could be 'There is no difference between children aged under or over seven in terms of their ability to conserve volume'. The null hypothesis is a statement of no difference.

Probability and chance

The aim of conducting research is to discover or demonstrate 'facts'. Some facts are discovered through direct verification – when I touch a piece of metal it is cold and hard. Other facts are discovered through indirect association. If we want to establish that A causes B, for example that loud noises make people jump, then we observe what happens every time there is a loud noise. If we find that individuals only jump 10 times in 100 trials, we would probably conclude that loud noises don't make people jump. On the other hand, if we observe that on 90 occasions people did jump, then we might think that it is pretty likely that loud noises cause jumping. If no one ever jumps, or every person tested jumps every time we still cannot be 100 per cent certain of the relationship (because the 101st trial might be different) but we would be pretty confident.

Our observations enable us to state the 'probable-ness' or *probability* of a relationship between the noise and jumpiness. In the first instance (people jumped 10 times) the probability is 10 in 100 or 10 per cent. When the probability is this low it seems reasonable to suspect that *chance* alone has brought about the link between the noise and jumping. But when the jumping response was seen 90 times out of 100 then the balance of doubt swings in the other direction; it is unlikely to be a random occurrence but some causal link between noise and jumping.

It is rare to find that 100 per cent of a set of observed cases behave in the same way and for this reason we say that a result has a certain probability of being true. Scientists use the word *significant*. If the association between A and B is very likely then the result is said to be highly significant, in other words it matters and is of some importance. When professional researchers have gathered their results, they will often perform statistical tests on the data in order to ascertain the probability that chance could have accounted for those results. This gives an objective idea of just *how* significant the results are. Such statistical tests are advanced stuff, however, and you may be relieved to find that we won't be looking at them in this chapter.

More about hypotheses

The null hypothesis is not simply the negation of H_1, it is the statement that *chance alone can account for the results obtained*. (You were wondering where the discussion about probability and chance came in.) So, in the example about noise and jumping above, the null hypothesis would be that 'any observed association between noise and jumping is due to chance factors alone'. And, in the case of cognitive development the null hypothesis could have been that 'any observed difference between children under and over the age of seven was is due to chance factors'.

It is tempting to write hypotheses in the future tense because they are predictions of what you expect to find, for example 'Young children *will* not be able to perform task A'. However, in terms of proof and disproof, it makes no sense to put this in the future. The hypothesis should be made as a statement of (presumed) fact.

One- and two-tailed hypotheses

The hypothesis may predict a direction for the results. 'School children are better at short-term memory tasks than adults over the age of 40' suggests a difference (between younger and older participants) and a direction (one group will do better than another).

'There is a difference in the short-term memory performance of younger and older participants' suggests only that there will be a difference but doesn't say which group will be better.

These are called *one-tailed hypotheses* and *two-tailed hypotheses*, respectively. A one-tailed hypothesis predicts the direction of the difference. A two-tailed hypothesis only states that there is a difference but does not predict which group will be better. A simple way to remember what one- and two-tailed hypotheses are is to think of 'Hypothesis the cat' (see opposite).

Does it matter? If your theory, or previous research, suggests that younger people are better at memory tasks than older people, then it would be reasonable to include this in your statement of expectation (a one-tailed hypothesis). However, if you find that the groups do differ in performance but in the unexpected direction, then you are in trouble! That is, if you

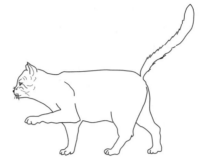

Hypothesis the cat

This is Hypothesis the one-tailed cat. You can tell which direction Hypothesis is going because of his single tail.

This is Hypothesis the two-tailed cat. Because Hypothesis has two tails you can't tell which direction he is going.

find that in fact the older participants do better than the younger ones, you can't accept H_1 and therefore have to accept H_0 even though you have found a difference.

It is thus usually preferable to use a two-tailed hypothesis in case the results are significant but not in the anticipated direction. However, if all previous research indicates that there should be a directional difference then it makes better sense to follow this trend and go for a one-tailed hypothesis.

Methods used in psychological research

Broadly speaking, there are two kinds of method used in psychological research: *experimental* or *non-experimental* methods.

You are probably familiar with the word 'experiment' because it is a term we all use. For example, you might say 'I think I'll experiment with this nail varnish' or a chef might try to experiment with a new recipe to see whether his customers will like it. The *Oxford Concise Dictionary* defines an experiment as 'a procedure undertaken to make a discovery, test a hypothesis, or demonstrate a known fact'. Scientists, and psychologists, use the term in a rather narrower sense. In an experiment, one *variable* is altered such that we can observe what effect this has on another variable. A variable is a thing that varies! For example, if we change the temperature of a room (variable 1) we can observe the effect this has on people's mood (variable 2). The second variable is called the *dependent variable* (DV) because any change in this is brought about by (or depends on) the first variable, called the *independent variable* (IV). In an experiment changes in the IV are brought about, or manipulated, by the experimenter.

This relationship between the IV and DV means that we can claim that any changes in the DV are due to the IV, and therefore demonstrate that one thing *causes* another. This is the essential difference between an experimental and a non-experimental method. Only experiments can demonstrate cause and effect relationships.

The other major distinction between experimental and non-experimental methods is the issue of *control*. In the case of the effect of a change in room temperature on people's mood, there might be a third variable such as how crowded the room is or how much coffee people have drunk. We call this an *extraneous* variable, one which is not the IV we are interested in, but which may nonetheless affect the DV. Such extraneous variables need to be *controlled* in order for the experimental results to have any meaning. One way to do this is to keep all known extraneous variables constant. In our room temperature experiment, we would make sure that everything that might affect people's mood apart from room temperature is kept constant.

Laboratory experiments

A laboratory is a place where an experimenter can control conditions as much as possible. However, the laboratory is also an idealised world. Experimental variables often behave differently in the real world, especially when the variables are aspects of human behaviour. The extent to which the results of a study can be generalised to natural settings is referred to as *ecological validity*. 'Validity' means how true or well-grounded something is. 'Ecological' refers to the study of things in the natural environment. Putting these terms together we get the concept of how true a study is to 'natural' (real) life. An experiment conducted in a laboratory may not be very true to real life and therefore it may not be appropriate to draw conclusions about how people behave in the real world.

Replication

The fact that a laboratory experiment is well-controlled also means that we can repeat or *replicate* the research. If a research result is 'true' (valid) then we should be able to repeat it. Replication is thus a very important way of demonstrating that a finding was not just a fluke. Think of the situation where one study found that going to school led to decreased IQ. We would want to have this confirmed by at least one other study before we would regard the finding as valid. The less controlled the research conditions the more difficult it is get the same result because the conditions vary, and the more factors might impinge on the results. In reality it is unlikely that conditions are ever exactly the same and, especially where humans are the experimental participants, behaviour is affected by their own expectations, as we shall see.

Experimenter bias

There are many ways that an experimenter may influence the behaviour of experimental participants. For example, their manner may be friendly or rude, and this might predispose a participant to behave well or act antagonistically. In both cases, the sample of behaviour which is produced may be untypical and biased. Experimenters have many personal characteristics, such as their sex and appearance, which also elicit stereotypical responses from participants.

There is one kind of *experimenter effect* called *experimenter bias*, which itself is an example of the *self-fulfilling prophecy*. This is the principle that things frequently turn out as one expected (or prophesied) not because of foresight but because one behaved in a manner which helped bring out these expectations. Rosenthal and Fode (1963) were the first to systematically demonstrate the self-fulfilling prophecy in an experimental setting. They gave two sets of students the task of training rats to run mazes, telling one group that their rats were high in intelligence and telling the other group that their rats were bred for dullness. In fact the rats were randomly assigned to the students. It was found that the 'maze-bright' rats were significantly faster than the 'maze-dull' ones in learning a T-maze.

Demand characteristics

In the experimental setting an experimenter may subtly and unconsciously convey expectations. The reason these expectations are especially effective is because participants are looking for cues about how to behave. The result is something we call *demand characteristics*. These are aspects of the experimental situation which prompt the participant to interpret the study in a specific way and then alter their behaviour in certain predictable ways. In other words, the experimental set-up makes certain 'demands' on all participants and these tend to produce a biased and similar set of responses from the participants.

Demand characteristics act as extraneous variables. They may affect the dependent variable in a way which makes it appear that the independent variable has had that effect. Participants react to demand characteristics in several ways:

- Participants may wish to please the experimenter. They want to appear normal and competent and therefore try to do what is expected of them.

- Or the opposite may occur, the 'screw you' effect. For some participants, a hint about what is expected of them may have the opposite effect.

- Social desirability. Most people want to display themselves in a good light and therefore they display desirable or good behaviour, which may nevertheless be untypical.

- Evaluation apprehension. Knowing that you are being observed and thus in some sense evaluated means that some people may suffer from anxiety which depresses their performance.

Attention

The attention given to participants in an experiment may cause some people to feel anxious, as in evaluation apprehension. But it also can act to improve performance. Psychologists call this *social facilitation*. The classic example of this is called the *Hawthorne effect*, so-called because it was first observed during research conducted at the Hawthorne works of the Western Electrical Company by Mayo (1933). Various aspects of the workers' working environment were investigated to see in what way productivity was affected. In one series of experiments they increased the level of lighting and found increases in output, but then they found the same happened when lighting levels were decreased! The eventual conclusion was that social factors were more important than physical ones and that, in the case of the lighting changes, the workers were responding to the interest being shown in them by the researchers rather than any physical changes made as part of the experiment. This applies to all experimental work – improved performance may be an artefact of experimental attention, particularly because participants assume that the experimental effect should be beneficial. One would hardly think that an experimenter is going to do something to you which will depress your performance.

for and against

the laboratory experiment

+ It identifies cause and effect relationships.

+ It permits good control of extraneous variables.

+ It permits replication because of high control.

− It can lack ecological validity.

− It is not suitable for certain kinds of research, such as investigating the effects of emotional deprivation on children. It would be unethical to manipulate such an IV.

The field experiment

A field experiment is an experiment that is not conducted in a laboratory. You can conduct a field experiment in places other than fields, in the same way that you can conduct laboratory experiments outside a laboratory. The two terms refer to the notion that some experiments are conducted in artificial and controlled environments (the laboratory experiment) whereas others take place in more natural surroundings where the participants are not aware that they are in fact in an experiment. One example is Bushman's (1988) study of obedience (see Chapter 6, page 182). This type of study takes place in more realistic surroundings and therefore is often described as high in ecological validity. However, this is not always the case. Consider Hofling *et al.*'s (1966) obedience experiment that involved doctors and nurses (see Chapter 6, *classic research*, page 183). This has been criticised for being *unrealistic* (i.e. lacking ecological validity) because doctors don't give orders over the telephone. The findings also can only be applied to the behaviour of doctors and nurses, or other people whose relationships are built on obedience. The study may tell us little about everyday obedience.

Field experiments have the advantage of allowing the experimenter to investigate causal relationships because one can still control the independent variable, but within a natural setting. However in a field experiment this control is obviously not as rigid as in a laboratory. The most obvious problem is that extraneous variables are more difficult to control so that we cannot be certain that observed changes in the dependent variable are due to the independent variable.

Field experiments have other design problems aside from weaker control. The experimenter still has to select a sample and this is most likely to be done using opportunity techniques, which are inevitably biased. Field experiments also tend to be more time-consuming and expensive than laboratory experiments. They also raise some rather serious ethical concerns. You can neither obtain informed consent from participants, nor is it always possible to debrief them afterwards because you might alert other potential participants to the ongoing experiment. There is also the question of privacy – individuals would not like to think that their behaviour was being observed and recorded without their knowledge.

for and against

the field experiment

+ It can identify cause and effect relationships because there is an IV and DV.

+ It is conducted in more natural surroundings and therefore may generalise better to real life.

+ There is no experimenter bias (effects of the experimenter's expectations) because participants are not aware they are in an experiment.

− It is harder to control extraneous variables and therefore the findings are less certain (we cannot be sure that observed changes in the DV were due to the action of the IV).

− Lack of control also makes replication more difficult.

− Sampling techniques tend to be biased because opportunity sampling is used.

− It is more expensive and time consuming than laboratory experiments.

− There are ethical issues such as no informed consent or debriefing, and invasion of privacy.

Natural or quasi-experiments

It is possible to observe naturally-occurring independent variables and measure their effects on a dependent variable. For example, we might investigate the hypothesis that intelligence is inherited by seeing whether identical twins have more similar IQ than non-identical twins. If this is true it would support the idea that intelligence is inherited. This is called a *quasi-experiment* because the researcher has not directly manipulated the independent variable (genetic relatedness) and also has not controlled the allocation of participants to the experimental conditions. This might mean that the groups of participants are not equivalent. Therefore a natural experiment is not a 'true' experiment but rather partly or seemingly an experiment (therefore 'quasi').

One might think that the results of natural experiments would have the same validity as 'real' experiments, however we are making an assumption that our independent variable (for example, inherited factors) has *caused* observed variations in the dependent variable (IQ test performance). In fact, cause and effect can only be stated when we have directly influenced the IV and therefore the conclusions from natural experiments should be regarded as 'speculative' (without firm factual basis). Piaget's research into cognitive development is an example of a natural experiment. In the conservation experiments (see Chapter 4) he showed that children under the age of seven could not cope whereas older children could. This is a natural experiment because the IV is the children's age which varies naturally. The DV is performance on the conservation task.

for and against

the natural experiment

+ It can speculate about cause and effect.

+ It allows research into variables which could not ethically be manipulated.

– There is reduced control in comparison with laboratory experiments.

– There can be some ethical problems such as invasion of privacy and confidentiality.

– Full conclusions about cause and effect are not justified because participants are not randomly allocated to conditions and the IV is not directly manipulated.

Correlational studies

To correlate means to establish a relationship between two (or more) things. The two variables vary systematically together, i.e. they co-vary. For example, it has been found that older people tend to have rather lower IQs than younger people. This relationship between age and IQ has led some people to the conclusion that aging *causes* a deterioration in cognitive functioning. However, it is more likely that older people tend to have lower IQ because, when the older people were younger, they had poorer diets and less stimulation. The relationship we see between IQ and age is thus probably related to a difference between generations rather than a change in individuals with age. This example illustrates how careful we need to be to avoid making assumptions about cause and effect when we observe correlations.

Correlation is a method of analysing data rather than a method of study so, strictly speaking, correlation is not a research method. However, a study which uses correlation to analyse the data is distinct from other methods of study so we should include it in this list of research methods.

Another common conception, or rather misconception, about correlation is that the two variables (*co-variables*) must increase together. For example, when we say that hay fever and pollen are correlated we mean more precisely that they are *positively* correlated – hay fever increases as

Types of correlation

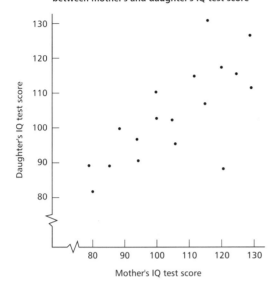

Scattergram showing the relationship between mother's and daughter's IQ test score

(y axis: Daughter's IQ test score — 80, 90, 100, 110, 120, 130)
(x axis: Mother's IQ test score — 80, 90, 100, 110, 120, 130)

Positive correlation. Mother's and daughter's IQs were recorded for 20 mother–daughter pairs. A point was plotted for each pair. The result is reasonable *positive correlation*. For perfect positive correlation the dots should be in a line at 45° to the *x* axis, starting at (0, 0)

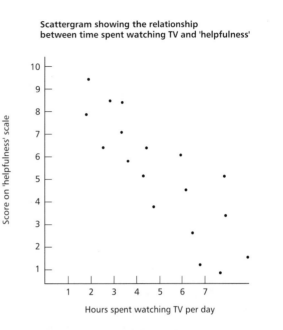

Scattergram showing the relationship between time spent watching TV and 'helpfulness'

(y axis: Score on 'helpfulness' scale — 1 to 10)
(x axis: Hours spent watching TV per day — 1 to 7)

A survey was carried out of the number of hours an individual spent watching TV per day, and an assessment was made of each individual's tendency to be helpful. A point was plotted for each individual. The result is almost perfect *negative correlation* – line going from top left to bottom right

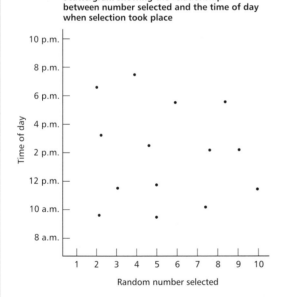

Scattergram showing the relationship between number selected and the time of day when selection took place

(y axis: Time of day — 8 a.m., 10 a.m., 12 p.m., 2 p.m., 4 p.m., 6 p.m., 8 p.m., 10 p.m.)
(x axis: Random number selected — 1 to 10)

This scattergram shows the results of asking 20 people to pick a number between 1 and 10 and to state the time of day. The result is a fairly random scatter, i.e. *no correlation*.

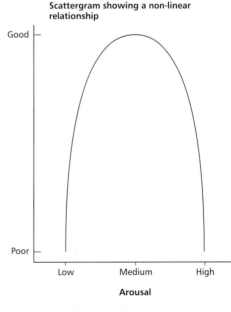

Scattergram showing a non-linear relationship

(y axis: Performance — Poor to Good)
(x axis: Arousal — Low, Medium, High)

The first two scattergrams show a *linear correlation* but sometimes variables may have a *non-linear* relationship. The Yerkes-Dodson law states that low arousal and very high arousal lead to impaired performance whereas moderate arousal leads to high performance the amount of pollen around increases. Shoe size and height are also positively correlated. However, it is possible to have a significant inverse or *negative* correlation, as is the case with amount of cloud cover and sunshine – the more clouds there are the less sunshine there tends to be.

Plotting correlations

We assign the numerical value of 1 to perfect correlation and 0 to no correlation. +1 is perfect positive correlation and –1 is perfect negative correlation. The clearest way to see this is on a *scattergram* – a graph consisting of lots of points, each point representing one observation. The exact numerical value for a correlation is calculated using a formula and will be a decimal lying between 0 and 1. Look at the examples on page 209.

for and against

using the correlational technique

+ It enables us to establish possible relationships between co-variables. Future experimental studies might try to establish whether one is a cause of the other.

+ It is an alternative when experimental manipulation would be unethical and/or natural experiments are not available. For example, studies of the relationship between heredity and intelligence.

– It cannot demonstrate cause and effect relationships, though this is often a mistaken interpretation. For example, if hours spent watching TV and aggressive are correlated this doesn't mean that TV has caused the aggressiveness – it could be the other way round, that more aggressive people have a need to watch more television, or there could be a third variable.

Observational studies

The term 'observation' is a broad one and refers to both a technique for gathering data (as in all research) or a method of study, as is the case when there is no manipulation of an independent variable. There are many different kinds of observational studies, but remember that all research involves some degree of systematic study and therefore all observation is conducted with careful planning. Observational studies generally do not have any hypotheses because the aims tend to be more open-ended, but one can state research questions.

Naturalistic observation

When you think of observational research it is perhaps naturalistic observation that you have in mind. A researcher sits in a field and watches a group of lions, recording what they do when hunting, eating, mating and looking after their young. It is fairly obvious that this is called 'naturalistic' because behaviour is being studied in its natural context. The first researchers to use this technique were *ethologists* who felt that laboratory studies failed to capture the essence and richness of real-life behaviour. Ethologists are scientists who are especially interested in trying to explain the function of behaviours in terms of how well they help an individual animal to survive. Ethologists felt that naturalistic observation was a preferable form of research because of the greater ecological validity. An important feature of naturalistic observations is that the observer should 'leave things as they found them'.

Disclosed and undisclosed observation

When someone knows they are being observed (*disclosed observation*) this may affect their behaviour. We have noted ways that participants react to an experimenter's interest, such as behaving in socially desirable ways or behaving unnaturally. In order to avoid this, an observational study may be designed for *undisclosed observation* such as using a one-way mirror. The weakness in this case is an ethical one. People may object to being observed without having given their permission. In some cases it may be possible to obtain consent afterwards but not if one were observing a large crowd of people.

Participant and non-participant observation

The observer may participate in the group being studied or may observe from the outside of the group. Being a participant gives the researcher some insights into the individuals being studied. However it is also likely to lead to biased observations.

An example of undisclosed participant observation comes from a memorable study by Festinger *et al.* (1956). They were intrigued by a small group lead by a Mrs Marian Keech who predicted that a great flood would destroy 'Lake City' on 21 December. Her knowledge was based on messages received from the planet Clarion. Festinger's theory of cognitive dissonance predicted that, when (if) the flood did not occur, Mrs Keech's followers would become even more fervent in their beliefs rather than less so. In order to find out what did happen Festinger *et al.* infiltrated the group. In other words, they were undisclosed but participant observers. This particular study had an amusing conclusion. When the flood failed to materialise and the world remained intact, the believers claimed that their prayers had saved the world!

Controlled or laboratory observation

It is possible to conduct observations in a laboratory. Clearly one loses naturalism but gains control. An example of such a study is one conducted by Ainsworth (1979) when looking at the behaviour of infants and their mothers during periods of separation. She developed the 'Strange Situation', a series of situations which enabled her to observe a child's behaviour when briefly separated from and later reunited with its mother. This was done in a controlled environment.

Content analysis

So far all methods of observation involve directly watching the participants. It is easier in some circumstances to use data already collected and make observations. For example, using a politician's diaries or a set of children's television programmes might form the basis of systematic study. Manstead and McCulloch (1981) studied 170 commercials and counted the differences in the way men and women were portrayed. They used behavioural categories such as *kind of role* (autonomous or dependent), *argument* (scientific or not), and so on.

for and against

observational studies

naturalistic observation

+ It is particularly suitable for studying non-human animals and children.

+ It gives a more realistic picture of spontaneous behaviour.

undisclosed observation

+ It avoids participant reactivity.

− It raises ethical issues of lack of informed consent and invasion of privacy.

participant observation

+ There is greater understanding of behaviour.

− There is a tendency to lack objectivity.

controlled observation

+ There is greater control over extraneous variables.

+ It maintains some degree of ecological validity.

content analysis

+ It gives easy access to large amounts of data.

+ There are no problems with participant reactivity.

+ It can be highly objective.

− It relies on good sampling. Extremely easy to get a biased sample.

all observational studies

+ They use more natural data.

− *Observer bias:* observations are influenced by the observer's prior beliefs and expectations. One way to reduce the effects of bias is to use more than one observer and compare observations, establishing *inter-observer reliability*. Ideally, research should be repeatable, so inter-observer reliability should be high.

The term 'content analysis' refers to the fact that we are analysing the content of something. Like other kinds of observation we need to decide on a set of categories and on a method of sampling. If we were going to investigate gender bias in children's books we might decide to look at the pictures (rather than the words) in the books, or compare adjectives used to describe males and females. We would then need to establish a list of categories for coding. We would not be able to look at all children's books and therefore would decide on a population (for example, books published after 1990) and work out a method of deriving a sample. Finally, we might want to avoid observer bias and therefore use more than one person to code the material. It might be useful for the observers to be unaware of the research hypothesis so that their observations were not affected by expectations.

Surveys

Another means of systematically collecting data is to ask the participant what they think! All such self-report methods are collectively called 'surveys'. These can be oral (an interview) or written (a questionnaire), they can be highly structured or very loose – in which case some of the questions may not even be written but instead only a generally topic decided on.

Structured surveys

A structured survey uses a very specific set of questions, rather than having a more general set of aims. This is most likely to be a questionnaire but could be a pre-set group of questions read out by an interviewer. The study by Poppe and Linssen (1999) in Chapter 6, page 171, is an example of a study using a highly structured questionnaire.

Unstructured surveys

It is difficult to have an unstructured questionnaire because the questions are pre-written. In an unstructured situation the interviewer develops the questions as she or he goes along in response to previous answers. Piaget used this method in his research (see Chapter 4), calling it the 'clinical method' because it is a method commonly employed by doctors and therapists. The interviewer starts with a predetermined set of questions, but as the interview proceeds these questions are adapted in line with some of the responses given. This allows for the possibility that the child, or adult respondent, will give unexpected answers and that questions generated from responses will lead to new discoveries about behaviour, thus maximising the amount of information that is gained. It is also true that the more informal atmosphere is good for some participants. However, it is highly susceptible to *interviewer bias*, where the interviewer affects the kind of responses given, and relies on the interviewer's skill in developing good questions on the spur of the moment.

for and
against

the survey method

+ They enable a large amount of data to be collected.

+ They give access to information which is not available through direct observation, such as what individuals feel.

− People often don't know what they think or do, and therefore are forced to rely on 'social desirability', meaning that they tend to answer a question in the way that seems most representative of 'good' behaviour. This produces a *social desirability bias*.

− Some people show a *response bias*, answering questions in consistent way such as preferring to disagree with the interviewer rather than to agree.

− Questionnaires rely on linguistic competence and are not suitable for children

− Interviewers may bias the responses given by the way that they ask questions.

− There may be *sampling biases*, for example only certain 'kinds' of people return postal questionnaires and only some people are willing to answer interviews.

Case study

A case study is, as you might expect, a study of a single case but this could be a case of one person, one family, one school or a particular event. The method is commonly used in the study of atypical behaviour because occurrences are rare. Examples include Freud's case study of Little Hans in Chapter 5, page 140. When a case study covers more than one individual it again may relate to something unusual, such as a school trying out a radical new curriculum.

Case studies offer more than insight into the unusual, they provide rich details grounded in real life. For example, Allport (1947) studied personality through an in-depth study of one individual called Jenny. In fact he never met 'Jenny' but had access to 300 letters she had written over a period of 12 years. This is referred to as an *idiographic* approach, one that is concerned with the individual rather than with general laws of behaviour. This is contrasted with the *nomothetic* approach that seeks to find out facts which can be applied to a whole population (this is the aim of all experiments and many non-experimental methods).

The case study approach can involve one or more of a number of research methods. The individual(s) might be interviewed to discover information about their past or about present attitudes and feelings; questionnaires or psychometric tests can be used to assess attitudes, abilities and personality;

and other parties might also be questioned about the target individual. The individual might be given experimental tasks or observed in relevant situations.

for and against

the case study

+ Case studies are good for rare behaviours and for providing information in-depth.

+ Case studies provide us with information regarding situations we would not wish to set up artificially for ethical reasons, for example in investigating the effects of child abuse.

− They are time-consuming because it is usual to follow the case over a period of time.

− Much of the data is collected retrospectively because we don't know that an individual would be an appropriate case to study until after many of the key events have taken place. For example, we might look want to at interview the family of an autistic child but can only begin the study when a diagnosis has been made, and then we would want to explore events from the child's birth and maybe even before. Recollected data is often unreliable because memory is never perfect and often biased by later knowledge.

− Case studies are not replicable.

− One cannot generalise from one case study.

− One cannot determine cause and effect relationships.

− There are ethical problems concerning the privacy of individuals whose life histories may be publicised after their death.

Ethics in human research

Ethical research is that which is deemed acceptable in the pursuit of certain goals or aims. It is not simply a question of 'right' or 'wrong', but considering the relative gains and costs. In order to make an ethical decision, you must always consider the balance between means and ends. In medical research this is easier because we can say that certain research ultimately may enable many lives to be saved. Psychological research rarely involves the saving of life or even the prevention of serious illness, but it often offers important insights into human behaviour, which could have important applications. In order to aid researchers who have to make ethical decisions professional organisations such as the British Psychological Society (BPS) and the American Psychological Association (APA) have produced ethical guidelines. We look here at the guidelines offered by the BPS.

BPS guidelines

The British Psychological Society ethical guidelines (1978) started with this preamble:

> 'The understanding of human behaviour ameliorates the human condition and enhances human dignity…The balance between the interests of the [participant] and the humane or scientific value of the research must be weighed carefully…A detailed list of prescribed and proscribed procedures would be impractical…The principles should not be a substitute for considered judgement.'

The British Psychological Society (1990) principles for psychologists conducting research is organised around the framework below.

1 *Introduction.* Guidelines are necessary to clarify conditions under which psychological research is acceptable.

2 *General.* The best people to judge whether an investigation is acceptable will be members of the sample population. This is because research may involve people of different ages, gender and background to the investigator.

3 *Consent.* As far as possible participants should be told the objectives of the investigation and be informed of any procedures that could influence their decision to participate. Participants should not be pressurised to take part, nor should any payment be used to induce them to take unnecessary risks.

4 *Deception.* It is unacceptable to withhold information or mislead participants if they are likely to feel unease when debriefed. Intentional deception should be avoided wherever possible, and any use of deception discussed thoroughly with colleagues.

5 *Debriefing.* Where participants are aware of being part of a psychological experiment, the investigator should discuss the findings with them once the research is completed. The investigator should also give the participant a chance to discuss his or her experiences so that any negative effects can be handled.

6 *Withdrawal from the investigation.* From the outset participants should be told of their right to withdraw. If this decision is taken after the research, the participant's data should be withdrawn from the sample.

7 *Confidentiality.* Any published data should not contain participant's names, and unless participants have given their permission, all data should remain confidential except where the law specifies that it must be disclosed (for example, if an act of terrorism had been committed).

8 *Protection of participants.* Participants should not be exposed to any physical or mental harm. Any risks must be no greater than in normal life. Any interventions should be positive rather than negative (for example, telling some participants that they have failed a test).

9 *Observational research.* Individuals have a right to privacy. Observations should only be made in situations where those being observed would expect to be observed by strangers, or where the participants have given their consent. Special attention should be paid to local cultural values.

10 *Giving advice.* If, during the course of an investigation, a researcher obtains evidence of physical or psychological problems which may affect the participant's future well-being, it is the researcher's duty inform the participant and offer advice about where to seek help.

11 *Colleagues.* Any psychologist who considers that another psychologist is not conducting ethical research should encourage that psychologist to re-evaluate their work.

Designing research

An investigator must pay particular attention to ethical considerations when designing a prospective piece of research. Certain of the ethical guidelines should not be breached under any circumstances, such as avoiding physical or mental harm or invading another person's privacy. However, it may not be clear from the outset that there will be harm, and if this arises during the study the investigator should stop at once. Distress includes feeling embarrassed, being angered, or feeling you may have harmed someone else. The prolonged testing used with case studies may also be stressful beyond the bounds of normality.

Investigators need to consider how they will select participants and, where appropriate, how to allocate them to experimental groups. This may be problematic for some research, such as investigating the effectiveness of a particular psychotherapy (see Chapter 5) – any control group would have to have treatment withheld at least for a period of time to enable comparisons to be made with and without treatment. The same objections might be raised if a new educational method was being tested on only some participants. If the method is thought to be beneficial, would it be ethical to withhold it from some members of the class for the sake of the research?

Selection which involves offering some recompense may put pressure on the participants to comply and the BPS guidelines explicitly advise against using money where there are potential risks.

Some of the guidelines are less straightforward, such as deception which is discussed below, and require discussion with colleagues to reach decisions about the ethical acceptability of the proposed procedures.

Consent and informed consent

It makes little sense to gain participants' consent unless they have some idea about what they are agreeing to. Participants should be informed about the research before being asked to give their consent. This means several things: being informed about what will be required, being informed about the purpose of the research, being informed of your rights (for example, the right to confidentiality, the right to leave the research at any time) and, finally, giving your consent.

It may be an unrealistic ideal to seek informed consent because most people will only understand after the research what they were actually being asked to do. Simply being informed doesn't guarantee comprehension, especially for a participant who has never studied psychology. When an investigator describes research procedures to prospective participants there is no certainty that the participants actually understand what will be involved. For example, in memory experiments a participant may find that they feel quite foolish when they are unable to remember many of the words presented. This could create distress and discomfort, and the participant may have preferred not to take part.

People often think of experiments as being unethical, but in fact they allow the researcher to put many ethical guidelines into place, whereas this is not possible outside the laboratory. In field experiments or observational studies it is not possible to gain informed consent, nor is it possible to debrief participants afterwards. In such cases, presumptive consent might be used, or the BPS guidelines relating to observational research should be followed, though this only relates to invasion of privacy.

Certain participants, such as children or individuals suffering from a psychological disorder, could not be asked to give informed consent because they would not understand what is required. In this case the consent of a guardian is sought as a substitute. This is a somewhat controversial area, however, and not everyone would feel that the practice of gaining 'secondhand' consent is acceptable.

Informed consent is a particular issue when deception is a necessary part of the research design, as in Milgram's experiment (1963; 1974).

Informed consent and deception

If an investigator seeks informed consent from participants this inevitably leads participants to form expectations which are likely to bias the results. The single blind technique aims to prevent such expectations forming by making the participant 'blind' as to the purpose of the research. However, if the investigator offers no explanation about the nature of his or her research, participants are likely to try to guess the research purpose. Therefore investigators usually offer a false description of the research. The use of confederates (stooges) is another form of deception. These procedures are especially common in social psychology, for example Milgram's study of obedience (see Chapter 6, page 100).

The BPS guidelines suggest that the ethical issues can be resolved by discussing any proposed deception with colleagues to determine that the procedure is unavoidable and justified in terms of the research aims. In addition to this, psychologists can compensate for the lack of informed consent and the use of deception through the following.

1   *Debriefing.* We could argue that often deception is only temporary and that, in cases when participants are eventually debriefed and informed about the true nature of the research, their ethical objections are minimised.

2   *Presumptive consent.* 'Presumptive' means 'grounds for assuming that something is true'. In cases where actual research participants cannot give informed consent, approval can be sought from the general public prior to the investigation; in other words the public are asked to provide 'presumptive consent'. The BPS guidelines suggest that if a procedure would be potentially acceptable to the general local population, we can regard it as ethical even when there has been no specific informed consent. Milgram (1963) surveyed a range of people prior to his classic study of obedience (see Chapter 6). The general opinion was that people were unlikely to administer the strongest level of shocks. He therefore presumed that his procedure would not lead to undue distress. When he found otherwise, he might have considered stopping the experiment, as has been done in some other experiments. A criticism of the presumptive consent approach is that people may 'say' they wouldn't mind perhaps because they wish to appear helpful. However, if they actually had to take part in the described procedures they may feel differently.

3   *Prior general consent.* Another roundabout route is to ask prospective participants to give their prior general consent without specifying the nature of the actual investigation.

4   *Argue that deception isn't unethical.* A further approach is to argue that participants don't actually mind being deceived. For example, Milgram's participants, when interviewed afterwards, said that they did not object to the deception. Gross (1996) suggested that many participants regard deception as a relatively minor issue and are more concerned about the quality of the experience in an experiment. Gross also suggested that participants don't seem to object to deception as long as it is not extreme.

5   *The use of role play.* It is possible to investigate the way people behave by asking them to act out certain roles. In this way their informed consent can be sought and the distress of behaving in anti-social ways can be avoided. There are two drawbacks to this approach. First, social desirability bias may affect the way individuals behave and therefore their role play will not be true to life. Second, even in role play individuals can be very distressed and their prior informed consent acts as little recompense.

The right to withdraw

Only once a participant is actually involved in the research procedures are they in a position to assess what they have agreed to do. For this reason the right to withdraw is included in the BPS ethical guidelines as follows.

1   *The right to withdraw may affect the research outcome.* Gardner (1978) found different results when participants were placed in a position of control. He was investigating the effects of noise on task performance, and in particular the effect of unpredictable noise. It is thought that noise affects performance most especially when it is unpredictable and uncontrollable. Gardner found that when participants were given consent forms (which included information about the right to withdraw) prior to the experiment their performance was not unduly affected by unpredictable noise. However, when they had no consent forms, they *were* affected by the noise. Gardner suggested that asking for consent gave the participants a better sense of control and influenced their behaviour.

2   *The social contract.* Some participants may feel they cannot withdraw because they have made a 'deal' with the investigator. In many experiments, such as Milgram's, participants are paid for taking part and this may enhance their feeling of having entered into a social contract. In other studies, participation is required as part of an undergraduate psychology course. Dion *et al.* (1972) actually gave their student participants extra points on their final exam grade! It may occur even where there are no tangible rewards; simply agreeing to be a research participants means taking on a particular social role and acting out expected behaviour (obeying the investigator).

3   *Using 'prods' denies participants' the right to withdraw.* Milgram claimed that his participants were free to leave at any time; they were explicitly told this at the start of the study. However, during the study if they said they didn't want to continue, the experimenter said the following four 'prods':

- Prod 1: Please continue.

- Prod 2: The experiment requires that you continue.

- Prod 3: It is absolutely essential that you continue.

- Prod 4: You have no other choice, you must go on.

Coolican (1990) has argued that this amounted to a denial of the right to withdraw. This raises the question as to how far an investigator may go to 'encourage' a participant to remain in the study before we would consider that undue force has been exerted.

Debriefing

The debriefing of participants may involve advising them of the true aims of the investigation. Debriefing also allows investigators to find out much useful information:

- The investigator can check to see if any deception worked, such as seeing whether participants were aware of the true nature of the investigation. In the case of some studies some participants do report that they were aware of the deception and therefore their data can be discarded.

- The investigator can counsel participants on any aspects of the research which worried them. Milgram provided such support for many of his participants.

- The investigator can gain further insights into the research topic through in-depth interviews.

Confidentiality

Confidentiality is especially important in student's research where it might be tempting to tell other people about your findings. This is acceptable as long as the performance of individual participants is not revealed. When psychometric tests are used, test scores are highly confidential and records must not be kept without informed consent. If psychologists did not adhere to this principle they might find that people become progressively less willing to take part in their studies.

Ethics and cost-benefit analysis

The concept of ethics as a cost-benefit analysis – weighing up the potential findings of the research (benefits) against the potential harm (costs) – would seem a logical way to assess the ethical implications of a study. It does however have drawbacks.

- First of all, it is easy to be critical once research is completed. Milgram claimed that he had no idea that participants would behave as they did, and his initial interviews (presumptive consent) supported these views. Therefore we cannot so easily criticise the stress created because it could not be anticipated. Milgram (1974) pointed out that 'understanding grows because we examine situations in which the end is not known' and Aronson (1988) argued that deception 'may be the best and the only way to get useful information about how people behave in most complex and important situations'.

- Second, it is hard to quantify costs and benefits. Individuals differ in what they regard as unacceptable and opinions vary over time so that, for example, Harlow's (1959) research is seen as unacceptable now but it wasn't viewed in the same way in the 1950s. Baumrind (1975) has made the point that cost-benefit analyses inevitably lead to moral dilemmas, yet the function of ethical guidelines is precisely to avoid such dilemmas.

Designing and planning your own study

Starting out

Where do you begin? You need to think about an area of psychology that you find interesting and identify a set of *research questions* related to the topic. For example, you might have found Piaget's research on cognitive development was intriguing and would like to investigate it further. What is it that you would specifically like to find out? 'Can children under the age of seven conserve volume?' 'Do younger children cope less well with being asked two questions rather than one?'

Out of all the questions you should select one to investigate and then translate this into your research hypothesis – the statement of what you expect to be true. For example, 'Children under the age of seven can conserve volume when asked only one question rather than two questions.' The null hypothesis for this experiment would be 'There is no difference in the performance of children under the age of seven years when asked either one or two questions in the conservation experiment. In this study the IV would be the number of questions asked, and the DV is the ability of children to demonstrate conservation.

The steps involved are:

1   Establish some research questions based on past research and/or theory.

2   Write a research hypothesis, and then a null hypothesis.

3   Identify the variables. (The IV is the one you will manipulate and the DV is the one that will be measured.)

Choosing the research method

In the above example, the method of study would be an experiment. In a different situation you might find that your research questions did not clearly lead to a hypothesis, in which case the observational or survey method might be the more suitable form of research. If you found that the hypothesis stated a *relationship* between variables then your method will be one using the correlational technique.

Next you need to decide on the *design* of the study, which is related to the method of research.

Designing an experiment

When designing an experiment we want to know if the independent variable (IV) had affected the dependent variable (DV). For example, we might want to know if caffeine (IV) affects recall on a test of short-term memory (DV). If we ask a group of people to drink a cup of coffee and then do a test of memory, we end up with a score on the test but no way of knowing whether the coffee had any effect. We need to establish a *baseline* of behaviour *without* the caffeine. There are three ways of doing this:

- *Related (repeated) measures.* You test each person's short-term memory, then give them each some caffeine and then re-test their memory. This means you can compare each participant's memory behaviour before and after what is called the experimental treatment (the caffeine).

- *Independent measures.* You test two separate groups of participants. One group receives the experimental treatment and the other group receives no treatment, acting as a *control group.* Both groups are tested once and their performance on the memory test is compared.

- *Matched participants.* Participants are paired according to key variables such as age, sex, intelligence, and experience. Each pair contributes one member to the experimental group and one to the control group. Thus the participants are both related and independent, and this enables us to avoid some of the problems that occur with related and independent designs.

With each method it is possible to compare the results from the experimental and control conditions/groups and see whether the IV did affect the DV.

Which method is better?

Order effects

With a repeated measures design you may give a person the same test twice. They are likely to do better the second time because of practice. This is called a *practice effect*. So in the memory example we would find that participants had improved performance after the caffeine but we could not be certain whether this was due to the caffeine or to practice. Therefore the practice is a extraneous variable. Practice effects are one kind of *order effect*. There may also be a *boredom effect*. Participants may do less well on the second test because they have become bored by the task and less motivated.

There are various ways in which we might tackle order effects. We might give participants two different tests which are as similar as possible. However, because they are similar, there may still be a practice effect. Therefore we would need to *counterbalance* the tests. We do this by dividing our participants into two groups and give group 1 test A first followed by test B (AB) and do the reverse for group 2 (BA). If test A was easier, the effect will be cancelled out.

Another way to overcome order effects is to leave a gap between the conditions. For example, test your participants on one day and then give them the caffeine on the following day, followed by another test. Of course, here you might have to consider extraneous variables such as the fact that the participants' mood has changed from one day to the next affecting their performance or that it is a colder day.

The problem of order effects does not occur with an independent measures design. We might investigate the effects of caffeine by giving one group of participants the experimental treatment (caffeine) while the other group gets none, and test everyone's short-term memory. The control group acts as a baseline. However, when we use independent groups we never know for sure whether differences between the groups of participants affected the results. It is therefore usually preferable to use a repeated measures design.

Problems that occur with independent measures

Independent measures design has different problems. First of all there is no control for *participant variables*. What if the experimental group happens to contain participants with better short term memories than the control group?

One way to try to make sure that the experimental and control groups are of the same ability is to use *random allocation*. We can use the 'names drawn out of the hat' technique as a means of placing participants in the experimental and control groups.

There is a further problem for independent measures design. It might be that participants in the experimental condition respond positively to the extra treatment they are being given and this alone could explain why they show improved performance. The same problem occurs when testing drugs in medical research. Patients often get better because they think they are being given a drug which will have a beneficial effect and it is this expectation alone that explains the patient's improvement. Pharmacological researchers use *placebos* as a means of separating the physical and psychological effects of drugs. A placebo is a preparation which has no relevant medicinal properties. The same procedure can be used in psychology experiments, this time separating the effect of expectations from the psychological effects. For example, participants might think that their performance will be improved by the intake of caffeine and therefore it might make the conditions more equivalent if we gave all participants a cup of coffee but the control group had decaffeinated coffee.

for and against

methods for establishing baselines

related (repeated) measures

+ They provide good control for participant variables.

+ Fewer participants are needed because each participant is in both conditions.

– There may be order effects (although these can be counterbalanced).

independent measures

+ They avoid order effects and the need for two tests.

– Participant variables are not controlled (but can use random allocation).

– They may require placebo treatments.

matched participants

+ Participant variables are controlled.

+ Order effects are avoided.

– Matching participants is time-consuming and not always effective.

Designing an observational study

Different issues concern us when designing an observational study. The main problem is how to record the observations that are made. Observational study is not just a matter of watching and writing; it is vital to structure your observations in some way. Some examples of how this might be done:

- *Behavioural categories.* If you were studying concerned aggressive behaviour in a children's playground then you would list the various behaviours that would indicate aggressiveness. For example, one child hits another, one child shoves another, one child raises fists. A set of behavioural categories are called *ethograms*. One researcher develops an ethogram for others to use in their research, as illustrated in the example below.

An ethogram to enable researchers to observe the behaviour of horses

Arnold, G.W. and Grassia, A. (1982) Ethogram of agonistic behaviour for thoroughbred horses. *Applied Animal Ethology*, 8 (1–2), 5–25

Arnold and Grassia recorded the social interactions within a group of horses (1 stallion and 11–16 mares) using the following categorisation scheme. The horses were observed for 20 minutes each day at the time they were fed and the behaviours were recorded for each horse in the group. This was done on 33 occasions.

Category	Behaviour
1 Leaves	A horse feeding by itself or with other horses leaves a heap of hay.
2 Is left	Horses left behind when one or more horses leave a heap.
3 Avoids	Horses that pass by other horses when seeking a place to feed.
4 Is avoided	Horses that are passed by.
5 Joins	A horse or horses is joined by one or more horses.
6 Is joined	The horses that are joined.
7 Chooses not to be alone	A horse that joins other horses rather than feeding alone.
8 Chooses to be alone	A horse that feeds alone (more than 30 m apart) rather than feeding with others.
9 Found alone	Horses observed to be feeding alone when all horses were feeding quietly.
10 Aggressive acts	Threats to kick or bite, and kicks and bites.

- *Behavioural codes* can be used for the sake of speed. When watching an animal (human or non-human) you might write down what you see rather than ticking a grid of categories.

- *Rating* behaviour may be appropriate when there are degrees of difference rather than all or nothing. For example, when studying aggression you might rate the amount of aggressiveness shown rather than just saying whether or not the animal was displaying aggressive behaviour.

- *Diaries* are useful for individuals to record self-observations, such as studies of everyday memory or sleep routines.

- *Sketches* are important for understanding how observations were made, and photographs enhance the detail of the observations.

A further issue, when designing research is to decide how much behaviour to record. The behavioural categories you use will limit the amount of behaviours that are recorded but there may still be too much data so it is necessary to use some systematic method of sampling:

- *Event sampling* – a list of behaviours is drawn up and a frequency count is kept of their occurrence. This is alright as long as there are not too many behaviours to record

- *Time sampling* – observations are made at regular intervals. For example, every 30 seconds you make a note of what your target participant is doing

- *Point sampling* –the observer concentrates on one individual until a sufficient record has been made of their behaviour and then moves on to another target individual. You could conduct time and point sampling at the same time.

Designing a survey

This sounds as if it should be relatively simple, but it isn't. You might think of a few questions off the top of your head but then stop at that. Once you see the results of your survey you'll find that the responses provide little insight into your topic of study. As with all other forms of research, design is critical.

The first step is to research the topic. This should provide you with relevant ideas on which to base your questions and also give breadth to your study. A top-down approach should be used in generating questions – start with broad questions and break each down into a number of different specific behaviours. It may be helpful to generate questions with a group of people because more varied ideas are produced (brainstorming). Each group member should put forward ideas, which are initially received uncritically by the group. Later, the group can select the best questions.

There are guidelines for writing the questions themselves:

- Avoid complex, ambiguous and or leading questions which use technical or emotive language and negative terms.

- Decide when to use open or closed questions. Open questions, such as 'what is your favourite pastime?' are best for gaining maximum information but such questions make the scoring and analysis of the data difficult. Closed questions can be forced-choice: binary (yes/no) or they may offer a number of possible answers. The inclusion of 'don't know' allows an escape for respondents especially because forced 'yes' answers may bias your results. However if too many people opt for the 'don't know' category this will produce unhelpful results. If this happens it suggests that the question is probably not a good one. An alternative and popular method in psychology is the use of *Likert scales*, as described below.

- How many questions? Not too many or the respondent may become bored, too few and the information you collect will be rather thin.

- Filler questions: it may help to include some irrelevant questions to distract the respondent from the main purpose of the survey. It also helps to have some easy, non-threatening questions which help the respondent relax, especially at the beginning of the survey.

- Lie detection questions: you might set some questions designed to deliberately 'trap' lies, such as asking 'Do you always tell the truth'. If a respondent answers 'yes' then it suggests that they are tending to portray themselves in a 'socially acceptable' way.

A *Likert scale*

If you wish to assess respondents' attitudes towards a topic then the Likert scale is a commonly used method.

1 Write an equal number of favourable and unfavourable statements about the topic.

2 After each statement offer the follow choice of answers, and ask respondents to circle their answer:

> 5   4   3   2   1
> *Strongly agree   Agree   Undecided   Disagree   Strongly disagree*

3 Calculate a score for each respondent by giving a value of 5 for strong agreement to a favourable item but a score of 1 to strong agreement to a negative item.

4 Add up all scores.

You can refine the questionnaire by removing all questions that lacked the ability to discriminate, i.e. those on which everyone scored around 3.

Sampling techniques

The participants who are selected for an experiment or any kind of research are a *sample* or selection of all members of the total *population*.

The aim of most research is to be able to make statements about groups of people, but we are only able to study a small number of the people, so we have to *generalise* from our sample to the wider population. In order to make such generalisations we need a good or *representative sample*.

How can we collect a representative sample?

The more examples looked at, the more confident we can feel about generalising from our results, but realistically any researcher has to minimise the number of participants in the study. Many studies use about 15 participants (or 30 for independent measures).

In order to select a representative sample, it is necessary to choose participants in some way so that every member of the population is equally represented. This avoids *sampling bias*, a partiality in the sample that may affect the results, such as more women than men or more people with good memory than is typical in the population. The most common sampling methods are:

- *Random sampling.* Every member of the total population has an equal chance of being selected. This is rarely possible because we do not know every member of the total population. We might take a random sample from a *sampling population*, by placing their names in a hat and selecting some of them at random.

- *Opportunity sample.* This kind of sample is obtained by selecting those people who are available (those participants who have the opportunity to be selected because of circumstances). You might think that a good way to achieve a sample for, say, your memory research would be to stand in the street on a Monday morning and ask the first 20 people you see. This is not a random technique (though many people think it is) for several reasons. First of all your sample is being selected from a specific sampling population (people not at work), second you may ignore certain individuals without being aware of doing so, and third not everyone has an equal chance of being selected – only those people who pass by you. However, this technique is the most commonly used and the easiest.

- *Volunteer sample.* Another common technique is to ask for volunteers. Milgram did this in his obedience study. This means that your sample is from a large but limited sampling population – in Milgram's case the population was all the readers of the newspaper, a distinct population. So you inevitably start with a biased sample. Furthermore, volunteers tend to be atypical, they are likely to be more motivated and perform at a higher level than the population in general. They may also be keen to please the experimenter, responding to demand characteristics and experimenter bias. However, volunteers are important if unusual behaviour, such as telepathy, is being studied.

- *Systematic sample.* A sample may be obtained using some system, such as selecting every tenth person walking along the street or every name that appears at the top of the right-hand page in the phone book. Systematic sampling is often mistakenly called random. It is equivalent, however, in its capacity to derive a representative sample.

- *Quota sampling.* In this case certain categories are designated in a population, such as people in age groups or classified in terms of their qualifications. The researcher then aims to collect a set quota from each category. This ensures that the typical categories in a population are equally represented in the research. This method is commonly used when conducting market research.

for and against

different methods of sampling

random sampling

+ It avoids bias.

− It is often impractical, because it relies on a representative sample population.

opportunity samples

+ They are easy to collect.

− They are biased.

volunteer sampling

+ It is a useful way to locate willing participants.

− The participants tend to have special characteristics.

systematic sampling

+ It is less biased.

− It is not truly random.

quota sampling

+ It ensures equal representation of key groups.

− It requires considerable organisation. There may be bias because the selection is an opportunity sample rather than a random one within the parameters of the quota.

Other design issues

Standardised procedures

It is important for replication that the procedures in a research study are standardised (made the same) so they can be followed on future occasions. An important element of this standardisation are the *standardised instructions*, the set of instructions which are given to each participant to tell them what to do. These are especially important in eliminating experimenter bias because they try to prevent the experiment unknowingly communicating expectations. Such instructions may be given in written form to avoid any unnecessary interaction between experimenters and participants. However, this doesn't prevent the participant trying to guess what the experiment is about.

The standardised instructions of any study can be divided into:

- *briefing* instructions, telling the participants what they are going to do, the experimental procedures

- *debriefing*, information passed on after they have participated. This usually consists of telling the participants about any deception which has taken place and offering them the chance of withdrawing their data from the experiment. Debriefing is an important ethical consideration.

Single and double blind procedures

An experimenter may not actually deceive participants but may simply not tell them anything. This is called a *single blind technique*. The problem is that participants may consciously or unconsciously seek to find out what the experiment is all about, and so be influenced by subtle cues in their interaction with the researcher. This is why deception may be a preferable technique from the experimenter's point of view. The term 'single blind' refers to the fact that the participant is kept blind to the aims of the experiment.

Double blind is when the person interacting with the participants is also blind to the experimental aims and does not know which group of participants is receiving which treatment. This minimises the extent to which participants are exposed to expectations and cues from the supervisor.

Pilot studies

If you have ever baked a cake (or followed any recipe) you will know that afterwards you can think of a number of things which you could have done better. You might regard your first effort as a 'trial run'. When researchers conduct large-scale (and expensive) projects it is clearly beneficial to try the design out on a small sample first, and then make useful adjustments to the design before embarking on the actual research. This first study is a *pilot*.

Control of variables

There are a number of variables in any research:

- *Independent* and *dependent variables*, in an experiment. The experimenter manipulates the IV and observes changes in the DV.

- *Participant variables*, such as age, gender, and abilities, as well as the participant's mood or how awake they are. These are controlled either by using a repeated measures design or, in an independent design, using random allocation to conditions.

- *Situational variables*. Certain features of the research situation such as noise or temperature may act as extraneous variables and need to be controlled.

Selection of materials

If an experiment requires that two different tests are given for the experimental and control condition, then it is imperative that both tests are equivalent. There are several things that may be worth considering:

- The words on both tests should be of equal length and familiarity. If the word 'hermaphrodite' appeared in one list it would be much more memorable than words such as 'table' and 'ocean'. There are word lists which show the frequency of occurrence for words, such as the Thorndike-Lorge word list (Thorndike and Lorge, 1944).

- The order of items in any test should be randomly distributed to avoid any bias. In the experiment on shallow and deep processing by Craik and Tulving (1975, see Chapter 3, page 76) it was important that the different conditions were randomly distributed throughout the test rather than having all the shallow sentences at the start which would have created an order effect.

Evaluating research

Validity

There are two aspects of the validity or 'trueness' of an experiment:

- The *internal validity* of an experiment is an assessment of the extent to which an experimental manipulation does the job it is meant to do. In other words, the extent to which we have controlled all extraneous variables and can be certain that any changes in the DV were due to manipulation of the IV. In order to maximise this validity we must be concerned with such things as experimenter bias, demand characteristics, order effects (in repeated measures designs), participant variables (in independent measures) and any other confounding variables. Internal validity is sometimes called *experimental validity*.

- The *external validity* of an experiment concerns the extent to which we can apply the results to other situations besides the one where the research was conducted. This is also referred to as *ecological validity* of the experiment, a concept that has already been discussed. It is often said that Milgram's study lacked external validity because it was a laboratory experiment whereas the obedience study by Hofling *et al.* (see page 183) had such validity because it was a field experiment. On the other hand, Milgram's findings have been replicated many times whereas no one has ever been able to produce the same findings as Hofling *et al.* In this sense Milgram's study is the one with external validity and Hofling's extremely high obedience rates may only apply to the specific situation of hospital nurses and therefore has low external (ecological) validity.

An experiment has low validity if it can tell us little about behaviour outside the experiment, i.e. how *generalisable* the research results are. Another aspect of external validity is the representativeness of the sample which was used and the sampling population from which it was drawn.

Experiments which have low external validity are said to lack *mundane realism*, i.e. they do not appear like real life. This can be compensated for by raising *experimental realism* which is the extent to which the experimental set-up engages the participants so that they behave as if it were real. Milgram's study may have lacked mundane realism but had experimental realism.

Reliability

Reliability is a measure of dependability or consistency, in the case of measurement we would regard a ruler as reliable if it reported the same measurement each time it measured the same thing.

The concepts of validity and reliability hang together. For something to be valid it must be reliable, though a test can be reliable without being valid. In the experimental setting we would consider a result to be both reliable and valid if it can be repeated with the same result.

Reliability can be established in various ways:

- In an observational study, it is useful to have more than one observer to avoid the bias of having only one person's observations. The observations from each observer can be compared and *inter-observer reliability* calculated.

- When psychological tests are used, reliability of the test can be established using the *test–retest* method where the same test is given to participants on two separate occasions to see if their scores remain relatively similar. The interval between testings must be long enough to prevent a *practice effect* occurring. Alternatively, the *split-half technique* can be used where one test is split in half and the scores on both halves are correlated to see if they are similar. If the test is reliable (consistent then there should be a high correlation between both halves.

Handling your data

Descriptive statistics

A statistic is a number or numbers used to represent findings or data. This includes graphical representations, which are numerical. Data can be measured at different levels (levels of measurement): nominal, ordinal, interval (quasi-interval) or ratio.

Descriptive statistics include:

- measures of central tendency (mean, median and mode) which express the most central value of a group of data

- measures of dispersion which describe the data in terms of how spread out individual results are

- graphical representation (tabulated data, pie and bar chart, pictogram, histogram, frequency polygon, line and curved graph, and scattergram) which expresses data in pictorial form.

It is important to select the right descriptive statistics for your data and to use them to get a 'feel' for what the results mean.

Levels of data

When we collect a sample of data, we use different scales or levels of measurement to represent the data.

- *The nominal scale.* Data is grouped in *named* (nominal) categories. This is the lowest level of measurement. No magnitude is represented. An example would be in a study which investigated how much violence there was on television, the data was represented in terms of different kinds of programmes: comedies, dramas, soap operas and so on, and for each category the frequency of violent acts was shown.

- *The ordinal scale.* Data is placed in order along some dimension or placed in terms of relative position in comparison with others (for example, 1st, 2nd, 3rd, etc.). This scale is limited in that true magnitude is not expressed, only *relative* magnitude is recorded. An example of this would be determining a sequence for programmes containing violence and listing the programmes in that order.

- *The interval scale.* The intervals between each item are of constant or equal size. The intervals on this scale reflect precise differences between the units. However the units are arbitrary and the zero point is not a true zero. In the case of the ordinal scale we know that items are in order but one item may be twice as violent as the next whereas the third item is four times as violent. On an interval scale we would rate the amount of violence in each programme and assign a value to that programme. Then we could represent the data on an interval scale.

IQ scores are sometimes called *quasi-interval scales*. They are not truly interval measurement because the intervals are not constant – we cannot say that the 'distances' between the score of 95 and 100, and 100 and 105 are the same. Therefore IQ scales, and all other data from psychometric tests, are at the ordinal level of measurement but, for the purpose of statistics we often regard them as almost (or *quasi*) interval scales.

- *The ratio scale.* The scale has constant intervals and a true zero point (the zero represents a state of nothing rather than an arbitrary zero point). These are rare in psychological measurement. An example would be the absolute zero scale for temperature.

Measures of central tendency

- The *mean* (or arithmetic mean). The mean is calculated by adding up all values, and dividing by the total number of values.

- The *median* is the middle or central value in an ordered list. It is calculated by placing all the values in order, and finding the mid-point or median. If the mid-point lies between two numbers you must work out the mean of these values.

- The *mode* or modal group is the most common value(s). Again you place all the values in order, and find the value or values which occur most frequently. If all the data values are equal in frequency then there is no mode. If two values share the highest frequency then the data is bimodal, or it may even be multi-modal if there are more than two modes.

Comparing the mean, median and mode

Consider the following set of data (they might be errors on a reaction time test):

$$3, 4, 4, 5, 6, 7, 8, 9, 9, 39$$

How can we describe this data?

- The mean would be 9.4. This does not represent the data very well – though it does use all the data.
- The median would be 6.5, which reflects the data better, in this particular case.
- There are two modes – 4 and 9. Again, in this case, the mode would not be a very useful measure.

Consider this data (colour preferences):

red, orange, blue, blue, red, yellow, red, green

- The mode would be the only way to represent this data as it is recorded at the nominal level of measurement.

Note that:

- The mean is rarely a whole number – this reflects the fact that it is mathematically calculated.

- The mode and median may bear no relation to the mean.

- For nominal data you must use the mode.

- The mean may be unduly affected by one extreme value (for example, the set of data used above plus an extreme value) and the median would be better in this situation.

- The median should be used for ordinal level data.

- The term *average* is not mathematically precise. The mean, median and mode are all averages.

Measures of dispersion: the range

The range is the distance between the lowest and highest value in the data sample. It is desirable to add 1 to the difference, to account for possible measurement error.

Graphical representation

A graph is the picture which uses lines, curves or figures to reflect the relationship between variables (Reber, 1995). To represent something graphically means to provide a visual or vivid illustration.

Some graphical methods are suitable for all levels of measurement whereas others can only be used with ordinal or interval data.

For all levels of measurement

- *Tabular data (tables).* Summarising raw data in a more readable form.

- *Bar chart.* Frequency is represented by the height of the bar. You can exclude empty categories.

- *Pie chart.* Frequency translated into degrees of a circle. This is especially suitable for nominal data.

Graphical methods suitable for ordinal and interval data

- *Histogram.* This is often confused with a bar chart because they look the same. In a histogram the area within the bars must be proportional to the frequencies represented, the horizontal axis must be continuous and any empty categories must be represented.

- *Frequency polygon.* The mid-point of each bar on a histogram is represented by a dot and the dots are joined together. The data must be ordered and continuous. (See page 237.)

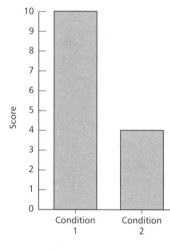

An example of a bar chart

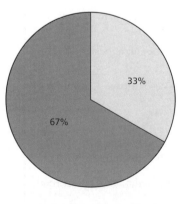

An example of a pie chart

- *Line graph.* A frequency polygon with ordinal rather than interval data. The data still shows a progression but it is not continuous.

- *Curved line graph.* It may be that the lines which join the plotted points are better linked as curves rather than straight lines. In this case a curved line should be sketched.

- *Scattergram.* When two sets of data are correlated (see earlier in this chapter), each pair of values is plotted against each other to determine if a consistent trend is apparent. You may draw a line to represent what looks like the 'line of best fit' but this phrase is reserved for the result of a statistical calculation.

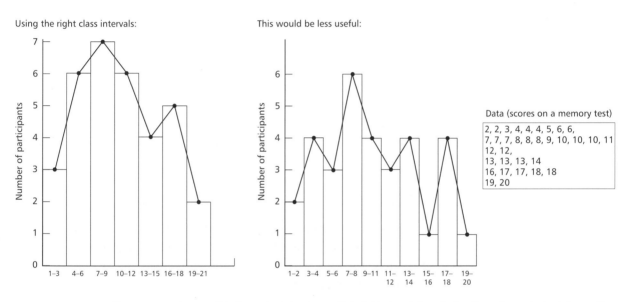

Data (scores on a memory test)

2, 2, 3, 4, 4, 4, 5, 6, 6,
7, 7, 7, 8, 8, 8, 9, 10, 10, 10, 11
12, 12,
13, 13, 13, 14
16, 17, 17, 18, 18
19, 20

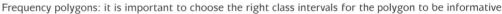

Frequency polygons: it is important to choose the right class intervals for the polygon to be informative

Things to remember when drawing graphs

- Write a clear title, and if necessary subtitle.

- Carefully label both axes.

- Mark all units on the graph.

- Use graph paper.

- Don't 'gild the lily' – one table of data and one graph will be enough for each set of data.

A few comments for those who are 'scared' of numbers

- Numbers can be quite comforting if you approach them in an organised and confident manner. I actually find it quite relaxing to do numerical calculations!

- Find a quiet corner, a clean sheet of paper, a calculator and a pencil.

- Write the numbers down carefully and neatly according to the instructions.

- You do not need to record all those decimal places – 3 decimal places is fine during calculations and the final answer should be given to one decimal place.

- Always look at your answer – is it in the right ballpark?

- If all else fails, throw away your piece of paper and start again. You'll probably get it right this time.

Writing the report

A critical part of any research is writing the report. This provides others with an opportunity to find out about your research and is also done in order to permit other researchers to try to repeat the study and verify the findings. If you are taking psychology AS-level, your report should total between 1,200 and 2,000 words, excluding tables, figures and appendices. You can use the following divisions.

Abstract

The abstract or summary gives the reader a chance to find out the bare essentials without going any further. It should include the basic details of the study: the topic investigated, aims and hypothesis; the method used including the design and participants; the findings and conclusions. You might mention the implications of your findings and suggestions for further research. In total, the abstract should be about 150 words.

Introduction (or literature review)

The purpose of this review of past research is to explain where your hypothesis comes from. Start with general theory and then narrow down to specific and relevant theory and research. In total the length should be about 600 words which leads logically into your research aims. It is important to be concise and selective. You should not write an essay. You also should not include research which contradicts your hypothesis because it then doesn't make sense to test that hypothesis. Save such information for the discussion.

Aims and hypothesis

The preceding literature review should lead logically into the aims, so they do not appear out of thin air. Explain what it is that you intend to investigate. Then formally state your expectation as the alternative hypothesis, followed by the null hypothesis. You should ensure that your hypothesis is clear and unambiguous. Operationalise all concepts. It is also customary to say whether this is a one- or two-tailed hypothesis, and explain why you choose this form of hypothesis.

Method

This section (sometimes called 'the study') should be about 600 words. The intention is to provide precise details of what you did, so that another person could replicate your study. The method is typically subdivided into the follow sections.

Research design

Describe what method has been used (for example, field experiment, participant observation) and why. If appropriate also explain the choice of design (for example, repeated or independent measures, or point or time sampling). You might also identify the IV and DV plus any potential extraneous variables that have been controlled. If single or double blind procedures were used, they should be described. If you carried out a pilot study prior to the main study say so here, and note any alterations you made to the design as a result.

Participants and sampling

Give full details of both researchers and participants, including number, age and sex, and the method of sampling and from what target population they were selected from. If participants were allocated to conditions, you should explain how this was done.

Apparatus and materials

Include descriptions of all materials used. The exact details should be placed in the appendices. Remember to include mark schemes for any tests or questionnaires. The reasons for the design of such materials can be explained.

Standardised procedures

Describe the exact steps taken in conducting the research. State where the research was undertaken, the instructions given to researchers and participants, details of debriefing, and any other relevant details which would be necessary for replication. It may be preferable to place some of these details in an appendix and refer to them here.

Special considerations

Any other information, such as ethical issues or the use of pilot studies should be mentioned.

Results

Present a summary of the data in the main text using descriptive statistics. Select those that are most appropriate to your data including information about central tendency and dispersion. You will need to use some way of presenting results clearly, such as a table and/or graphs. Any raw data (such as the actual test scores from all participants) and calculations should be placed in the appendices. You do not need to include details such as the names of participants. In fact such information should be regarded as confidential. Depending on the study, you may also wish to make some observations on findings that cropped up in the study that seemed interesting and relevant, but were not included in your table of results. Draw some conclusions about what the descriptive statistics show about the data.

Discussion

This final section should be about 600 words. Discuss the theoretical significance of your findings, with reference to the introduction and aims/hypotheses. If your hypothesis appears not to be supported by the data you might consider reasons to explain this such as flaws in your design. Even if your study produced expected results, you might still feel that there were design flaws and these should be discussed. Propose possible modifications to the design of your study in the light of your criticisms. In addition you might consider ideas for future research.

Finally you should state your conclusion, including a consideration of the implications of the study for psychological theory and/or applications to real-life situations.

Appendices

Some details are better in an appendix so that they do not interrupt the flow of text. Examples would include working out of any results you did by hand.

References and bibliography

This section should contain a bibliography (a list of books you used), but should also the reference of any studies that have been mentioned, such as Fields (1997), even if you have not personally looked at it. If you do not have the original you can find all the necessary details in the reference list at the back of the book which did mention the source. Look at the way references are used in this book.

The recommended style for a textbook reference is:

Fields, W.C. (1997) *An Introduction to Psychology*. London: Thomas and Co. (i.e. author, date, title in italics or underlined, place of publishing, publisher's name)

The recommended style for a journal reference is:

Fields, W.C. (1997) How to pass A level. *Psychology Review*, 2, 23–45 (i.e. author, date, title of article, title of journal in italics or underlined, volume number, page numbers)

You should ideally have one subheading for your bibliography, under which you list the books or articles you read yourself (in name alphabetical order), and another subheading for references, under which you need to list the original publication details for every person you referred to in your literature review or discussion (also in name alphabetical order).

where to now?

▶ **Banister, P., Burman, E., Parker, I., Taylor, M. and Tindall, C. (1994)** *Qualitative Methods in Psychology: A Research Guide*. **Buckingham: Open University Press** – a comprehensive and relatively accessible guide to conducting qualitative research, including observation and interviews

▶ **Coolican, H. (1996)** *Introduction to Research Methods and Statistics in Psychology*, **2nd edition. London: Hodder & Stoughton** – very popular with A-level students. Well written with useful exercises to try

▶ **Flanagan, C. (1996)** *A Resource Pack for 'A' level Psychology*. **Crewe: Hartshill Press (available through Hodder & Stoughton)** – good variety of ideas for coursework, plus summaries of journal articles with questions on research methodology

▶ **Foster, J.J. and Parker, I. (1995)** *Carrying Out Investigations in Psychology: Methods and Statistics*. **Leicester: BPS Books** – very clear explanations of research methods and techniques

▶ **Searle, A. (1999)** *Introducing Research and Data in Psychology*. **London: Routledge** – part of a series of books written for A-level students. Very readable and clear text.

references

Abernathy, E.M. (1940) The effect of changed environmental conditions upon the results of college examinations. *Journal of Psychology*, 10, 293–301

Adam, K. (1977) Body weight correlates with REM sleep. *British Medical Journal*, 1, 813

Adams, H.E., Wright, L.W. and Lohr, B.A. (1996) Is homophobia associated with homosexual arousal? *Journal of Abnormal Psychology*, 105 (3), 440–5

Adorno, T.W., Frenkel-Brunswick, E., Levinson, D.J. and Sanford, R.H. (1950) *The Authoritarian Personality*. New York: Harper & Row

Aggleton, J.P. and Waskett, L. (1999) The ability of odours to serve as state-dependent cues for real-world memories: Can Viking smells aid the recall of Viking experiences? *British Journal of Psychology*, 90, 1–7

Ainsworth, M.D.S. (1979). Attachment as related to mother–infant interaction. In Rosenblatt, J.G., Hinde, R.A., Beer, C. and Busnel, M. (eds) *Advances in the Study of Behaviour*, Vol. 9. Orlando, FL: Academic Press

Ainsworth, P.B. and King, E. (1988) Witnesses' perceptions of identification parades. In Gruneberg, M.M., Morris, P.E. and Sykes, R.N. (eds) *Practical Aspects of Memory: Current Research and Issues*, Vol. 1. Chichester: Wiley

Alex, J.A. and Ritchie, M.R. (1992) School-aged children's interpretation of their experience with acute surgical pain. *Journal of Pediatric Nursing*, 7 (3), 171–80

Allport, G.W. (1947) *The Use of Personal Documents in Psychological Science*. London: Holt, Rhinehart & Winston

Amir, S. and Stewart, J. (1996), quoted in 'Clocked off', *New Scientist*, 8 November 1997, 29

Andrews, B., Morton, J., Beckerian, D.A., Brewin, C.R., Davies, G.M. and Mollon, P. (1995) The recovery of memories in clinical practice. *The Psychologist*, 8, 209-14

Anon (1994) Crime waves. *2600 The Hacker Quarterly*, 11 (1), 4–5

Arendt, J. (1985) The pineal: a gland that measures time? *New Scientist*, 1466, 36–8

Arnold, G.W. and Grassia, A. (1982) Ethogram of agonistic behaviour for thoroughbred horses. *Applied Animal Ethology*, 8 (1–2), 5–25

Aronson, E. (1988) *The Social Animal*, 5th edition. New York: Freeman

Aronson, E., Wilson, T.D. and Akert, R.M. (1994) *Social Psychology*. New York: Harper Collins

Asterinsky, E., Lynch, J.A., Mack, M.E., Tzankoff, S.P. and Hurn, E. (1985) Comparison of eye motion in wakefulness and REM sleep. *Psychophysiology*, 22, 1–10

Asterinsky, N.E. and Kleitman, N. (1955) Regularly occurring periods of eye motility and concommitant phenomena during sleep. *Science*, 118, 273–4

Atkinson, R.C. and Shiffrin, R.M. (1968) Human memory: A proposed system and its control processes. In Spence, K.W. and Spence, J.T. (eds) *The Psychology of Learning and Motivation*, Vol. 2. London: Academic Press

Atkinson, R.C. and Shiffrin, R.M. (1971) The control of short-term memory. *Scientific American*, 224, 82–90

Avis, J. and Harris, P.L. (1991) Belief–desire reasoning among Baka children: evidence for a universal conception of theory of mind. *Child Development*, 62 (3), 460–7

Ayensu, E.S. and Whitfield, P. (eds) (1982) *The Rhythms of Life*. London: Book Club Associates

Baddeley, A.D. (1990) *Human Memory*. Hove, East Sussex: Lawrence Erlbaum Associates Ltd (2nd edition, 1996)

Baddeley, A.D. (1995) *Your Memory: A User's Guide*. London: Penguin

Baddeley, A.D. and Warrington, E.H. (1970) Amnesia and the distinction between long- and short-term memory. *Journal of Verbal Learning and Verbal Behaviour*, 9, 176–89

Bagby, R.M., Schuller, D.R., Levitt, A.J., Joffe, R.T. and Harkness, K.L. (1996) Seasonal and non-seasonal depression and the five factor model of personality. *Journal of Affective Disorders*, 38 (2–3), 89–95

Baillargeon, R. and DeVos, J. (1991) Object permanence in young infants: further evidence. *Child Development*, 62, 1227–46

Bancroft, D. and Carr, R. (1995) *Influencing Children's Development*. Milton Keynes: Open University

Bandura, A. (1977) *Social Learning Theory*. Englewood Cliffs, New Jersey: Prentice-Hall

Bandura, A., Ross, D. and Ross, S.A. (1961) Transmission of aggression through imitation of aggressive models. *Journal of Abnormal and Social Psychology*, 63, 575–82

Banister, P., Burman, E., Parker, I., Taylor, M. and Tindall, C. (1994) *Qualitative Methods in Psychology: A Research Guide*. Buckingham: Open University Press

Baron, R.A. and Byrne, D. (1994) *Social Psychology: Understanding Human Interaction*. Boston: Allyn & Bacon.

Baron-Cohen, S. (1995) *Mindblindness: An Essay on Autism and Theory of Mind*. Cambridge: MIT Press

Bateman, A. and Fonagy, P. (1999) Effectiveness of partial hospitalisation in the treatment of borderline personality disorder: a randomised control trial. *American Journal of Psychiatry*, 156, 1563–9

Bateman, A. and Holmes, J. (1995) *Introduction to Psychoanalysis*. London: Routledge

Baum, M. (1969) Extinction of an avoidance response following response prevention: some parametric investigations. *Canadian Journal of Psychology*, 23, 1–10

Baumrind, D. (1975) Metaethical and normative considerations governing the treatment of human subjects in the behavioural sciences. In Kennedy, E.C. (ed.) *Human Rights and Psychological Research: A Debate on Psychology and Ethics*. New York: Thomas Y. Crowell

Beaumont, G. (1988) General practitioner prescribing for the driving patient. In Burley, D. and Silverstone, T. (eds) *Medicine and Road Safety*. London: CNS

Bellezza, F.S. and Bower, G.H. (1981) Person stereotypes and memory for people. *Journal of Personality and Social Psychology*, 41 (5), 856–65

Benjamin, J., Li, L., Patterson, C., Murphy, D.L. and Hamer, D.H. (1996) Population and familial association between the D4 receptor gene and measures of novelty seeking. *Nature Genetics*, 12, 81–4

Bentley, E. (1999) *Awareness*. London: Routledge

Bergin, A.E. and Garfield, S.L. (eds) (1994) *Handbook of Psychotherapy and Behaviour Change*. New York: Wiley

Bergin, A.E. and Lambert, M.J. (1971) The effectiveness of psychotherapy. In Bergin and Garfield, S.L. (eds) (1994) op. cit.

Bifulco, A., Brown, G.W. and Alder, Z. (1991) Early sexual abuse and clinical depression in later life. *British Journal of Psychiatry*, 159, 115–22

Borich, G.D. and Tombari, M.L. (1997) *Educational Psychology: A Contemporary Approach*. New York: Longman

Bower, G.H. (1981) Mood and memory. *American Psychologist*, 36, 129–48

Bower, G.H. and Karlin, M.B. (1974) Depth of processing pictures of faces and recognition memory. *Journal of Experimental Psychology*, 103, 751–7

Bowlby, J. (1969) *Attachment*. London: Pimlico

Bradmetz, J. (1999) Precursors of formal thought: a longitudinal study. *British Journal of Developmental Psychology*, 17, 61–81

Brenner, V. (1996) An initial report on the online assessment of Internet addiction: The first 30 days of the Internet usage. Marquette University Counselling Center and SUNY-Buffalo.
http://www.ccsnet.com/prep/pap/pap8b/638b12p.txt

Brigham, J.C. and Malpass, R.S. (1985) The role of experience and contact in the recognition of faces of own and other-race persons. *Journal of Social Issues*, 41, 139–55

British Psychological Society (1978) Ethical principles for research with human subjects. Statement at Annual General Meeting, April 1978

British Psychological Society (1985) A code of conduct for psychologists, *Bulletin of the BPS*, 38, 41–3

British Psychological Society (1990) *Ethical Principles for Conducting Research with Human Participants*. Leicester: The British Psychological Society

Brown, D. and Pedder, J. (1991) *Introduction to Psychotherapy*. London: Routledge

Brown, G.W. and Harris, T.O. (1978) *The Social Origins of Depression: A Study of Psychiatric Disorder in Women*. London: Tavistock

Brown, N.R., Rips, L.J. and Shevell, S.K. (1985) The subjective dates of natural events in very long-term memory. *Cognitive Psychology*, 17, 139–77

Brown, R. and Kulik, J. (1977) Flashbulb memories. *Cognition*, 5, 73–99

Brown, R., Cazden, C.B. and Bellugi, U. (1969) The child's grammar from 1 to 3. In Hall, J.P. (ed.) *Minnesota Symposium on Child Psychology*, Volume 2. Minneapolis: University of Minnesota Press

Bruner, J. (1971) The course of cognitive growth. In Richardson, K. and Sheldon, S. (eds) (1985) *Cognitive Development to Adolescence*. Hove: Lawrence Erlbaum Associates Ltd

Bruner, J.S. (1963) *The Process of Education*. New York: Vintage Books

Bruner, J.S. (1966) *Towards a Theory of Instruction*. New York: Norton

Bruner, J.S. and Kenney, H. (1966) *The Development of the Concepts of Order and Proportion in Children*. New York: Wiley

Bryant, P. (1998) Cognitive development. In Eysenck, M. (ed.) (1998) op. cit.

Burns, A. (1998) 'Pop' psychology or 'Ken behaving badly'. *The Psychologist*, 11 (7), 360

Burr, V. (1995) *An Introduction to Social Constructionism*. London: Routledge

Bushman, B.J. (1988) The effects of apparel on compliance: a field experiment with a female authority figure. *Personality and Social Psychology Bulletin*, 14, 459–67

Carey, S. (1978) The child as a word learner. In Halle, M., Bresnan, J. and Miller, G.A. (eds) *Linguistic Theory and Psychological Reality*. Cambridge, MA: MIT Press

Carlson, N. (1977) *The Physiology of Behaviour*. New York: Allyn & Bacon

Cave, S. (1999) *Therapeutic Approaches*. London: Routledge

Child, D. (1997) *Psychology and the Teacher*. London: Cassell

Chodorow, N. (1996) Reflections on the authority of the past in psychoanalytic thinking. *Psychoanalytic Quarterly*, 65, 32–51

Chorney, M.J., Chorney, K., Seese, N., Owen, M.J., Daniels, J., McGuffin, P., Thomson, L.A., Detterman, D.K., Benbow, C.P., Lubinski, D., Eley, T.C. and Plomin, R. (1998) A quantitative trait locus (QTL) associated with cognitive ability in children. *Psychological Science*, 9, 159–66

Clamp, A. and Russell, J. (1998) *Comparative Psychology*. London: Hodder & Stoughton

Cohen, G. (1991) *Memory in the Real World*. Hove: Lawrence Erlbaum Associates Ltd

Cohen, N.J. and Squire, L.R. (1980) Preserved learning and retention of pattern-analysing skill in amnesia: Dissociation of knowing how from knowing that. *Science*, 210, 207–10

Coolican, H. (1990) *Research Methods and Statistics in Psychology*. London: Hodder & Stoughton

Coolican, H. (1996) *Introduction to Research Methods and Statistics in Psychology*, 2nd edition. London: Hodder & Stoughton

Cory, T.L., Ormiston, D.W., Simmel, E. and Dainoff, M. (1975) Predicting the frequency of dream recall. *Journal of Abnormal Psychology*, 84, 261–6

Craik, F.I.M. (1979) Levels of processing: overview and closing comments. In Cermak, L.S. and Craik, F.I.M. (eds) *Levels of Processing in Human Memory* (pp. 447–61). Hillsdale, NJ: Erlbaum

Craik, F.I.M. and Lockhart, R.S. (1972) Levels of processing: a framework for memory research. *Journal of Verbal Learning and Verbal Behaviour*, 11, 671–84

Craik, F.I.M. and Tulving, E. (1975) Depth of processing and retention of words in episodic memory. *Journal of Experimental Psychology: General*, 104, 268–94

Crick, F.I. and Mitchison, G. (1986) Sleep and neural nets. *Journal of Mind and Behavior*, 7, 229–50

Crook, C. (1994) *Computers and the Collaborative Experience of Learning*. London: Routledge

Czeisler, C.A. *et al.* (1990) *New England Journal of Medicine*, 1322: 1253. Quoted in Taylor, S. (1990) Scientists make light work of night work. *New Scientist*, 2 June, 32

Czeisler, C.A., Kronauer, R.E., Allan, J.S., Duffy, J.F., Jewett, M.E., Brown, E.N. and Ronda, J.M. (1989) Bright light induction of strong (type O) resetting of the human circadian pacemaker. *Science*, 244, 1328–33

Dalenberg, C. (1996) The prediction of accurate memories of trauma. Paper presented at the NATO Advanced Study Institute of Recollections of Trauma, France, 15–25 June

Deary, I.J. and Tait, R. (1987) Effects of sleep disruption on cognitive performance and mood in medical house officers. *British Medical Journal*, 295, 1513–16

Delfabbro, P.H. and Winefield, A.H. (1999) Poker-machine gambling: an analysis of within session characteristics. *British Journal of Psychology*, 90, 425–39

Dement, W. and Kleitman, N. (1957) The relation of eye movements during sleep to dream activity: an objective method for the study of dreaming. *Journal of Experimental Psychology*, 53, 339–46

Dement, W.C. (1960) The effect of dream deprivation. *Science*, 15, 1705–7

Dement, W.C. (1965) Studies on the function of rapid eye movement (paradoxical) sleep in human subjects. In Jouvet, M. (ed.), *Aspects Anatomo-fonctionnels de la Physiologie du Sommeil*. Paris: Editions du Centre Nationale de la Recherche Scientifique

Dement, W.C. (1978) *Some Must Watch While Others Must Sleep*. New York: Norton

Deutsch, M. and Collins, M.E. (1951) *Interracial Housing*. Minneapolis: University of Florida Press

Dion, K., Bersheid, E. and Walster, E. (1972) What is beautiful is good. *Journal of Personality and Social Psychology*, 24, 285–90

Duck, J.M. (1990) Children's ideals: the role of real life versus media figures. *Australian Journal of Psychology*, 42, 19–29

Ebstein, R.P., Novick, O., Umansky, R., Priel, B., Osher, Y., Blaine, D., Bennett, E.R., Nemanov, L., Katz, M. and Belmaker, R.H. (1995) Dopamine D4 receptor (DRD4) exon III polymorphism associated with the human trait of novelty seeking. *Nature Genetics*, 12, 78–80

Elliott, D.M. (1995) Delayed recall of traumatic events: correlates and clinical implications. Paper presented at the annual meeting of the American Psychological Association, New York

Emmelkamp, P. and Kuipers, A. (1979) Agoraphobia: a follow-up study four years after treatment. *British Journal of Psychiatry*, 134, 352–5

Emmelkamp, P.M. (1994) Behaviour therapy with adults. In Bergin, A.E. and Garfield, S.L. (eds) (1994) op. cit.

Empson, J. (1993) *Sleep and Dreaming*. Hemel Hempstead: Harvester Wheatsheaf

Eng, L. (1995) Internet is becoming a very useful tool for campus radicals. *The Journal Star*, 22 Jan, 8

Ennis, E. (1997) Seasonal variations in mood and behaviour and pre-menstrual syndrome. *Proceedings of the British Psychological Society*, 5 (1), 9

Erikson, E.H. (1959) *Identity and the Lifecycle*. New York: Norton

Eysenck, H.J. (1952) The effects of psychotherapy: an evaluation. *Journal of Consulting Psychology*, 16, 319–24

Eysenck, M. (1993) *Principles of Cognitive Psychology*. Hove: Lawrence Erlbaum Associates Ltd

Eysenck, M. (1994) How many memory stores? *Psychology Review*, 1, 1–4

Eysenck, M. (1998) Memory. In Eysenck, M. (ed.) (1998) op. cit.

Eysenck, M.W. (ed.) (1998) *Psychology: An Integrated Approach*. Harlow: Longman

Eysenck, M.W. and Keane M. T. (1997) *Cognitive Psychology: A Student's Handbook*. Hove: Psychology Press Ltd

Fairbairn, W.R.D. (1952) *Psychoanalytic Studies of the Personality*. London: Routledge

Fancher, R. (1995) *Cultures of Healing*. New York: Freeman

Faulkner, D. (1995) Teaching and learning. In Bancroft, D. and Carr, R. (eds) *Influencing Children's Development*. Milton Keynes: Open University

Faulkner, D., Littleton, K. and Woodhead, M. (1998) *Learning Relationships in the Classroom*. London: Routledge

Fawcett, S.B. (1991) Some values guiding community research and action. *Journal of Applied Behaviour Analysis*, 24, 621–36

Ferenczi, M. (1997) Seaonal depression and light therapy. http://nimnet51.nimr.mrc.ac.uk/mhe97/sad.htm

Ferguson, E. and Cassidy, H.J. (1999) The Gulf War and illness by association. *British Journal of Psychology*, 90, 459–75

Festinger, L., Riecken, H.W. and Schachter, S. (1956) *When Prophecy Fails*. Minneapolis: University of Minnesota Press

Flanagan, C. (1996) *A Resource Pack for 'A' level Psychology*. Crewe: Hartshill Press

Fonagy, P., Steele, M., Moran, G., Steele, H. and Higgit, A. (1993) Measuring the ghost in the nursery: an empirical study of the relation between parents' mental representations of childhood experiences and their infants' security of attachment. *Journal of the American Psychoanalytic Association*, 41 (4) 957–81

Foot, H., Morgan, M. and Shute, R. (eds) (1990) *Children Helping Children*. Chichester: Wiley

Foster, J.J. and Parker, I. (1995) *Carrying Out Investigations in Psychology: Methods and Statistics*. Leicester: BPS Books

Fox, D.K., Hopkins, B.L. and Anger, W.K. (1987) The long-term effects of a token economy on safety performance in open pit mining. *Journal of Applied Behaviour Analysis*, 20, 215–24

Frankland, A. and Cohen, L. (1999) Working with recovered memories. *The Psychologist*, 12, 82–3

Freeling, N.R. and Shemberg, K.M. (1970) The alleviation of test anxiety by systematic desensitization. *Behavior Research and Therapy*, 8, 293–9

Freeman, N., Lloyd, S. and Sinha, C. (1980) Hide and seek is child's play. *New Scientist*, 304–5

Freud, S. (1900) *The Interpretation of Dreams* (A.A. Brill trans., 1913). London: George Allen & Unwin

Freud, S. (1900) *The Interpretation of Dreams*. London: Hogarth

Freud, S. (1905) *Three Essays on Sexuality*. London: Hogarth

Freud, S. (1909) Analysis of a phobia in a five-year-old boy. *Collected Papers*, Volume III. London: Hogarth

Freud, S. (1917) Mourning and melancholia. *Collected Works*, Volume 14. London: Hogarth

Freud, S. (1924) The dissolution of the Oedipus complex. *Collected Works*, Volume 19. London: Hogarth

Freud, S. (1933) *New Introductory Lectures on Psychoanalysis*. London: Hogarth

Frith, U. and Happe, F. (1994) Autism: beyond theory of mind. In Messer, D. and Dockrell, J. (1999) *Developmental Psychology: A Reader*. London: Arnold

Gaertner, S.L., Mann, J.A., Dovidio, J.F., Murrell, A.J. and Pomare, M. (1990) How does cooperation reduce intergroup bias? *Journal of Personality and Social Psychology*, 59, 692–704

Gaertner, S.L., Mann, J.A., Murrell, A.J. and Dovidio, J.F. (1989) Reducing intergroup bias: the benefits of recategorisation. *Journal of Personality and Social Psychology*, 57, 239–49

Gaertner, S.L., Rust, M.C., Divisio, J.C., Bachman, B.A. and Anastasio, P. (1993) The contact hypothesis: the role of a common in-group identity on reducing intergroup bias. *Small Business Research*

Garcia, J. and Koelling, R.A. (1966) Relation of a cue to consequence in avoidance learning. *Psychonomic Science*, 4, 123–4

Garcia, J., Hankins, W.G. and Rusiniak, K.W. (1974) Behavioral regulation of the milieu interne in man and rat. *Science*, 185, 824–31

Gardner, G.A. (1978) The effects of human subject regulations on data obtained in environmental stressor research. *Journal of Personality and Social Psychology*, 36, 317–49

Gay, P. (1989) *The Freud Reader*. New York: Norton

Geyer, A.L.J. and Speyrer, J.M. (1997) Transformational leadership and objective performance in banks. *Applied Psychology: An International Review*, 46

Gilboa, N. (1996) Elites, lamers, narcs and whores: exploring the computer underground. In Cherny, L. and Weise, E.R. (eds) *Wired Women: Gender and New Realities in Cyberspace*. Seattle: Seal Press

Gildea, J.H. and Quirk, T.R. (1977) Assessing the pain experience in children. *Nursing Clinics of North America*, 1, 631–7

Glanzer, M. and Cunitz, A.R. (1966) Two storage mechanisms in free recall. *Journal of Verbal Learning and Verbal Behaviour*, 5, 351–60

Godden, D. and Baddeley, A.D. (1975) Context dependent memory in two natural environments: On land and under water. *British Journal of Psychology*, 66, 325–31

Gomez, L. (1997) *An Introduction to Object Relations*. London: Free Association Books

Goren, C.C., Sarty, M. and Wu, R.W.K. (1975) Visual following and pattern discrimination of face-like stimuli by new-born infants. *Paediatrics*, 56, 544–9

Gottesman, I. (1991) *Schizophrenia Genesis: The Origins of Madness*. New York: Freeman

Griffiths, M. (1999) Internet addiction: fact or fiction. *The Psychologist*, 12, 246–50

Groblewski, T.A., Nunez, A. and Gold, R.M. (1980). Quoted in Carlson, N.R. (1996) *Physiology of Behavior*. Boston: Allyn & Bacon

Gross, R. (1996) *Psychology: The Science of Mind and Behaviour*, 3rd edition. London: Hodder & Stoughton

Gross, R. (1998) *Key Studies in Psychology*, 3rd edition. London: Hodder & Stoughton

Gross, R., Humphreys, P. and Petkova, B. (1997) *Challenges in Psychology*. London: Hodder & Stoughton

Gulevich, G., Dement, W.C. and Johnson, L. (1966) Psychiatric and EEG observations on a case of prolonged (264 hours) wakefulness. *Archives of General Psychiatry*, 15, 29–35

Hammen, C. (1997) *Depression*. Hove: Psychology Press

Harlow, H.F. (1959) Love in infant rhesus monkeys. *Scientific American*, 200, 68–74

Harma, M., Laitinen, J., Partinen, M. and Suvanto, S. (1994a) The effect of four-day round trip flights over 10 time zones on the circadian variation of salivary melatonin and cortisol in airline flight attendants. *Ergonomics*, 37 (9), 1479–89

Harma, M., Suvanto, S. and Partinen, M. (1994b) The effect of four-day round trip flights over 10 time zones on the sleep-wakefulness of airline flight attendants. *Ergonomics*, 37 (9), 1462–78

Harris, R.J. (1973) Answering questions containing marked and unmarked adjectives and adverbs. *Journal of Experimental Psychology*, 97, 399–402

Hartley, J. (1998) *Learning and Studying*. London: Routledge

Hayes, N. (1998) *Foundations of Psychology*, 2nd edition. Walton-on-Thames: Nelson

Hebb, D.O. (1949) *The Organization of Behaviour*. New York: Wiley

Henderson, J. (1999) *Remembering and Forgetting*. London: Routledge

Herbert, M.J. and Harsh, C.M. (1944) Observational learning by cats. *Journal of Comparative Psychology*, 37, 81–95

Herman, J. and Roffwarg, H. (1983) Modifyinig oculomotor activity in awake subjects increases the amplitude of eye movement during REM sleep. *Science*, 220, 1074–6

Heston, L.L. (1966) Psychiatric disorders in foster home reared children of schizophrenic mothers. *British Journal of Psychiatry*, 112, 819–25

Hetherington, A.W. and Ranson, S.W. (1939) Experimental hypothalamohypophyseal obesity in the rat. *Proceedings of the Society for Experimental Biology and Medicine*, 41, 465–6

Hofling, K.C., Brotzman, E., Dalrymple, S., Graves, N. and Pierce, C.M. (1966) An experimental study in the nurse–physician relationship. *Journal of Nervous and Mental Disorders*, 143, 171–80

Hogan, R.A. (1968) The implosive technique. *Behavior Research and Theory*, 6, 423–31

Holm-Hadulla, R., Kiefer, L. and Sessar, W. (1997) Effectiveness of psychoanalytically founded brief and dynamic psychotherapy. *Psychotherapy and Psychosomatic Medicine*, 47 (8), 271–8

House, R.J., Spangler, W.D. and Woycke, J. (1991) Personality and charisma in the US presidency: a psychological theory of leader effectiveness. *Administrative Science Quarterly*, 36, 364–96

Hunter, C.E. and Ross, M.W. (1991) Determinants of health-care workers' attitudes towards people with AIDS. *Journal of Applied Social Psychology*, 21, 947–56

Hurley, A. and Whelan, E.G. (1988) Cognitive development and children's perception of pain. *Pediatric Nursing*, 14 (1), 21–4

Illnerova, H., Buresova, M., Nedvidkova, J. and Dvorakova, M. (1993) Maintenance of a circadian phase adjustment of the human melatonin rhythm following artificial long days. *Brain Research*, 626 (1–2), 322–6

Inhelder, B. and Piaget, J. (1958) *The Growth of Logical Thinking from Childhood to Adolescence*. London: Routledge & Kegan Paul

Jacobs, M. (1992) *Sigmund Freud*. London: Sage

Jilge, B. (1991) Restricted feeding: a nonphotic *zeitgeber* in the rabbit. *Physiology & Behavior*, 51, 157–66

Jones, E. (1951) *The Life and Works of Sigmund Freud*. London: Hogarth.

Jung, C.G. (1923) *Psychological Types*. New York: Harcourt Brace & Co.

Kagan, J., Kearsley, R.B. and Zelazo, P.R. (1978) *Infancy: Its Place in Human Development*. Cambridge: Harvard University Press

Kahn, S., Zimmerman, G., Csikszentmihalyi, M. and Getzels, J.W. (1985) Relations between identity in young adulthood and intimacy at midlife. *Journal of Personality and Social Psychology*, 49, 1316–22

Kassin, S.M. and Kiechel, K.L. (1996) The social psychology of false confessions: compliance, internalization, and confabulation. *Psychological Science*, 7 (3), 122–8

Katz, J (1997) The digital citizen. *Wired*, December, 68–82, 274–5

Kelly, C. and Breinlinger, S. (1996) *The Social Psychology of Collective Action: Identity, Injustice and Gender*. London: Taylor & Francis

Kessler, R.C. and Magee, W.J. (1993) Childhood adversities and adult depression: basic patterns of association in a US national survey. *Psychological Medicine*, 23, 679–90

Kiesler, S., Siegel, J. and McGuire, T.W. (1984) Social-psychological aspects of computer-mediated interaction. *American Psychologist*, 39, 1123–34

Koulack, D. and Goodenough, D.R. (1976) Dream recall and dream failure. *Psychological Bulletin*, 83, 975–84

Kramarski, B. and Mevarech, Z.R. (1997) Cognitive-metacognitive training within a problem-solving based Logo environment. *British Journal of Educational Psychology*, 67 (4), 425–46

Krane, V. (1998) Lesbians in sport. *Proceedings of the BPS Annual Conference*, 6 (2), 109

Kuczaj, S. (ed.) (1982) *Language Development: Volume 1, Syntax and Semantics*. Hillsdale, New Jersey: Erlbaum

Lacan, J. (1966) Function et champ de la parole et du language en psychoanalyse. *Ecrits*. Paris: Seuil

Latane, B. and Bourgeois, M.J. (1996) Experimental evidence for dynamic social impact: the emergence of subcultures in electronic groups. *Journal of Communication*, 46 (4), 35–47

Lee, V. and Das Gupta, P. (1995) *Children's Cognitive and Language Development*. Oxford: Blackwell

Lemma, A (1996) *Introduction to Psychopathology*. London: Sage

Lemma-Wright, A. (1995) *Invitation to Psychodynamic Psychology*. London: Whurr

Leslie, A. (1994) ToMM, ToBy and agency: core architecture and domain specificity. In Hirschfield, L. and Gelman, S. (eds) *Mapping the Mind: Domain Specificity in Cognition and Culture*. Cambridge: Cambridge University Press

Leslie, J.C. and O'Reilly, M.F. (1999) *Behaviour Analysis: Foundations and Applications to Psychology*. Amsterdam: Harwood Academic Publishers

Lindsay, R.C.L., Lea, J.A., Nosworthy, G.J., Fulford, J.A., Hector, J., LeVan, V. and Seabrook, C. (1991) Biased lineups: sequential presentation reduces the problem. *Journal of Applied Psychology*, 76, 741–5

Linton, M. (1982) Transformations of memory in everyday life. In Neisser, U. (ed.) *Memory Observed: Remembering in Natural Contexts*. San Francisco: W.H. Freeman & Co.

Littleton, K. (1995) Children and computers. In Bancroft, D. and Carr, R. (eds) (1995) op. cit.

Loehlin, J.C. (1992) *Genes and Environment in Personality Development*. Newbury Park: Sage

Loftus, E.F. (1979) *Eyewitness Testimony*. Cambridge, MA: Harvard University Press

Loftus, E.F. (1983) Whose shadow is crooked. *American Psychologist*, 38, 576–77

Loftus, E.F. (1986) Ten years in the life of an expert witness. *Law and Human Behaviour*, 10, 241–63

Loftus, E.F., Carry, M., Manning, C.G. and Sherman, S.J. (1996) Imagination inflation: Imagining a childhood event inflates confidence that it occurred. *Psychonomic Bulletin and Review*, 3 (2), 208–14

Loftus, E.F. and Marburger, W. (1983) Since the eruption of Mount St Helens has anyone beaten you up? Improving the accuracy of retrospective reports with landmark events. *Memory and Cognition*, 11, 114–20

Loftus, E.F., Miller, D.G. and Burns, H.J. (1978) Semantic integration of verbal information into a visual memory. *Journal of Experimental Psychology: Human Learning and Memory*, 4 (1), 19–31

Loftus, E.F. and Palmer, J.C. (1974) Reconstruction of automobile destruction: An example of the interaction between language and memory. *Journal of Verbal Learning and Verbal Behaviour*, 13, 585–9

Loftus, E.F. and Pickrell, J.E. (1995) The formation of false memories. *Psychiatric Annals*, 25, 720–5

Loftus, E.F. and Zaani, G. (1975) Eyewitness testimony: The influence of the wording of a question. *Bulletin of the Psychonomic Society*, 5, 86–8

Loftus, G. (1974) Reconstructing memory: The incredible eyewitness. *Psychology Today*, December, 116–19

Luce, G.G. and Segal, J. (1966) *Sleep*. New York: Coward-McCann

Luria, A.R. (1968) *The Mind of a Mnemonist*. New York: Basic Books

Luria, A.R. and Yudovich, F.I. (1971) *Speech and the Development of Mental Processes in the Child*. Harmondsworth: Penguin

Main, M. (1996) Introduction to the special section on attachment and psychopathology: 2. Overview of the field of attachment. *Journal of Counselling and Clinical Psychology*, 64, 237–43

Malan, D. (1995) *Individual Psychotherapy and the Science of Psychodynamics*. London: Butterworth-Heinemann

Manstead, A.R. and McCulloch, C. (1981) Sex-role stereotyping in British television advertisements. *British Journal of Social Psychology*, 20, 171–80

Maquet, P. *et al.* (1997) from the *Journal of Neuroscience*, 17, 2807. Reported in Motluk, A. (1997) Emotions need forty winks. *New Scientist*, 10 May, 20

Marcia, J.E. (1993) The relational roots of identity. In Kroger, J. (ed.) *Discussions on Ego Identity*. Hillsdale: Lawrence Erlbaum

Marks, I.M. (1987) *Fears, Phobias and Rituals*. New York: Oxford University Press

Marks, I.M. and Rachman, S.J. (1978) Interim report to the Medical Research Council

Masur, E.F. (1995) Infants' early verbal imitation and their later lexical development. *Merrill-Palmer Quarterly*, 41, 286–306

Matute, H. (1996) Illusion of control: detecting response–outcome independence in analytic but not in naturalistic conditions. *Psychological Science*, 7, 289–93

Mayer, J.D., Gayle, M., Meehan, M.E. and Haarman, A. (1990) Toward better specification of the mood-congruency effect in recall. *Journal of Experimental Social Psychology*, 26, 465–80

Mayo, E. (1933) *The Human Problems of an Industrial Civilisation*. New York: Macmillan

McCafferey, M. (1972) *Nursing Management of the Patient with Pain*. Philadelphia: Lippincott

McGarrigle, J. and Donaldson, M. (1974) Conservation accidents. *Cognition*, 3, 341–50

McIlveen, R. and Gross, R. (1998) *Biopsychology*. London: Hodder & Stoughton

McKenna, K.Y.A. and Bargh, J.A. (1998) Coming out in the age of the Internet: identity demarginalisation through virtual group participation. *Journal of Personality and Social Psychology*, 75 (3), 681–94

McKnight, J. and Sutton, J. (1994) *Social Psychology*. Sydney: Prentice Hall

Meddis, R. (1977) *The Sleep Instinct*. London: Routledge & Kegan Paul

Memon, A. (1998) Recovered memories: psychological issues and legal questions. In Memon, A., Vrij, A. and Bull, R. (eds) (1998) op. cit.

Memon, A., Vrij, A. and Bull, R. (eds) (1998) *Psychology and Law, Truthfulness, Accuracy and Credibility*. London: McGraw-Hill

Memon, A. and Wright, D.B. (1999) Eyewitness testimony and the Oklahoma bombing. *The Psychologist*, 12 (6), 292–5

Messer, D. and Millar, S. (eds) (1999) *Exploring Developmental Psychology*. London: Arnold

Mevarech, Z., Silber, O. and Fine, D. (1991) Learning with computers in small groups: cognitive and affective outcomes. *Journal of Educational Computing Research*, 7 (2), 233–43

Michel, S., Geusz, M.E., Zaritsky, J.J. and Block, G.D. (1993) Circadian rhythms in membrane conductance expressed in isolated neurons. *Science*, 259, 239–41

Mickelson, K.D. (1997) Seeking social support: parents in electronic support groups. In Kiesler, S. (ed.) *Culture of the Internet*. Mahwah: Lawrence Erlbaum Associates

Miles, L.E., Raynal, D.M. and Wilson, M.A. (1977) Blind man living in normal society has circadian rhythm of 24.9 hours. *Science*, 198, 421–3

Milgram, S. (1963) Behavioural study of obedience. *Journal of Abnormal and Social Psychology*, 67, 371–8

Milgram, S. (1974) *Obedience to Authority*. New York: Harper & Row

Miller, G.A. (1956) The magical number seven, plus or minus two: Some limits on our capacity for processing information. *Psychological Review*, 63, 81–97

Mineka, S. and Cook, M. (1988) Social learning and the acquisition of fear in monkeys. In Zentall, T.R. and Galef, B.G., Jr (eds), *Social Learning Psychological and Biological Perspectives*. Hillsdale, NJ: Lawrence Erlbaum Associates Inc.

Mistleberger, R.E. (1991) Scheduled daily exercise of feeding alters the phase of photic entrainment in Syrian hamsters. *Physiology & Behavior*, 50, 1257–60

Mitler, M. (1988) Catastropes, sleep and public policy: consensus report. *Sleep*, 11, 100–9

Molnos, A. (1995) *A Question of Time*. London: Karnac

Monk, T.H. and Aplin, L.C. (1980) Spring and autumn daylight saving time changes: Studies of adjustment in sleep timings, mood and efficiency. *Ergonomics*, 23, 167–78

Moore-Ede, M. (1993) We have ways of keeping you awake. *New Scientist*, 13 November, 30–5

Morris, P.E., Gruneberg, M.M., Sykes, R.N. and Merrick, A. (1981) Football knowledge and the acquisition of new results. *British Journal of Psychology*, 72, 479–83

Mrosovsky, N. (1988) Phase response curves for social entrainment. *Journal of Comparative Physiology*, 162, 35–46

Mukhametov, L.M., Supin, A.Y. and Polyakova, I.G. (1977) Interhemispheric asymmetry of the encephalographic sleep patterns in dolphins. *Brain Research*, 134, 581–4

Muller, D.J., Harris, P.J. and Wattley, L. (1986) *Nursing Children: Psychology, Research and Practice*. London: Harper & Row

Myers, L.B. and Brewin, C.R. (1994) Recall of early experience and the repressive coping style. *Journal of Abnormal Psychology*, 103 (2), 288–92

Neisser, U. and Harsch, N. (1992) Phantom flashbulbs: false recollections of hearing the news about Challenger. In Winograd, E. and Neisser, U. (eds) *Affect and Accuracy in Recall: Studies of 'Flashbulb Memories'*. New York: Cambridge University Press

Nelson, K. (1973) Structure and strategy in learning to talk. *Monographs of the Society for Research in Child Development*, 38 (1–2, serial no. 149)

Nichols, J.D. (1996) Cooperative learning: A motivational tool to enhance student persistence, self-regulation, and efforts to please teachers and parents. *Educational Research and Evaluation*, 2 (3), 246–60

Nicol, C.J. and Pope, S.J. (1999) The effects of demonstrator social status and prior foraging success on social learning in laying hens. *Animal Behaviour*, 57, 163–71

Ohman, A., Fredrikson, M., Hugdahl, K. and Rimmo, P. (1976) The premise of equipotentiality in human classical conditioning: conditioned electrodermanl responses to potentially phobic stimuli. *Journal of Experimental Psychology: General*, 105, 313–37

Oller, D.K. (1981) Infant vocalizations: Exploration and reflectivity. In Stark, R.E. (ed.) *Language Behavior in Infancy and Early Childhood*. New York: Elsevier North-Holland

Oswald, I. (1969) Human brain protein, drugs and dreams. *Nature*, 223, 893–7

Oswald, I. (1980) *Sleep*. Harmondsworth: Penguin

Overton, D.A. (1972) State dependent learning produced by alcohol and its relevance to alcoholism. In Kissin, B. and Begleiter, H. (eds) *The Biology of Alcoholism 2: Physiology and Behaviour*. New York: Plenum Press

Papert, S. (1980) *Mindstorms: Children, Computers and Powerful Ideas*. Brighton: Harvester Press

Parry, G. (1996) *NHS Psychotherapy Services in England*. Wetherby: National Health Service Executive

Pavlov, I.P. (1927) *Conditioned Reflexes: An Investigation of the Physiological Activity of the Cerebral Cortex*. New York: Dover Publications Inc.

Pennington, D.C. (1986) *Essential Social Psychology*. London: Edward Arnold

Phillips, J.L. (1975) *The Origins of Intellect: Piaget's Theory*. San Fransisco: Freeman

Piaget, J. (1952) Logic and psychology. In *Series of lectures at Manchester University*, Basic Books (1957)

Piaget, J. (1963) *The Origins of Intelligence in Children*. New York: Norton

Piaget, J. (1971) The theory of stages in cognitive development. In Green, D.R., Ford, M.P. and Flanner, G.B. (eds) *Measurement and Piaget*. New York: McGraw-Hill

Piaget, J. (1972) Intellectual evolution from adolescence to adulthood. *Human Development*, 15, 1–12

Piaget, J. and Inhelder, B. (1956) *The Child's Conception of Space*. London: Routledge & Kegan Paul

Pinker, S. (1994) *The Language Instinct*. London: Penguin

Piontelli, A. (1992) *From Fetus to Child*. London: Routledge

Platow, M.J., McClintock and Liebrand, W.B. (1990) Predicting intergroup fairness and ingroup bias in the minimal group paradigm. *European Journal of Social Psychology*, 20, 221–39

Plomin, R., DeFries, J.C., McClearn, G.E. and Rutter, M. (1997) *Behavioural Genetics*. New York: Freeman

Poppe, E. and Linssen, H. (1999) In-group favouritism and the reflection of realistic dimensions of difference between national states in Central and Eastern European nationality stereotypes. *British Journal of Social Psychology*, 38, 85–102

Ralph, M.R., Foster, T.G., Davis, F.C. and Menaker, M. (1990) Transplanted suprachiasmatic nucleus determines circadian period. *Science*, 247, 975–8

Raven, B.H. and Haley, R.W. (1982) Social influence and compliance in hospital nurses with infection control policies. In Eiser, J.R. (ed.) *Social Psychology and Behavioural Medicine*. Chichester: Wiley

Ray, J.J. (1972) A new balanced F-scale and its relation to social class. *Australian Psychologist*, 7, 155–66

Ray, J.J. (1989) Authoritarianism research is alive and well and in Australia: a review. *The Psychological Record*, 39, 555–61

Reber, A.S. (1995) *Dictionary of Psychology*. London: Penguin

Rechtschaffen, A., Gilliland, M.A., Bergmann, B.M. and Winter, J.B. (1983) Physiological correlates of prolonged sleep deprivation in rats. *Science*, 221, 182–4

Reicher, S. and Hopkins, N. (1996) Self category constructions on political rhetoric: an analysis of Thatcher's and Kinnock's speeches concerning the British miner's strike (1984–5). *European Journal of Social Psychology*, 26, 353–71

Reinsel, R., Wollman, M. and Antrobus, J.S. (1986) Effects of environmental context and cortical activation on thought. *Journal of Mind and Behavior*, 7, 259–76

Resnick, M.N. (1984) *The Nuremberg Mind Redeemed: A Comprehensive Analysis of the Nuremberg War Criminalsí Rorschach Records*. Unpublished doctoral dissertation. The Professional School of Psychology, San Francisco

Rideout, B. (1979) Non REN sleep as a source of learning deficients induced by REM deprivation. *Physiology and Behavior*, 22, 1043–7

Roberts, R.D. and Kyllonen, P.C. (1999) Morningness-eveningness and intelligence: early to bed, early to rise will make you anything but wise! *Personality and Individual Differences*, 27, 1123–33

Rokeach, M. (1960) *The Open and Closed Mind*. New York: Basic Books

Rose, S., Kamin, L.J. and Lewontin, R.C. (1984) *Not in Our Genes*. Harmondsworth: Penguin

Rosenthal, R. and Fode, K.L. (1963) The effect of experimenter bias on the performance of the albino rat. *Behavioural Science*, 8 (3), 183–9

Rubin, D.C., Wetzler, S.E. and Nebes, R.D. (1986) Autobiographical memory across the lifespan. In Rubin, D.C. (ed.) *Autobiographical Memory*. Cambridge: Cambridge University Press

Russell, M.J., Dark, K.A., Cummins, R.W., Ellman, G. Callaway, E. and Peeke, H.V.S. (1984) Learned histamine release. *Science*, 225, 733–4

Rutter, M. *et al.* (1998) Developmental catch-up and deficit, following adoption after severe global early privation. *Journal of Child Psychology and Psychiatry*, 39, 465–76

Sanders, G.S. (1984) Effects of context cues on eyewitness identification responses. *Journal of Applied Social Psychology*, 14, 386–97

Savory, T.H., Joselin, F.E. and Walton, J. (1943) *Seven Biologists*. Oxford: Oxford University Press

Schaie, K.W. and Willis, S.L. (1996) *Adult Development and Ageing*. New York: Harper Collins

Schneidermann, N., Fuentes, I and Gormezano, I. (1962) Acquisition and extinction of the classically conditioned eyelid response in the albino rabbit. *Science*, 136, 650–2

Schultz, N.V. (1971) How children perceive pain. *Nursing Outlook*, 3 (6), 670–3

Searle, A. (1999) *Introducing Research and Data in Psychology*. London: Routledge

Shapiro, C.M. Catteral, J.R., Warren, P., Oswald, I., Trinder, J., Paxton, S. and East, B.W. (1986) Lean body mass and non-rapid eye movement sleep. *British Medical Bulletin*, 294, 22

Sherman, L.W. (1992) The influence of criminology on criminal law: evaluating arrests for misdemeanour domestic violence. *Journal of Criminal Law and Criminology*, 83, 1–45

Skellington, R. (1995) *Race in Britain Today*, 2nd edition. London: Sage

Skinner, B.F. (1938) *The Behavior of Organisms*. New York: Appleton-Century-Crofts

Skinner, B.F. (1948) Superstition in the pigeon. *Journal of Experimental Psychology*, 38, 168–72

Skinner, B.F. (1957) *Verbal Behavior*. New York: Prentice-Hall

Smith, C. (1995) Sleep states and memory processes. *Behavioral and Brain Research*, 69 (1–2), 137–45

Smith, C. (1996) Sleep states, memory processes and synaptic plasticity. *Behavioral and Brain Research*, 78 (1), 49–56

Smith, P.K., Cowie, H. and Blades, M. (1998) *Understanding Children's Development*. London: Blackwell

Snyder, M. and Uranowitz, S.W. (1978) Reconstructing the past: Some cognitive consequences of person perception. *Journal of Personality and Social Psychology*, 36, 941–50

Stephan, F.K. and Zucker, I. (1972) Circadian rhythms in drinking behaviour and locomotor activity in rats are eliminated by hypothalamic lesion. *Proceedings of the National Academy of Science*, 69, 1583–6

Sternberg, S. (1966) High speed scanning in human memory. *Science*, 153, 652–4

Stevens, R. (1983) *Freud and Psychoanalysis*. Milton Keynes: Open University Press

Stiles, B. (1990) in 'Is winter the saddest time of year?'. *New Scientist*, 1740, 23

Stirling, J. (1999) *Cortical Functions*. London: Routledge

Straub, R.E., Maclean, C.J., O'Neil, F.A., Burke, J., Murphy, B., Duke, F., Shinkwin, R., Webb, B.T., Zhang, J., Walsh, D. and Kendler, K.S. (1995) A potential vulnerability locus for schizophrenia on chromosome 6p24-22: evidence for genetic heterogeneity. *Nature Genetics*, 11, 28–93

Suler, J. (1996) Why is this thing eating my life? Computer and cyberspace addition at the 'Palace'. http://wwwl.rider.edu/~suler/psycyber/eatlife.html

Suvanto, S., Harma, M., Ilmarinen, J. and Partinen, M. (1993) Effects of 10 hour time zones changes on female flight attendants' circadian rhythms of body temperature, alertness and visual search. *Ergonomics*, 36 (6), 613–25

Tajfel, H. and Turner, J.C. (1979) An integrative theory of intergroup conflict. In Austin, W.G. and Worchel, S. (eds) *The Social Psychology of Intergroup Relations*. Cambridge: Cambridge University Press

Tajfel, H.(1970) Experiments in intergroup discrimination. *Scientific American*, 223, 96–102

Tauber, E.S., Rofas-Ramire, J. and Hernandez-Peon, R. (1968) Electrophysiological and behavioural correlates of wakefulness and sleep in the lizard Ctenosaura pectinata. *Electroencephalograpy and Clinical Neurophysiology*, 24, 424–33

Terman, M., Amira, L., Terman, J.S. and Ross, D.C. (1996) Predictors of response and nonresponse to light treatment for winter depression. *American Journal of Psychiatry*, 153 (11), 1423–9

Thorndike, E.L. (1911) *Animal Intelligence: Experimental Studies*. New York: Macmillan

Thorndike, E.L. and Lorge, I. (1944) *The Teacher's Word Book of 30,000 Words*. New York: Teacher's College, Columbia University

Tienari, P. (1992) Implications of adoption studies on schizophrenia. *British Journal of Psychiatry*, 161, 52–8

Tilley, A.J. and Empson, J.A.C. (1978) REM sleep and memory consolidation. *Biological Psychology*, 6, 293–300

Torrey, E., Fuller, E., Edward, H., Bracha, H. and Bowler, A.E. (1994) Prenatal origins of schizophrenia in a subgroup of discordant monozygotic twins. *Schizophrenia Bulletin*, 20, 423–32

Totterdell, P. (1995) Effects of depressed affect on diurnal and ultradian variations in mood in a healthy sample. *Chronobiology International*, 12 (4), 278–89

Tulving, E. (1972) Episodic and semantic memory. In Tulving, E. and Donaldson, W. (eds) *Organisation of Memory*. London: Academic Press

Tulving, E. (1974) Cue-dependent forgetting. *American Scientist*, 62, 74–82

Tulving, E. (1983) *Elements of Episodic Memory*. Oxford: Oxford University Press

Tulving, E. (1985) How many memory systems are there? *American Psychologist*, 40, 385–98

Tulving, E. and Pearlstone, Z. (1966) Availability versus accessibility of information in memory for words. *Journal of Verbal Learning and Verbal Behaviour*, 5, 381–91

Twycross, A. (1998) Children's cognitive level and perception of pain. *Professional Nurse*, 14 (1), 35–7

Vrij, A. (1998) Psychological factors in eyewitness testimony. In Memon, A., Vrij, A. and Bull, R. (eds) (1998) op. cit.

Wagenaar, W.A. (1986) My memory: a study of autobiographical memory over six years. *Cognitive Psychology*, 18, 225–52

Wallace, P. (1999) *The Psychology of the Internet*. Cambridge: Cambridge University Press

Walther, J.B. (1993) Impression development in computer-mediated interaction. *Western Journal of Communication*, 57, 381–98

Waugh, N.C. and Norman, D. (1965) Primary memory. *Psychological Review*, 72, 89–104

Webb, W.B. and Cartwright, R.D. (1978) Sleep and dreams. *Annual Review of Psychology*, 29, 223–52

Wells, G.L. (1993) What do we know about eyewitness identification? *American Psychologist*, 48, 553–71

Wertsch, J.V. (1991) *Voices of the Mind: A Sociocultural Approach to Mediated Action*. Cambridge: Harvard University Press

Wertsch, J.V. and Tulviste, P. (1996) L.S. Vygotsky and contemporary developmental psychology. In Faulkner, D., Littleton, K. and Woodhead, M. (1998) op. cit.

Wetherall, M. (1997) *Identities, Groups and Social Issues*. Milton Keynes: Open University

Whitbourne, S.K., Zuschlag, M.K., Elliot, L.B. and Waterman, A.S. (1992) Psychosocial development in adulthood: a 22-year sequential study. *Journal of Personality and Social Psychology*, 63, 260–71

Wimmer, H. and Perner, J. (1983) Beliefs about beliefs: representations and constraining function of wrong beliefs in young children's understanding of deception. *Cognition*, 13, 103–28

Winnicott, D.W. (1965) *The Family and Individual Development*. London: Tavistock Publications

Wolpe, J. (1969) Basic principles and practices of behavior therapy of neuroses. *American Journal of Psychiatry*, 125, 1242–7

Wortman, C.B. and Loftus, E.E. (1985) *Psychology*, 2nd edition. New York: Knopf

Wright, S., Taylor, D. and Moghadden, F. (1990) Responding to membership in a disadvantaged group: from acceptance to collective protest. *Journal of Personality and Social Psychology*, 58, 994–1003

Young, K.S. (1998) *Caught in the Net: How to Recognise the Signs of Internet Addiction and a Winning Strategy for Recovery*. New York: John Wiley

Zepelin, H. and Rechtschaffen, A. (1974) Mammalian sleep, longevity and energy metabolism. *Brain, Behaviour and Evolution*, 10, 425

Zillmer, E.A., Harrower, M., Ritzler, B.A. and Archer, R.P. (1995) *The Quest for the Nazi Personality: A Psychological Investigation of Nazi War Criminals*. Hillsdale, New Jersey: Lawrence Erlbaum Associates

Zinbarg, R.E., Barlow, D.H., Brown, T.A. and Hertz, R.M. (1992) Cognitive-behavioural approaches to the nature and treatment of anxiety disorders. *Annual Review of Psychology*, 43, 235–67

index

Page numbers in **bold** indicate where these terms are defined